SO YOU THINK YOU KNOW FOOTBALL?

SO YOU THINK YOU KNOW FOOTBALL?

THE ARMCHAIR REF'S
GUIDE TO THE OFFICIAL RULES

BEN AUSTRO

TAYLOR TRADE PUBLISHING
Lanham • Boulder • New York • London

Published by Taylor Trade Publishing
An imprint of Rowman & Littlefield
4501 Forbes Boulevard, Suite 200, Lanham, Maryland 20706
www.rowman.com

Unit A, Whitacre Mews, 26-34 Stannary Street, London SE11 4AB

Distributed by NATIONAL BOOK NETWORK

British Library Cataloguing in Publication Information Available

Library of Congress Cataloging-in-Publication Data is available on file.

ISBN 978-1-63076-043-4 (paperback)
ISBN 978-1-63076-044-1 (electronic)

The paper used in this publication meets the minimum requirements of
an National Standard for Information Sciences—Permanence of Paper for
Library Materials, ANSI/NISO Z39.48-1992.

the United States of America

Dedicated to the tens of thousands of men, women, girls, and boys who wear the stripes every weekend during the season for the love of the game.

CONTENTS

CONTENTS

FOREWORD

Each football season, all thirty-two NFL teams begin the quest for the prestigious Vince Lombardi Trophy, sparking optimism from every corner of the football world. Fans watching their favorite teams feel any close call, especially any that goes against their beloved team, is incorrect. Every call can have an effect on the chance their team has at achieving that Super Bowl dream. They listen to the TV announcers and the so-called rules experts on broadcasts and social media. They may even complain to a friend who may have worn the stripes and blown a whistle at some point or at some level who will attempt to clarify what the officials ruled on the field. "Is that the rule? Was the ref correct or did he blow another one?"

It's a fact: NFL officiating consistently draws the ire of football fans throughout the stadiums, TV rooms, and sports bars around the country. I heard it all through my career as an official. In fact, in my very first NFL game, I was summoned to the sideline by Houston Oilers coach Jerry Glanville. His salty response to my call was legendary: "This is the NFL, which means 'not for long' if you make them [. . .] calls." I stood my ground. I knew I was right. (It turned out NFL Films picked up the whole conversation through a wireless microphone. To this day, the clip surfaces on TV from time to time.) The fact remains that NFL officials are accurate more than 98 percent of the time. And the reason is they have spent countless hours every week and many years studying and understanding the rules and philosophies of this game.

I have thoroughly enjoyed reading *So You Think You Know Football?*. In this book, Ben Austro does a great job explaining rules to the NFL fan in a manner that is easy to understand. Although you may not always agree with his explanations—or those of the official making the call on the field—you will understand a lot more than you ever had before if you read this book. Ben has simplified each rule and has done a fantastic job of giving a historical background as to the specific plays or situations that helped put these rules in place.

As I read this book, I felt it could have been titled *Everything You Wanted to Know About NFL Rules, But Didn't Know Who to Ask*, since so many rules and questions are addressed. Not only that, and perhaps more importantly, they are explained in a manner that anyone will be able to understand.

So You Think You Know Football? is a great resource to help educate its readers and answer many of those questions that football fans discuss each and every week of the NFL season. It won't stop fans from complaining, but this book can certainly settle a few arguments.

—Jim Daopoulos

About Jim Daopoulos:
Jim is a former NFL official, having worked as a back judge and an umpire during his time on the field. He moved up to an officiating supervisor in the NFL office, which entailed analyzing game film and grading officials on all the calls they made or missed. He has offered his rule analysis on controversial calls for NBC Sports, ESPN, and several sports-talk radio shows, in addition to the author's website *Football Zebras*. Currently he is a consultant for the American Athletic Conference and *Monday Night Football*. On Sundays during the football season, he can usually be found offering his opinion and answering questions on Twitter as @RefereeJimD.

PREFACE

Perhaps it is a little unfair to cast one person's fleeting mistake as an opportunity. But, one call in Week 2 of the 2008 season led to an interesting chain of events that I could never have imagined.

It was a cool, late-summer afternoon in Denver as the Broncos were hosting their division rivals, the San Diego Chargers. After trailing the Broncos by 18 points early in the second quarter, the Chargers clamored back to seize a seven-point lead with a few minutes remaining. But the Chargers defense was unable to stop the offensive march of the Broncos with quarterback Jay Cutler at the helm. The Chargers were literally on the goal line when it appeared they finally stopped the Broncos drive short.

Cutler fumbled the ball on second down, which was recovered by linebacker Tim Dobbins at the 10-yard line. Dobbins is not listed in the statistics as having made a fumble recovery because when the ball was loose, a whistle echoed through the gasps of the crowd at Mile High. Referee Ed Hochuli had ruled it an incomplete pass but immediately realized this was in error. As much as Hochuli wanted to take back that whistle, the play is dead and the fumble recovery nullified. There was no recourse to right the wrong.

The press coverage of that game centered on the inadvertent whistle by Hochuli. Obviously it was an incorrect call, but I was curious if the crew further compounded the error in a replay review, since the ball was then declared dead at the 10-yard line, instead of returning to the original line of scrimmage for the incomplete pass. I was seeking analysis of the call, but there was very little to be found other than complaints about the call and about the rule that kept the Chargers from getting possession. There was no discussion about which rule applies to such situations, and all I got was nothing but a sports radio stew of complaints and rants. As for the few websites that discussed officiating, most were blogs whose authors churned out post after post about officials who were alleged to be visually impaired.

I decided that if I could not find the site I was looking for, I was going to create it. My interest in being an armchair official started when I requested a rulebook from the league office in 1988. I think it was $5 to cover the shipping, and it was worth much more than that. It was the same rulebook all the officials receive: a solid, battleship-grey cover with ordinary black, sans-serif capital letters in black; the only splash of color was the red and blue in the inch-high NFL logo. After updating the book with various margin notes of rule changes, I saw the rulebook for sale in the bookstore, now with a cover that had much more shelf appeal, but the same content, nonetheless.

I started the *Football Zebras* blog for a trial run for Super Bowl XLIII at the end of the 2008 season. The first post covered a pre–Super Bowl press conference by commissioner Roger Goodell, in which he floated the possibility that the sudden-death format of overtime might need to be tweaked. I argued against changing the decades-old format, which I also did in a post the following year when the owners followed through and passed the modified sudden-death format.

I felt I knew my rules well enough to roll out the site with weekly updates, but I made a very deliberate editorial choice from the very beginning to avoid being critical of the officials. I rationalized that less than 2 percent of the calls an official makes in a season are deemed incorrect or at least have some shade of an error; therefore, I believed the coverage should reflect that percentage. I do hand out criticism when it is warranted, but there are plenty of websites available to the football fan who is only interested in a rant against the officiating.

As I started to cover my first full season, I quickly learned that there was more to report than just the rules. Yes, there were the "armchair" officials such as myself, but there were also the many people who put the stripes on Friday and Saturdays who were watching their professional cohorts on Sunday. The black-and-white rulebook with the grey cover was only a part of officiating, and I soon expanded to cover the procedural aspects—the "mechanics"—of officiating with the indispensable help of Mark Schultz, a high-school official and the moderator of an Internet discussion board that is now under the *Football Zebras* umbrella.

I found a greater respect for the job that the officials do to call a fair game, not only at the NFL level, but all the way down to the pee-wee games. Rules knowledge is of utmost importance, but I appreciated the fuller package that is a football official: the agility, the concentration, the stamina, the authority, the control, the teamwork, the indifference to the weather, the tolerance of wanton criticism, and, above all, the anonymity. The bane of officiating is to be known. There can be no greater appreciation for a participant in any sport than to be an official, because it is all about the purity of the competition and essence of fair play. Teams play to win. Officials can have the personal satisfaction of a perfectly called game, yet they never record that victory.

One of the tools available to football officials, particularly in the NFL, is the casebook. The rulebook can only go so far to delineate the parameters of any particular rule. Practical hypotheticals are presented in a parallel guide that provides examples of what the correct call is in each situation, should an official be faced with a similar scenario. The casebook employs a very dry read of assigning "Team A" to the offense and "Team B" to the defense and designating players and yard-lines by letter-number combinations. For example, the *2014 Official Casebook* has the following scenario (Approved Ruling 3.2) for an intentional forward fumble on fourth down:

> Fourth-and-10 on B35. With 0:17 left in the game, and Team B ahead 21-20, A1 scrambles to the B21 and intentionally fumbles the ball forward to the B20 where it is recovered by B1 who returns it to the B22.

In this case, the B team gets to keep the ball, but not where you might expect. Because the forward fumble was not caught, it is an incomplete pass. Since the foul by A brought the ball short of a first down by one yard, the loss-of-down penalty means that Team A was short on fourth down. It is B's ball at the 26-yard line with the option to enforce a ten-second runoff.

It's not very easy for the casual fan to visualize the A's and the B's, and it doesn't make for a compelling read. I compiled this collection of unusual plays and situations in games spanning from a 1921 contest in the NFL's second season through the end of the 2014 season. Much like the football couch potato of the 1980s was implored by the "You Make the Call" segments produced by NFL Films, these chapters will provide you the opportunity to see if you would make the same call as the officials did—and if you are right.

Some rules may change from year to year that affect the interpretations in this work. I will update any of these situations online at thinkyouknow football.com.

I owe a great debt of gratitude to those who helped me along the way. It started with my dad, Ben Sr., who imparted the foundations of the rules as we froze during so many games from the top row of the upper deck of Giants Stadium. (I'm sure it must have been warm at *some* point, but I don't remember when.) My friends Scott Diller, Jeff Wakeman, and Craig Hall have always been ready for a spirited debate over the rules. Mark Schultz, David Root, and Josh Lewis all have enthusiastically contributed to *Football Zebras* with the same passion that I have felt and helped carry the site when I needed more time with the book. My researcher, Brian Flood, was indispensable for gaps in a fading memory, and Danny Corbalis was able to share his design gifts by creating the formation illustrations in Chapter 4.

Two of the kindest men you will ever meet have helped me immensely as *Football Zebras* grew: Jim Daopoulos and Larry Upson. Both are former NFL officials and officiating supervisors under Mike Pereira when he was the NFL's vice-president of officiating. They have always been a phone call away to offer their expert interpretations or to validate my own. They are fantastic mentors to have. I also appreciate the network of officiating contacts who have provided some opinion and suggestions and who have chosen to remain—as true officials feel most comfortable—anonymous.

I also extend thanks to Dan Bial, who proposed this book concept to me and found the right match for a publisher, and to my agent Regina Ryan who has been magnificent navigating a first-time author through the process. The incredible patience of Flannery Scott and Karie Simpson and the entire staff at Taylor Trade Publishing was welcome as deadlines became nothing more than highway roadkill as I zoomed past them.

This book is also possible through the support and inspiration of the woman who I turn into a football widow for six months out of the year—and twelve months when I am writing a book. To my wife, Karen, I thank you for everything you have done to encourage me to fulfill a dream. And, I guess it is now *my* turn to make sure I keep the kids out of your hair.

AUTHOR'S NOTE

All numbered references and rules passages that are quoted in this work are from the *2014 Official Playing Rules of the National Football League.* The rules for high school, college, and minor professional leagues will differ.

Each year at the league's annual meeting, the team owners vote on rules proposals brought by the Competition Committee and the teams themselves. Thus, the NFL rulebook is constantly evolving compared to the rulebooks of other major professional sports. Some of the interpretations in this book may not be valid in future seasons. As passages are added, deleted, or moved, sections of the rulebook are renumbered in sequence and may cause some of the references in this work to mismatch with the latest version of the rulebook.

Please note, also, that *flagrant* is a term derived from the official rules to describe a degree of an action and is not meant to imply that the players referenced had any premeditated or deliberately harmful intentions.

The final arbiter for the rules is the official rulebook and the companion *Official Casebook of the National Football League*, and they supersede any conflict with this work.

ONE

PREGAME

Gentlemen, let's play football.

—Referee Red Cashion, after conducting numerous coin tosses

For a 1 p.m. kickoff, the officiating crew is escorted on a shuttle bus from their hotel, arriving at the stadium around 10:30 a.m. The officials enter a private locker area where a sign warns passers-by POSITIVELY NO VISITORS. The rulebook is unequivocal about this:

> By order of the Commissioner, from the time any official first enters the dressing room, and until all officials have left it at the end of the game, no person other than clubhouse attendants or those invited by the Referee shall be allowed to enter it. This prohibition includes coaches, players, owners, and other management personnel.

The pregame responsibilities for the crew are almost as long as the game itself, and they are rigidly timed:

> 135 minutes to kickoff—The crew has a brief meeting in the dressing room. Game balls are handed over to crew from each team.

120 minutes—The referee goes to the 50-yard line of the home-team bench side to perform a check for his wireless microphone (and a backup microphone) over the public-address system.

100 minutes—Officials have assumed formal game jurisdiction. The referee receives a security briefing about any unusual circumstances or inclement weather forecast.

90 minutes—The officials meet with the public relations directors of both teams and the sideline coordinators for television in the officials' locker room. Participants sync their watches. The home team PR director (who functions as a communications coordinator during emergencies) sets a "code name" with the referee to authenticate him if he needs to call the press box. Teams identify players approved to have coach-to-player radios in their helmets and players who will wear microphones for television or NFL Films.

85 minutes (approximately)—Two officials each meet with the head coaches. This occurs after the meeting at the 90-minute mark.

80 minutes—Officials must be on the field during the teams' warm-up period.

35 minutes—The referee conducts a second microphone check for the television network.

20 minutes—Officials signal the end of the warm-up period, and teams must return to their respective locker rooms.

(The remainder of the times vary slightly for primetime games to allow player introductions and the national anthem to occur at specific times. While the times vary, they are set at the 90-minute meeting.)

13 minutes—Side judge must knock on the visiting team locker door and announce, "Two-minute warning—two minutes until you leave the locker room."

11 minutes—Umpire gives the home team its two-minute warning. This is done separately to avoid teams walking together in the stadium concourse area.

10 minutes—Officials appear on the field for the game.

3 minutes—The referee conducts the coin toss.

1 minute—Both teams are on the field.

For the early Sunday games, kickoff is actually scheduled for 1:02 p.m. eastern time to allow the television network to begin the broadcast. This is monitored for compliance back at the command post in the league headquarters; any games that kick off at 1:03 or later are noted on the game reports.

During the pregame warm-ups of a *Monday Night Football* game on September 12, 2005, Philadelphia Eagles linebacker Jeremiah Trotter pushed Atlanta Falcons cornerback Kevin Mathis, who then punched Trotter. This created a swarm of players, and the officiating crew intervened to separate both teams.

1. What actions should the crew take?

Both Trotter and Mathis were ejected from the game. Even though Mathis was not the instigator, his actions were flagrant enough to warrant the disqualification. Since the officials had assumed authority over the game at the 100-minute mark—before the warm-up period—fouls and disqualifications could be administered.

2. What if Mathis had not thrown a punch?

If Trotter was the only player penalized for his actions, not only would he be ejected, but also a 15-yard penalty would be assessed on the opening kickoff. But, in this game, the offsetting penalties negated any yardage to be assessed on the kickoff.

3. Because pregame warm-ups encompass the entire field, the officiating crew did not see the start of the fight. What can they do to determine that the penalties are properly assessed?

Since it is not typical for there to be an incident in pregame, the warm-up period is not closely monitored. An official can call only what is seen, and not what is believed to have occurred, which creates a potential enforcement gap that a player can surreptitiously exploit.

For that reason, the referee is allowed to use the replay equipment to determine who should be assessed a penalty. Once the video assistant has booted up and tested the equipment, it may be used for any pregame infractions that warrant an extra look. Typically, the television networks use the warm-up period to collect footage and to help camera operators identify players. If there is video that shows the extent of the major participants' role in the altercation, the referee may use that to call unsportsmanlike conduct and disqualification fouls.

Once the game begins, replay is not permitted for these types of fouls. If an instigative action is missed during the course of the game and the retaliator is penalized, there is no recourse unless another official sees the initial foul. However, this does not preclude the league office from fining players who commit unsportsmanlike actions during the game, even if a penalty is not assessed.

GAME BALLS

Each team must provide a set of game balls to the officials' locker room two hours and 15 minutes prior to kickoff. In addition, the crew receives special kicking balls directly from the manufacturer.

4. How many game balls are prepped for a typical game?

Counting the supply from the home team, the visiting team, and the kicking balls, there can be anywhere from 30 balls for an indoor game up to 54 for an outdoor game. Each ball must be inflated to 12½ to 13½ pounds per square inch and examined for defects. The crew then applies an imprint on the balls that pass inspection. Each crew has a different imprint: The crews for Ed Hochuli and Bill Vinovich use an ink stamp with the referee's uniform number in a circle—85 and 52, respectively. *Sports Illustrated* writer Peter King shadowed Gene Steratore's crew in 2013, and he noted that the crew marks each ball with the letter *L* in a silver marker, the initial of the crew chief's wife, Lisa. The marking on the ball keeps practice balls from getting mixed in with the game-ball supply.

The home team is responsible for supplying five game-ball attendants, and the visiting team may provide up to two attendants if it wishes.

In a single season, Wilson Sporting Goods is contracted to provide over 27,000 game balls, as well as a large supply of balls for promotional and charity purposes.

5. The kicking balls are subject to a separate procedure. How are the kicking balls handled?

In 1999 the league instituted a procedure requiring that balls designated for kicking plays—known as the K balls, for their special marking—be shipped directly from the manufacturer to the officials' hotel. This became necessary after revelations that equipment managers were baking footballs in ovens and using belt sanders and vises to slightly deform the shape to be favorable to kickers.

The officials must break the seal on the carton, and the balls are given to each team's equipment staff after the air pressure is checked. Both teams can use only cloths or soft horsehair brushes to remove the waxy surface off the balls. The K balls were once ruled to remain out of the team's possession entirely, but a concession was made after the 2006 season. In an NFC Wild Card Playoff game that season, the Dallas Cowboys lost to the Seattle Seahawks after quarterback Tony Romo was unable to handle the slippery new K ball on a potential game-winning field goal.

One of the five ball attendants is responsible for the K balls throughout the game; this person is monitored by a league-hired K-ball coordinator. The balls are numbered one through six, and the K-ball handler will use the lowest-numbered ball throughout the game as long as possible. (Generally one team is assigned even numbers and the other odd numbers.) If a ball becomes unusable, goes into the stands, or is removed for historical preservation (a milestone field goal or a kickoff return), the attendant will go to the next numbered ball in sequence.

6. On November 29, 2009, the Baltimore Ravens were deadlocked 17–17 against the visiting Pittsburgh Steelers. The Ravens had the ball on fourth down with the clock running at 20 seconds, unable to stop the clock. In the chaos of the mass substitution by both teams to bring out their field goal units, the officials were trying to get a K ball out for the field goal kick and inadvertently did not spot it correctly. The field goal was short, and the game went into overtime. Under current protocols, what are officials supposed to do differently?

In this game, the crew inadvertently did not apply the two-minute fumble rule on the third-down dead-ball spot because the officials had only a few seconds to race to their standard field goal positions, count the players, and make sure that the offense was set properly. As a result of this play, the officiating department stated that, going forward, the crew should spot the first available ball, even if it is not a K ball, when there is a time element added to the field goal setup. This officiating mechanic was established because there would be no time for an attendant to select a particularly favorable ball for a kicker from the standard ball supply.

If there is not a time element of a clock running out, the crew will just reset the play clock to 25 seconds and stop the game clock only if there is an undue delay.

7. What happens if there aren't enough playable balls during the game?

There will always be an ample supply of footballs available for a game, but it is theoretically possible for a collection of game balls to suddenly become unplayable or have a foreign substance inadvertently or deliberately placed on them. If the home team ball supply is exhausted or unusable, there is a provision for the referee to "secure a proper ball from the visitors and, failing that, use the best available ball."

Because the kicking balls are to be delivered directly to the officials for game day, there is a provision for shipping problems. Each team has two games' worth of kicking balls in sealed cartons as a contingency.

In the 1940 NFL Championship game, Chicago defeated Washington 73–0 by scoring 11 touchdowns. Because there was no net behind the goalposts as there is today, many of the game balls were going into the stands as souvenirs. The officials told the Bears in the third quarter that they could not kick for a point-after-touchdown because the ball supply was dwindling. There was no two-point conversion rule at the time, so all successful runs and passes were still one point each.

8. It was a frigid day at TCF Bank Stadium in Minneapolis on November 30, 2014. Vikings home games were played at the University of Minnesota while a new stadium was being built. At the start of this contest against the Carolina Panthers, the kickoff temperature was 12 degrees with a wind chill of −7. The ball attendants were seen on television warming the footballs in front of a sideline heater. Is this legal?

Although this practice was being carried out on both sidelines, one of the league supervisors stopped it during the game. The NFL's policy is that sideline heaters cannot be used to warm the footballs once they are inspected by the officials before the game. Although the goal was to be helpful to both teams, it is not something that can be done on a consistent basis throughout the game, which could disadvantage one team.

There is no distance penalty assessed, but the league can fine a team as much as $25,000 for the infraction. In this case both teams were informed that this was not an acceptable practice, and it stopped immediately.

Incidentally, this was the first season that the Vikings had a home game scheduled outdoors (not including a relocated game in 2010) since the Metrodome opened in Minneapolis in 1982, so this was new territory for the ball attendants.

About a month and a half later in the AFC Championship game, the New England Patriots were accused of deliberately deflating their team's game balls after the pressure was checked by referee Walt Anderson. Anderson is one of the few referees who personally checks the air pressure prior to the game, rather than delegating the duties to another official.

In the second quarter, Colts linebacker D'Qwell Jackson intercepted a pass from Patriots quarterback Tom Brady, and Jackson handed the souvenir ball to the equipment staff for safe keeping. The Colts, already suspicious that the Patriots let air out of game balls in previous games, checked the air pressure and found it to be below the minimum 12.5 pounds per square inch. The Colts bench brought the underinflated ball to the attention of alternate referee Clete Blakeman.

9. What can Blakeman do in this situation?

There are only two provisions in the rules regarding the condition of the game balls. First, the visual and pressure inspection is handled during pregame, and, second, the officials can remove a ball from the game at any time at their discretion. The only thing Blakeman can do is remove the ball from circulation, but seeing as Jackson was saving the ball, that was, in effect, already done.

The officials are not permitted to re-check the pressure in the footballs or to reinflate them once the game has started. Al Riveron, the senior supervisor of officiating and second in command in the officiating department, made an executive decision to have the game balls examined at halftime, which was in his authority to do so. (Separately, the Football Operations personnel had also reached the same conclusion to check the game balls.) Blakeman and fellow alternate Dyrol Prioleau found the Patriots game balls below the league minimum, while ones selected from the Colts supply were in compliance. Riveron had Blakeman and Prioleau pump the balls up to the correct size.

While there was no yardage penalty assessed, the NFL's independent investigator issued a scathing report that led to the forfeiture of a first- and fourth-round draft choice and a fine on the Patriots franchise of $1 million. The investigator also found "more probable than not" that Brady "was at least generally aware of the inappropriate activities of [the equipment staff] involving the release of air from Patriots game balls." Brady was suspended for the first four games of the 2015 season.

GROUND RULES

Of the popular professional sports played in America, Major League Baseball has an unparalleled and extensive set of ground rules to account for the various peculiarities specific to each of its 30 ballparks. For example, Petco Park in San Diego has these specific rules for fly balls to right field:

> Ball in flight strikes the top of the spectator rail at the Right Field Porch and bounds into the stands: Home Run.
> Ball strikes padded Right Field wall and then bounds over the higher spectator rail at the Right Field Porch: Two Bases.

The NFL, on the other hand, has very few considerations to make for the 31 home stadiums and the facilities used for the occasional games played in London and Toronto. Stadiums are now built to exacting standards set by the NFL to make the necessity of ground rules a thing of the past.

A minor ground rule tweak that was once more common: stadiums that the NFL shared with baseball would not have the 6-foot boundary stripe around the field during baseball season. The stripe instead was outlined at its inner and outer limit, but then made solid white once the baseball team's season was over. Only one stadium remains that is a shared facility: O.co Coliseum in Oakland is home to the Raiders and the Athletics.

The only major consideration that is currently made specific for certain stadiums concerns the operation of retractable roofs. The teams that have a retractable roof on their stadium are the Arizona Cardinals, Indianapolis Colts, Dallas Cowboys, and Houston Texans; the Atlanta Falcons will join that list when their new stadium opens (scheduled for 2017). The operation of the retractable roof is not covered in the rulebook; rather it is contained in the *Policy Manual for Member Clubs: Volume II—Game Operations*.

Ninety minutes prior to kickoff, the home team has to decide whether the roof will be open or closed for the game. For a postseason game or the Super Bowl, the league makes the decision on the roof position 90 minutes before the kickoff. If the home team has a written policy for regular season games—for example, the roof will be closed when the temperature falls below 50 degrees—the league will defer to that policy for wild card and divisional playoff games. Conference championship games and the Super Bowl are fully controlled by the league, and the decision is made independent of the local policy.

10. If the roof is open and it starts to rain, can the roof be closed?

The roof is closed if it begins to rain, upon the signal of the referee, at any point in pregame or during the game up to the five-minute mark of the fourth quarter. While any rain is the trigger for the roof to be closed, the referee can delay the closing of the roof if there is a competitive issue, such as completing a drive or a quarter that is nearing an end. If there is a dangerous situation occurring or imminent, such as lightning or high winds, the closing of the roof may be done immediately by the highest-ranking league representative in attendance.

The game continues while the roof is being closed.

After the five-minute mark of the fourth quarter and in overtime, the roof cannot be closed unless a dangerous situation is present.

The first stadium to have a retractable roof was Houston's NRG Stadium, which opened as Reliant Stadium in 2002. A 2013 study by the *Atlanta Journal-Constitution* found that retractable stadiums had the roofs closed for two out of every three NFL games out of an abundance of caution. The retractable-roof policy has never been invoked to close the roof after the 90-minute pregame mark.

Some stadiums also have a retractable wall at one end of the stadium, and a decision to close the roof does not necessarily mean the wall will be closed also. However, the decision to close the wall is subject to the same restrictions as the roof.

11. If the skies at the 90-minute deadline are threatening and the roof is closed, but the weather clears up prior to the game, can the roof be opened?

Once a decision has been made to close the roof—either before the game or during the game—it must remain closed for the duration of the game, even if the weather improves. This has caused some difficulties in game-day planning. Three of the four retractable roof stadiums are in the central time zone, meaning a noon kickoff requires a decision at 10:30 a.m. local time, when the temperature might be cooler than desired for an open-roof game. Jim Irsay, owner of the Indianapolis Colts, proposed a modification to the league policy in 2014 that would allow for the possibility of opening the roof at halftime. The owners approved that proposal—with specific protocols for opening the retractable roof—for the 2015 season only. It will require another vote by the owners to extend this policy or to make it permanent.

12. AT&T Stadium in Dallas is not a Western Hemisphere Stonehenge, but teams that have a late-afternoon game in October against the Cowboys have had to contend with sun glare. This is due to the sun streaming through the glass walls in the west end zone. The stadium has a curtain that can be drawn, but does this follow the same policy as the roof?

Actually, the policy on curtains is slightly more restrictive. If a stadium has a curtain that covers the retractable wall, the home team must make the decision at the 90-minute pregame mark whether the curtain is open or drawn, and must put it in that position no later than an hour before kickoff. However, if the sun starts streaming through the glass in the middle of the game, the curtain, unlike the roof, cannot be closed. It must remain in place throughout the game.

Sun glare has been an issue at least five times since the opening of the stadium, in games against the Falcons in 2009, the Rams in 2011, the Giants in 2012 and 2014, and the Broncos in 2013. The Cowboys played a combination of away and night games in 2010 and had no issue that year.

13. The Green Bay Packers played 126 home games in Milwaukee between 1933 and 1994 in an effort to expand their fan base to a large city and to play some games in a larger stadium. Beginning in 1953, those games were played in Milwaukee County Stadium, the home of the Milwaukee Brewers, which was largely built to accommodate baseball. What adjustments did the NFL have to make in order to fit the football field inside the stadium?

Milwaukee County Stadium was a logistical nightmare at best. The warning track for the baseball configuration cut across the back of the end zone, and the corner of the 6-foot-wide end line disappeared under the left-field wall. In the opposite end zone, players who overshot the end zone sometimes disappeared into the baseball dugout.

Because there was not enough room to accommodate the bench areas on opposite sides of the field, both teams' benches were positioned on the east sideline. The chain crew, which normally switches sidelines at halftime, operated on the west sideline for the duration of the game. Typically, the benches are placed between both 35-yard lines; when they are on the same sideline, each bench area spans from the goal line to the 45-yard line, leaving a 10-yard gap between the benches.

After their December 18, 1994, game against the Atlanta Falcons, the Packers never played another game in Milwaukee, opting to play all of their games in the newly refurbished Lambeau Field.

14. Who makes the decision to place the benches on the same sideline?

It is entirely the option of the home team, by Rule 1-4, but league policies prohibit an arbitrary change to a bench location. Each team must declare the location of the home and away benches to the league in the off-season. If there is a need to make an emergency alteration or if the game is relocated to another site, there are provisions to guide bench positioning.

15. Can the owner change the color of the field as long as it isn't too similar to the color of the team's jersey or the ball?

In March 2011 the league amended the rulebook to mandate, "The surface of the entire Field of Play must be a League-approved shade of green." It is hard to miss, as it is right inside the front cover in Rule 1–1.

This means that Boise State University could never host a neutral-site or relocated NFL game. The field at the university's Albertsons Stadium is dyed a deep blue and is colloquially known as the "Smurf Turf." While the NFL rule excludes this and a handful of other college venues, its purpose is to head off the temptation of an owner to paint the field with a sponsor's colors.

16. What if a stadium or a city presents any other situation where ground rules must apply?

It is up to the commissioner to establish ground rules based on fixed conditions that cannot be remedied. If the situation occurs prior to a game, it is up to a mutual decision by both coaches, and if they cannot come to an agreement, the referee makes the final call.

Some other notable instances of ground rules that the NFL had to use:

- An impromptu playoff game in Chicago to determine the 1932 champion had to be moved indoors due to a blizzard. The Chicago Bears and Portsmouth Spartans played on an 80-yard field, with the ball returned to the 20-yard line each time a team crossed midfield. (At the time, there were no championship games, and the team with the best record was declared champion. The Bears and Spartans were tied, so both teams agreed to a playoff game.)
- The Baltimore Colts could not schedule a kickoff earlier than 2 p.m. on a Sunday due to local blue laws. The restriction was removed from the city charter in 1982, but the team hastily moved to Indianapolis days later.
- The 1960 and 1963 NFL Championship games were moved to a noon kickoff, local time, because Philadelphia's Franklin Field and Chicago's Wrigley Field, respectively, did not have lights. Because championship games had an overtime provision, there was a concern the game could stretch to dusk.

COIN TOSS

The coin toss procedure is, for the most part, identical for the start of the game and at the start of overtime. However, the more notable coin tosses seem to come after regulation time.

On December 22, 1962, in the third year of the American Football League, the championship game held at Jeppesen Stadium in Houston would take more than one overtime period to decide. The 1962 title was up for grabs between two Lone Star State teams: the Dallas Texans and the Houston Oilers. (Today, these teams are the Kansas City Chiefs and the Tennessee Titans.)

At the beginning of overtime, with 40-mile-per-hour winds whipping through the outdoor stadium, Texans coach Hank Stram told Abner Haynes, the team captain, that they wanted the wind to their backs, so they should kick off to the scoreboard clock in the south end zone.

Because ABC Sports sideline reporter Jack Buck brought a microphone onto the field, the entire exchange during the coin toss was broadcast. This was unusual for its time; it would be another 12 years before referees wore wireless microphones to announce penalties and broadcast the coin toss.

17. When the Texans won the overtime coin toss, Haynes told referee Harold Bourne, "We will kick to the clock." How is this properly assessed?

The winner of the coin toss is given two options: (a) whether they want to *receive or kick*, or (b) which end zone they wish to defend. The losing team chooses the other option. By saying "kick to the clock," Haynes was indicating he wanted to defend the north end zone, but as a literal matter, his first choice was "We'll kick."

Bourne seemed to accept Haynes's selection by reiterating it: "You're going to kick? To the clock?" Bourne even gave a signal to show the Texans were going to have the wind at their backs. After consulting with another official, Bourne realized he had to ask the Oilers for their option. Since the Texans took choice A, that left the Oilers with choice B, the option of which goal to defend. The Texans essentially wound up missing out on both options.

The Texans eventually were able to get the wind at their backs, as the two teams switched sides at the start of the second overtime period. The Texans, in their final game before their move to Kansas City, won the title on a field goal in the third minute of the second overtime.

In a case like this, where a captain has given an invalid response, the referee is in a position to clarify the choice. Although Rule 4–2–2 states that the captain's first choice "is final and not subject to change," this is widely interpreted that once a captain has made a clearly understood choice, it is irrevocable.

On Thanksgiving Day in 1998, the Pittsburgh Steelers were visiting the Detroit Lions, and the game went into overtime tied 16–16. The Steelers captain calling the toss was Jerome Bettis, and referee Phil Luckett asked Bettis to call heads or tails while the coin was in the air.

Television viewers heard Bettis say "tails." Luckett said, as the coin landed, "Heads. The call is heads."

The coin came up tails, and the Lions won the toss and scored a field goal on their first possession.

18. After Pittsburgh TV station KDKA enhanced the audio, Bettis was heard to say "heh-tails." Luckett took this to be "heads." Was Luckett correct?

Despite his status as a perennial punchline and being put in a media pillory for years to come, one thing is certain: Phil Luckett was right.

Luckett may accept only the first call of the coin, and in this case he heard "heads" first. Even though Bettis retracted his choice midsyllable, he communicated an intent to call heads first. Since the coin was in the air, there was no time for deliberation about the choice.

19. Could Luckett have voided the coin toss and reflipped the coin for a clearer response?

That option was available to Luckett, but he believed he had a call of heads first, so he was convinced he made the correct call. The rulebook supports his judgment, but if he thought there was ambiguity, the rulebook does not preclude a second coin flip.

In failing to acknowledge its support of Luckett, the NFL did not tamp down the controversy. The officials' union implored the league to back the call, but the league refused to do so publicly. Luckett even qualified for a playoff assignment that year; he was assigned as an alternate official but paid the higher amount he would have earned if he had been on the field.

Between Thanksgiving Day and the remaining Week 13 games on Sunday, the league office revised the coin-toss procedure to have the captain call heads or tails and the referee to confirm the choice prior to the toss. Also, at least two officials are to be present at the coin toss.

Fifteen years later, Hall of Fame Jets quarterback Joe Namath was given the honors to conduct the coin toss at Super Bowl XLVIII. (It is now typical procedure for a football celebrity to do the honors at the championship game, rather than it being a referee duty.) Namath prematurely flipped the coin before the Seattle Seahawks captain declared his choice. Referee Terry McAulay quickly snatched the errant coin out of the air. If one of the Seahawks had declared heads or tails while the coin was in the air, McAulay would have voided the coin toss.

20. On December 8, 2013, in a driving snowstorm at Philadelphia's Lincoln Financial Field, referee Ed Hochuli told the Lions' and Eagles' captains prior to the toss that if the coin landed in the snow on its edge and not flat on one side, he would reflip the coin. Is this correct?

If the coin does not clearly land on one side, it may be flipped again. In Hochuli's case, it was good foresight to mention this: the coin landed on its edge in the snow.

The referee is also allowed to redo the coin flip if it lands on a player's shoe, but it is considered a clean toss if the coin bounces off the shoe.

21. How many players are allowed from each team to participate in the coin toss ceremony?

Each team may have up to six captains participate in the pregame ceremony. Before the 2012 season, all captains had to be players on the active roster. The rules now allow for "active, inactive, or honorary" captains. Only one of the captains from either team is permitted to choose heads or tails and to declare the team's option after the toss.

22. If a coach sends the entire 11-man starting offensive unit onto the field for the coin flip and declares, "We do everything together as a team," what should the referee do?

There are two officials that assist the referee in the coin toss. The official who escorts the offending team's sideline should intervene and state that only six representatives may meet at midfield.

If the team refuses to comply with the limit of six captains, or if an unnecessary delay ensues, a 15-yard penalty is assessed on the first-half kickoff. In addition, the opposing team is awarded the first choice of options for the first half, second half, and overtime.

23. In the 1986 NFC Championship game played at Giants Stadium, a blustery January wind swirled through the stadium, making passing and kicking very difficult. The Giants won the opening coin toss. They chose to defend the end zone with the wind to their backs. Washington chose to receive the kickoff for the first half. Do the Giants automatically get to receive at the beginning of the second half?

No. Since the Giants were able to have first choice in the first half, Washington gets first choice in the second half. Because Washington chose to receive in the second half (and the Giants, again, defended the goal with the wind), the Giants kicked off to begin both halves. Since Washington never scored, they never kicked off for the entire game.

An important distinction: the Giants did not defer their choice after the coin toss. (The option to defer was added to the rulebook in 2008.) The defer option allows the coin-toss winner to declare the first option in the second half, rather than the first. In this case, the Giants selected field position in both halves.

Deferring on a coin toss in overtime is technically allowed for postseason games, but it is essentially useless. The team that won the toss would have the option at the start of an unprecedented third overtime period; in the regular season, there is only one overtime period, so there is no period in the game to defer to.

EQUIPMENT

The Baltimore Ravens and the Denver Broncos were scheduled to kick off the first game of the 2013 season on a Thursday night, and the early September weather in the Mile High City wound up extending the off-season by about another hour. The kickoff was delayed due to a severe thunderstorm.

While attempting to kill time during the delay, the NBC cameras caught a glimpse of a pregame ritual that occurs when the teams exit the locker room. Back judge Greg Yette was seen patting down several players as they came through the door.

24. What are the officials checking for, and how many players does it involve?

This random uniform check is performed at the start of every game. When the official gives a team a two-minute warning to exit the locker room, he informs a team representative of the players who are subject to this check.

The officiating department gives each crew a random list of four offensive and defensive line positions to check for slippery substances, such as silicone. During the meeting with the public relations representatives at the 90-minute mark, the officials use the flip card (a two-sided lineup card media use for spotting) to determine which players at the randomly selected positions would be appropriate for a uniform check. Obviously, a starter is more likely to be checked than a third-string player, which is why it is not solely based on uniform number.

The same procedure is performed at halftime with a new list of four positions; however, a player who is checked in the pregame might be checked again at halftime. There are four players—two on offense, two on defense—patted down for each team at both times.

At Tulane Stadium in New Orleans on November 8, 1970, the Saints were trailing the Detroit Lions when Tom Dempsey was sent on to kick a game-winning field goal. Dempsey stood on the 35-yard line awaiting the snap—the *Saints'* 35-yard line. (In 1970 the goalposts were on the goal line.) Dempsey won the game with his 63-yard kick, shattering the previous record of 55 yards set by Bert Rechichar in 1953 for the Baltimore Colts. Dempsey was equaled by four other kickers before being surpassed by Broncos kicker Matt Prater by 1 yard in 2013.

However, Dempsey's shoe would be a continuing source of controversy. Born without toes and fingers on the right side of his body, Dempsey had a San Diego orthopedist design a $200 custom-made shoe that resembled the head of a polo mallet. (Adjusted for inflation, that would cost over $1,200 today.) The toe area was flattened off, and the laces were strung down the ankle side of the shoe.

25. Was Dempsey's modified shoe allowed under the rules?

The league office had examined Dempsey's shoe a year earlier when he signed with the Saints as a free agent in the hapless franchise's third season. (When with the Chargers, Dempsey was in the American Football League.) It was noted that the shoe was lighter than a traditional one, but that there was nothing illegal about the shoe.

Dallas Cowboys president and general manager Tex Schramm, who headed the league's competition committee, disagreed. "I have great admiration for Dempsey in overcoming his physical disability," Schramm said three days after the record-setting kick, "but I believe he should use the same surface to meet the ball that other kickers use."

Figure 1.1.   Saints kicker Tom Dempsey kicks a 63-yard field goal which re-mained in the record books as the longest field goal for 43 years. Dempsey was not born with a fully formed foot or hand on the right side of his body, so he wore a specially designed shoe on his kicking foot, which generated some controversy.
© Bettmann/Corbis / AP Images

Schramm argued that the league office did not have the authority to ap-prove a shoe that was not standard manufacturer's stock available for retail sale, and thus unacceptable under the policies set by the commissioner. This policy was intended to address metal inserts and other enhancements to the standard shoe.

Schramm eventually won his argument, as the owners approved a rule change in 1977 that stated that "any shoe that is worn by a player with an artificial limb on his kicking leg must have a kicking surface that conforms to that of a normal kicking shoe."

26. Could Dempsey have used a detachable toe for kicking plays?
The rules specifically prohibit a detachable kicking toe to be used on a player's shoe. If the attachment came flying off during a kick, it would be a player-safety issue.

27. On October 20, 2002, Rams kicker Jeff Wilkins kicked three field goals and three extra points against the Seattle Seahawks at the Edward Jones Dome in St. Louis. He did not have a shoe on his kicking foot. Is the practice of kicking barefoot currently legal?

Barefoot kicking was a bit of a novelty item in the NFL, particularly in the 1980s. New England Patriots kicker Tony Franklin began the practice in 1979, and since then a small number of full-time barefoot kickers are known to have kicked in the league. A few punters and kickoff specialists still had a bare kicking foot into the late 1990s, and Wilkins revived the practice at the start of the 2002 season. Barefoot kicking is still allowed under the current rules, as long as the kicker or punter has a shoe on the nonkicking foot.

After the game against the Seahawks, the Rams had a bye week. When they faced the Arizona Cardinals the following week, Wilkins had two shoes on his feet. While there are no official statistics kept, it appears that there has not been a barefoot kicker since then, reducing this kicking practice in the annals of the NFL to a footnote.

TWO

KICKOFFS

Ambush.

—Saints head coach Sean Payton calling for a surprise onside
kickoff to start the second half, Super Bowl XLIV,
February 7, 2010

When Princeton and Rutgers assembled their respective teams on November 6, 1869, the game they played only slightly resembled modern football, looked a little like rugby, and was a lot like soccer. Nonetheless, the emphasis on kicking and the prohibition on throwing the ball gave the game the name *football*. Historians have labeled this the first intercollegiate football game, although that designation, much like the origins of baseball, is up for debate.

The early game featured continuous play, just like soccer, but the remaining relic of the era was the start of play via a deep kickoff to the other team. Now, nearly a century and a half later, the kickoff has been subject to scrutiny by the NFL as a high-risk play when injury rates from it are compared to those from other types of plays. This link to the past could be phased out entirely, as commissioner Roger Goodell openly pondered in a cover story that appeared in *Time* magazine December 17, 2012.

When the brash, nonconformist XFL league formed in 2001, it removed the kickoff entirely. The initial possession of the game was awarded after two opposing players charged for the ball at midfield, which looked like it was going to cause a compressed spinal column every time it happened.

For now, the kickoff is here to stay. The ball initially was placed at the 40-yard line, then moved back incrementally through the years to the 30 before returning to the 35 in 2011. Other reforms have eliminated the oncoming-locomotive-type hits like a wedge—three or more players in a line converging on blocking members of the kicking team. Now an illegal wedge is a 15-yard penalty.

The rulebook uses the term *free kick* to denote any kickoff following any score (including a safety) and to begin either half or overtime. The free kick after a safety, however, has specific restrictions.

1. A team's placekicker is injured making a tackle earlier in the game, and the punter has to substitute for him. For the kickoff to start the second half, can he punt the kickoff?

For all kickoffs, except those that follow a safety, the ball can be put into play only by a placekick or a dropkick. The kicker also has the choice of using a tee or not. The punted kickoff is a 5-yard penalty; the receiving team can accept that penalty at the dead-ball spot (assuming the receiving team does not lose possession during the play) or force a rekick 5 yards back.

2. On a kickoff, if the kicker kicks the ball after the wind blows the ball off the tee, is it a live ball?

No, the play will be whistled dead as soon as the ball falls off the tee. This is a dead ball because the ball falling off the tee could result in the ball rolling forward, which would inadvertently have the ball beyond the kicking team's restraining line. It is not a penalty, because there is no deliberate action by the kicking team to place the ball beyond that line. The play clock will reset to 25 seconds to allow the kicking team to respot the ball.

If the ball falls off the tee a second time, the kicking team is required to have one of its players hold the point of the ball while it's on the tee.

3. Tennessee Titans kicker Rob Bironas was attempting an onside kick in a November 14, 2013, game against the Indianapolis Colts. Bironas placed the ball on the ground without a tee in such a way that the long axis of the ball was parallel to the 35-yard line. What is the proper call in this situation?

A. Once Bironas has left the ball on the ground, the back judge blows his whistle to have Bironas set the ball correctly.
B. When the ball is kicked, a flag is thrown for an illegal kick penalty.
C. When the ball is kicked, a flag is thrown for an illegal formation for not having a holder holding the ball when there is no tee.
D. This is a legal placement for the kick.

Even though there is no tee involved in Bironas's kickoff, there is no requirement that someone has to hold a placekick. He can legally place the ball flat on the ground, so D is the correct answer. Since this game was played outdoors at LP Field in Nashville, the wind could have made the holder necessary, but it would not have been required on the first attempt.

4. In the same situation, would it be legal if Bironas lays the ball on the ground and props up one point of the ball on the tee?
The kicker may place the ball on or off the tee in any manner he chooses, so long as the tee itself is in its standard upright position and the ball is not beyond the free kick line. The other restriction on the kicker is that once the ball is placed on the tee, the tee may not be moved. If he moves the tee, the officials will stop the play clock and reset it to 25, informing the kicker of the restriction without penalty.

The 25-second play clock starts after the back judge hands the kicker the ball.

5. If Bironas is kicking on a grass field, can he prop up the ball on a chunk of grass that came up from a divot?
When the NFL determined, in 1932, that it would keep a rulebook separate from college football, the league initially adopted seven rules that would differ from the college game. One of those rules permitted a kicker to elevate the ball by building a "natural tee made from the soil in the immediate vicinity of the point of kickoff." By 1939 the kicker was limited to a 3-inch elevation of the ball.

Artificial tees were permitted starting in 1948, and with the proliferation of artificial turf fields, the natural tee was abolished in 1983. In 1994 the height of the tee was standardized to 1 inch.

6. What is the minimum number of players a kicking team must have on the field for a legal kickoff?

In order to have a legal formation at the kickoff, there must be nine players lined up for the kicking team. Rule 6–1–3 states that there must be at least four players in formation on either side of the ball. If there are fewer than nine players on the field, it results in an illegal formation penalty.

If one of the kicking-team players is holding the ball on the tee, he counts toward the four-player minimum for either side of the kicker. It does not matter which side of the ball the holder is on, since his position is not strategic, but instead mandated by necessity.

To reduce injuries, all kicking-team players, with the exception of the kicker, can line up no farther than 5 yards behind the restraining line. They must also be spread apart: at least three players must be outside of the hash marks on the field, and at least one of those three must be outside the yard numerals painted on the field.

7. What is the correct spot on these onside kick attempts, assuming the kick was made from the 35-yard line?

    A. The receiving team touches the ball at the 44, and the kicking team recovers at the 42.

    B. The kicking team touches the ball at the 42, and the receiving team recovers at the 44.

    C. The receiving team touches the ball at the 44, and the ball goes out of bounds at the 42.

    D. The ball rolls untouched to the 42, where it stops in the field of play, and no player from either team makes an attempt to recover.

The kicking team is entitled to recover the kickoff once it has gone 10 yards, or to the receiving team's restraining line. Once the ball is kicked, the receiving team may cross that restraining line to recover the kick; however, once they touch the ball, either team may recover. In situation A, the ball did not need to go 10 yards, so the kicking team gets the ball at the 42.

The 10-yard prohibition on the kicking team applies equally to recovering or touching the ball. If the receiving team gets possession of the ball, it is a 5-yard penalty from the dead-ball spot, or, regardless of which team takes possession, the receiving team may take possession at the spot of the illegal touch. In situation B, the 5-yard penalty would give the receiving team the ball at the 39.

It is a foul if the ball goes out of bounds from the kick or if a kicking-team player is the last one to touch the ball before it goes out of bounds. However, if the receiving team was the last to touch it, there is no foul, as in scenario C; the receiving team gets the ball at the 42.

If neither team attempts to recover the ball before it has traveled 10 yards, and provided it stays in bounds, it is a short free kick. The ball is spotted at the 30-yard line for a rekick.

FREE KICK AFTER A SAFETY

After a safety, the team that was scored against will kick off to the other team. This free kick after a safety is taken from the 20-yard line (unless there was a penalty enforced between downs that moves the line), and the receiving team can line up no closer than 10 yards away.

Late in a game between the New England Patriots and the Pittsburgh Steelers on October 30, 2011, the Patriots fumbled the ball out of bounds in their own end zone, resulting in a safety for the Steelers. Down by eight points with eight seconds to go in the game, Patriots kicker Stephen Gostkowski drop-kicked the free kick in an onside-kick attempt.

8. Was this kick legal?

First, an onside kick may be attempted on a free kick following a safety. Typically, the ball is punted in this situation, but the drop kick is perfectly legal. He also may placekick the ball, but the use of a tee is prohibited on the free kick following a safety. Because of the lack of a kicking tee, most teams opt to punt the ball following a safety.

The free kick after a safety is treated just like any standard kickoff, in that the ball must go at least 10 yards or be touched by the receiving team before the kicking team is allowed to touch the ball.

9. Gostkowski's kick went out of bounds without a player from the receiving team touching the ball. Is this a penalty?

As in a standard kickoff, it is a foul to kick the ball out of bounds, but the penalty yardage is slightly different. While a regular kickoff penalty is 25 yards from the kickoff spot, a safety kick is 30 yards from the spot of the kick. In both instances, however, the receiving team may take the ball at the out-of-bounds spot if it is more advantageous, which is what the Steelers opted for.

If one of the Steelers touched the ball prior to it going out of bounds, then it would be Steelers ball at the out-of-bounds spot, but not a foul.

10. Another onside safety kick was attempted by a punt in a game to decide the NFC North title on December 28, 2014, at historic Lambeau Field. The Detroit Lions committed a safety with 2:32 remaining in the fourth quarter, trailing the Green Bay Packers 30–14. Punter Sam Martin kicked the safety kick high in the air about 20 yards. What must the officials be watching for specific to this situation?

With the ball popped straight up in the air, three Packers players signaled for a fair catch. This means that all of the Packers get an unimpeded chance to catch the ball. Typically on an onside kick, players from both teams attempt to occupy the same physical space to get the loose ball; here, the Lions may not make contact and must give the Packers the opportunity to make a fair catch.

If the ball is caught by the Packers, the play is dead immediately, and it does not matter if the player who signaled for a fair catch made the catch.

However, on this play, the ball hit the ground, which made it a live ball for either team to recover. Even though the ball was punted for the safety kick, the kick has *kickoff* properties, not punt properties. Once the ball hits the grass, the fair-catch restrictions are off, and the Lions are able to recover the loose ball, which they did after a scramble.

A legal fair-catch signal is very unusual for an onside kick. For typical kickoffs from a tee, an onside kick would be kicked into the ground, which allows the ball to hop up if kicked skillfully. Because of the contact with the ground, there cannot be a fair catch on that type of kick. If the receiving team makes a fair-catch signal in this case, it is ignored, but it is neither a valid nor invalid fair-catch signal.

RECOVERY OF A FREE KICK

It was a bizarre day on September 30, 1984, in Anaheim Stadium when many once-in-a-lifetime situations happened in a single game.

The Los Angeles Rams hosted the New York Giants for a game that saw the Rams score the NFL single-game record of three safeties (all in the third quarter!), Giants All-Pro kicker Ali Haji-Sheikh miss two extra points and a field goal, and one of the goalposts collapse when the backstop net tangled around one of the uprights.

If you missed this game, there is little chance you will ever see any of those things happen. But it all started with an equally rare situation on the kickoff.

Haji-Sheikh kicked the opening kickoff to A. J. Jones of the Rams, who allowed the ball to bounce next to him. Jones thought the ball was going to go out of the end zone for a touchback, but instead it bounced straight up into the air. Phil McConkey of the Giants raced downfield and recovered the ball in the end zone.

11. What is the correct call?

Once a kickoff travels 10 yards, either team is allowed to recover the ball and get possession. Because the recovery is in the end zone, the Giants are awarded the touchdown. (Don't celebrate too much, because Haji-Sheikh is about to shank the point-after-touchdown kick.)

Compare this to a kickoff on October 22, 1990, at San Francisco's Candlestick Park. Barry Foster of the Pittsburgh Steelers was deep to receive the kickoff from 49ers kicker Mike Cofer. The ball bounced inside the 10-yard line, and Foster did not make an attempt to recover the ball. Mike Wilson of the 49ers recovered at the 5-yard line.

12. Can Wilson score a touchdown?

On all kicking plays, the kicking team is able to recover *and* advance only if the receiving team has actually possessed the ball. If a kickoff has traveled 10 yards (or if it is touched but not possessed by the receiving team), it can be recovered by either team, but it is a dead ball on the recovery by the kicking team. The guiding principle is that on all kicks—whether kickoffs, punts, or field goal attempts—it is a dead ball the instant the kicking team takes possession of the ball. If Foster had muffed the ball and not recovered it, the 49ers recovery still would have made the ball dead immediately, because the receiving team had not yet possessed the ball.

The only way the 49ers would be entitled to an advance on the play is if Foster established possession of the ball and subsequently fumbled it. In this case, the play ceases to be a kick when the receiving team recovers, and everything from that point essentially becomes a running play.

In the recovery by the Giants, they are entitled to the touchdown because the dead ball and the touchdown occur simultaneously.

BOUNDARIES

The Tennessee Titans kicked off to the Green Bay Packers to start the second half on December 23, 2012. The ball bounced at the 4-yard line, and receiver Randall Cobb had to recover the ball. On the bounce on the icy cold turf of Lambeau Field, the ball made a left turn toward the sideline and slowed down. Cobb recovered the ball at the 4, but his right foot was out of bounds.

13. Where is the correct spot of the ball?

Cobb's actions seemed to have his team—and CBS announcer Greg Gumbel—flabbergasted, because it appeared the Packers were going to be pinned deep in their own territory. However, it was a heads-up play by Cobb, which Gumbel's color commentator, Dan Dierdorf, took note of as soon as he saw the penalty flag fly.

The important thing to remember, based on some of the previous plays illustrated here, is how all kicks are ruled: A *kick* remains a *kick* until it is *possessed.*

When the kickoff is touched by Cobb, the ball is dead immediately because it touched something out of bounds. It is irrelevant that the entirety of the ball is in the field of play; Cobb makes the kickoff out of bounds, which is a penalty on the kicking team. It also would be ruled out of bounds if Cobb stepped back in bounds with one foot down and the other in the air, even though Cobb's body is completely within the boundary lines. An out-of-bounds player remains out of bounds until two feet are down in bounds, an act referred to as "reestablishing in bounds."

The penalty for the kickoff out of bounds is 25 yards from the spot of the kickoff, which is the Packers' 40-yard line. Cobb essentially gave his team a "double touchback" for his efforts.

(Credit where it is due: Leon Washington had a similar play when he was with the New York Jets in 2008, but there was no video of the play available and very little description of the play. One account in the *New York Daily News* says that the officials were initially remiss in giving the Jets the ball at the 40 before they corrected the spot.)

KICKOFFS AND THE CLOCK

The NFL once avoided counterprogramming the World Series on Sunday nights, so it deliberately scheduled some Thursday night games in mid-

October. One such game was at the Pontiac Silverdome as the Detroit Lions hosted the Packers on October 15, 1998. The Packers scored a touchdown with three seconds remaining in regulation but still trailed 27–20. Ryan Longwell kicked the inevitable onside kick, which went past the Lions' front line untouched. Packers special teamer Roell Preston scooped up the ball at the Packers' 49-yard line and ran about 20 yards with the ball before he was tackled. The clock still had three seconds, as it was when the ball was kicked.

14. How should the crew fix this situation?

On a kickoff, the clock runs as soon as the ball is touched by any player in the field of play, but in this case, once the Packers possess the ball, the play is over. As long as the Packers cleanly recover the ball without bobbling it, the clock remains at three seconds. Some crews prefer to have the clock operator hold the clock in onside kick situations, and will make any appropriate adjustment, rather than signal for a quick start-and-stop. This would be discussed when the clock operators meet with the side judge and the back judge prior to the game.

Referee Bernie Kukar announced that, by rule, the Packers would have time for one more play. ESPN analyst Joe Theismann could not believe that, with all the running Preston did on the play, there would be *any* time remaining and openly questioned the competency of the crew. But by the time Preston had the ball, the play was already dead.

15. With three seconds on the clock, assess these hypothetical kickoff situations to determine the time that should remain on the clock:

A. The receiving team player catches the ball at the 45-yard line and immediately kneels to "give himself up."
B. The receiving team player is on the ground and covers the ball at the 45 with no effort to advance the ball.
C. The receiving team player signals for and makes a fair catch at the 45.
D. The kicking team player is the first to touch the ball at the 45, and it takes two seconds for him to secure possession of the ball.
E. The ball goes into the end zone, where the kicking team recovers and does not attempt to advance.
F. The ball goes into the end zone, and the receiving team player recovers and runs around in the end zone to run out the clock.

G. The ball is muffed at the 2-yard line by the receiving team and rolls into the end zone, where it is downed for a touchback. The ball is in the field of play for about one second and in the end zone for four seconds before it is declared dead.

The first five scenarios present a situation where the ball becomes dead almost immediately, but not quite. Once the ball is touched by either team in the field of play, or is in the possession of the receiving team in the field of play, the nearest official will give the signal to wind the clock. Even if the kickoff is a squib kick that takes several seconds before anyone touches the ball, the clock will remain stopped while it bounces around. By definition, the "field of play" includes any part of the field in bounds between the goal lines, so a ball touched or possessed in the end zone still does not start the clock.

For situations A through C, the receiving team's intention is to down the ball immediately. However, when a player surrenders his opportunity to advance—by either taking a knee or going straight to the ground—there is a recognized time element that must occur between the moment the possession is secured and when the dead-ball determination can be made. The rulebook makes specific provisions for cases such as this, and any immediate surrender by a receiver will result in one second being taken off the clock. Typically, this is done as a clock adjustment, rather than a start/stop as it occurs. If the crew feels that the surrendering action was delayed, the officials can adjust the clock accordingly.

Since a fair catch does not require an additional action to create a dead ball, the clock does not run in this situation. In order to be a valid catch, the ball must not touch the ground first.

The kicking team's actions in D will differ slightly than the scenario of the Packers' onside kick recovery. The clock runs when there is a touch in the field of play by either team, unless it is an immediate recovery. If the kicking-team player is having trouble securing the ball or if he muffs the recovery attempt, the clock begins to roll at that point. Only a clean recovery of the loose ball will keep the clock from running.

When the end zone is involved—as it is in the final three scenarios—the clock does not start if the ball enters the end zone untouched, and it remains stopped until the ball is carried out of the end zone by the receiving team. In situation F, the receiving player is expending precious energy for no advantage, as the clock will remain stopped. However, a ball that is touched in the field of play before entering the end zone will result in a running clock, and it will continue to run while the ball is in the end zone.

The clock in these scenarios, which shows three seconds at the kick, will read as follows:

Situations A and B: two seconds
Situations C, E, and F: three seconds
Situation D: one second
Situation G: end of the quarter.

THREE

CLOCK

It's complete to Dyson at the one yard line and he's stopped short! The clock strikes triple zero.

—*Westwood One radio announcer Howard David, on the final play as Mike Jones tackles Kevin Dyson, Super Bowl XXXIV, Tennessee Titans vs. St. Louis Rams, January 30, 2000*

For the first 50 years of its existence, the NFL kept the official game time on the field, leaving spectators and announcers to guess at the time remaining in the quarter. Many times in that era, football was played in baseball parks, which had no need for clocks. For instance, Cleveland Municipal Stadium (home of the Browns) and Yankee Stadium (where the New York Giants played for 18 seasons) had modified analog clocks numbered 0–14. Tiger Stadium posted only the minutes remaining on the scoreboard for Detroit Lions home games.

When stadiums were equipped with clock displays, this timing was unofficial. This led to occasions where there was still time displayed on the stadium clock, but the officials declared the game over. A vestigial rule of that era is that each half of the game has a two-minute warning; without an official clock display, it was the only indication of the time remaining.

When the American Football League began play in 1960, it brought in several innovations that ushered the sport into the television era, including a rule that the stadium clock was the official time. After the AFL merged with the NFL in 1970, the NFL adopted this rule, ending five decades of final-second futility.

1. With the clock running, the side judge notices that the time on the scoreboard clock jumps from 4:00 to 5:00, and counts down from there. What happens next?

The referee and the side judge will check with the clock operator to determine if the clock is malfunctioning. If it is not working properly, or if the clock operator is not working it properly, then the stadium clock is to be turned off and the official time is kept on the field by the side judge. The referee will typically announce the time remaining in the quarter during stoppages in play.

In 2014 the officiating crews were all outfitted with wireless headsets. When the game clock malfunctioned at Chicago's Soldier Field on November 16 that year, referee Ronald Torbert was able to announce the time after each play after the two-minute warning, as the side judge was able to relay that information to Torbert.

2. During a November 11, 2012, game between the St. Louis Rams and the San Francisco 49ers, the clock was stopped at 13:32 to measure for a first down. The clock then started to run during the measurement, and eventually it stopped at 12:20. What must the crew do next?

As of 2013, the game clock is primarily under the supervision of the side judge, matching the NCAA's rules. Prior to that, the line judge was responsible for the game clock.

When the referee's timeout is called for the measurement, it is the side judge's duty to note the time on the clock; however, all officials make it routine to also check the clock after each play. In the Rams–49ers game, at least one official seemed to notice a clock discrepancy, and the line judge (who had responsibility in 2012) called the clock operator via the sideline phone. The clock operator apparently said there was no clock error. The line judge was not aware that 72 seconds had ticked off the clock, so the clock remained at 12:20. The rules prohibit the replay official from intervening to set the clock correctly.

Once the ball is next snapped, the game clock can no longer be corrected.

3. At the end of the second quarter of a game on December 13, 2009, New York Giants kick returner Domenik Hixon fumbled the ball, and Moise Fokou of the Philadelphia Eagles recovered. It appeared that the recovery occurred with approximately two seconds on the clock, but time eventually expired on the play. How is this ruled, and can the time be ascertained by a replay review?

The answer depends on the observable elements when the play is live. If any official has declared the ball dead, and if he observes that there was time remaining on the clock, then the referee can announce that the game clock will be adjusted to that time. The covering officials did not see any time remaining on the clock when they declared the ball dead, so no adjustment was made.

In the case of a fumble recovery when a pileup develops, a covering official cannot immediately whistle the play dead. The official must ascertain that the ball is in a player's possession and not loose. Obviously, when a ball enters a pile, the ball is not observable, but a quick whistle would be a huge problem if the ball suddenly squirted out of the pile. That means the whistle comes only after the ball has disappeared in the pile for enough time that it is unquestionably a dead ball. This is up to the official's discretion, but it is safe to assume that it can be one or two seconds from the point when the official loses a visual on the ball.

The reaction times for the official to visibly signal the play dead and for the clock operator to stop the clock also serve to slightly delay the stoppage of the clock. But this, again, may be corrected only if the official observes time left on the clock.

By watching the replay on television, we potentially could pare down the dead-ball determination to 1/30 of a second, with the addition of hindsight that there was no loose ball once it was subsumed under the pile. If the video is paused at that point, we can examine the clock, but this would cause this fumble to be treated differently than others. There must be some time consumed to declare the ball dead under the pile. Unless possession is clearly visible, the clock must keep running under the assumption that the ball is still loose.

Under the rules at the time, the clock by itself is not a reviewable element that can be confirmed by video replay. For the Fokou play, the officials did not feel there was any time remaining at the point when they judged the ball to be dead. The half was over.

The league instituted a quick midseason rules change to make the clock reviewable in very limited circumstances at the end of a half for the 2009 postseason. It is very unusual for the league to make a rule change during the season, but when it does, the new rule must be reapproved in the following off-season to be made permanent. The league's Competition Committee found this hasty rule change to be very difficult to implement on a consistent basis, and the league owners allowed the rule change to expire without voting on it. The rule was never implemented in the limited number of games that it was in effect for.

Beginning in the 2015 season, the game clock is subject to very limited replay reviews at the expiration of either half. The rule only applies if the game clock operator was remiss in stopping the clock, particularly when a timeout signal occurs far away from the action of the play. The rule, however, will not afford the opportunity for the officials to refine their call to stop the clock, as the signal of an official will be the deciding factor in the review. Also, there is no correction to the clock if the difference is fewer than two seconds, nor in a situation where there is an insurmountable lead at the end of the game.

Incidentally, the clock operators are not hired by the teams, although they typically are nearby residents. As of the 2007 season, the clock operators are employees of the league's officiating department, which is responsible for training and evaluations. For playoff games, the league will send in out-of-town clock operators, which are usually determined regionally and with respect to the conference if the operators' home team is still active in the playoffs.

PLAY CLOCK

4. What is the minimum height of the numbers on the play clock: 20 inches, 28 inches, 36 inches, or 42 inches?

The answer is at the end of this subsection.

5. On October 5, 2014, the New York Jets were visiting the Chargers at San Diego's Qualcomm Stadium. During the fourth quarter, the officials noticed that there was a discrepancy between the two play clocks positioned at the back of opposite end zones. The clocks were stopped, with one showing 32 seconds and the other 28 seconds. How does the referee fix this situation?

Referee Ronald Torbert ordered the play clocks to be shut down, and the back judge assumed timing duties on the field. The back judge is positioned downfield and in the middle, so the quarterback is able to clearly see the back judge's signals showing 10 seconds, and then a countdown from 5.

If the league's game operations manager determines that the play clock malfunction has been rectified later in the game, the digital play clock may be reinstated. However, to avoid a potential recurring error and competitive disadvantage issues, it usually remains shut down for the duration of the game.

Oddly enough, Torbert and his crew would have the same game clock issue at Soldier Field in Chicago six weeks later.

When there is a stoppage between downs for some reason—for example, an officials' conference to confirm the spot of the ball or if a replay review is called—the game clock and play clock are stopped where they are, and resume from that point when time is back in. The play clock will reset to 25 for certain administrative stoppages:

A. Penalty, accepted or declined
B. Change of possession
C. Replay reversal
D. End of the quarter
E. Two-minute warning
F. Charged team timeout

After the two-minute warning, a replay reversal will reset the play clock to 25, but if replay upholds the call on the field, the play clock resumes counting when the ball is ready for play.

6. In Baltimore's M&T Bank Stadium, the Ravens were attempting to erase a 41–24 deficit against the Seattle Seahawks on November 23, 2003. After Baltimore narrowed the score to 41–38, the Seahawks had the ball when a penalty flag was thrown with 58 seconds remaining, stopping the clock. Referee Tom White conferred with his crew, and they decided there was no foul on the play. What is the proper restart procedure?

Once there is a penalty flag, the game clock stops on the conclusion of the play, and since the 40-second play clock has not yet started, the timekeeper will reset it to 25 seconds. It does not matter if the penalty is accepted or declined; with a few exceptions that address deliberate time-conserving tactics, the play clock starts at 25, and the game clock starts on the snap.

However, the flag in the Seahawks–Ravens game was picked up, so there is no accepted or declined penalty. None of the other restart exceptions apply to the situation, so the crew must restart the game as if the stoppage had not occurred. This means the play clock starts counting at 40, and the referee will wind both clocks as soon as the ball is ready for play.

The game clock inadvertently was not started, and the Seahawks missed an opportunity to run 40 seconds off of the game clock. The Ravens also were able to conserve a timeout they might have used in that situation. As a result, the Ravens got the ball back (with the timeout they saved) and scored a field goal to force overtime. The collapse of the Seahawks' two-touchdown lead was complete when the Ravens kicked a field goal to win the game in the extra period. Because of the pivotal error, White was fined $2,600, or half of a game check.

7. At Paul Brown Stadium in Cincinnati on October 6, 2013, referee Gene Steratore called for a referee's timeout, which froze the play clock at six seconds. After a conference with his crew, they adjusted the game clock, but left the play clock at six. Steratore then signaled the ball ready for play and wound the play clock. The Bengals were still in their huddle and were forced to take a timeout. Was this handled correctly?

The Bengals were unfortunate in having to call timeout, and probably could have gotten the timeout back if head coach Marvin Lewis had cited Rule 4–6–3. That rule states that the play clock resumes counting from the point where it stopped unless the clock shows less than 10 seconds; in that case it will restart at 10 seconds.

There were more clock issues that day, as the official scorekeeper noted that when the ball was snapped on a third-down play, the game clock operator inadvertently stopped the running clock. The play was an incomplete pass, so not much time was lost, but consecutive plays were listed in the statistics books as occurring at the same time.

8. Tensions were high as the Dallas Cowboys and Philadelphia Eagles played for the NFC East division title at AT&T Stadium in Arlington, Texas, on December 29, 2013. In the fourth quarter, the Cowboys seemed confused as the play clock expired before they were ready to run a play. After Dallas was assessed a delay-of-game penalty, NBC rolled a replay that revealed the play clock was erroneously reset to 25 seconds instead of the required 40 seconds. Can this clock error be corrected?

There are several ways this could have been corrected, which would have picked up the delay-of-game flag and placed 15 seconds on the play clock—the difference between the 40- and 25-second counts.

First, the back judge has play clock responsibilities, and if he notices an erroneous reset, he should stop the clock immediately. At the time, the back judge was involved with the spotting of the ball and did not see the reset.

The crew could also have discerned that the time between downs was too short by conferencing with the side judge. Since the side judge is responsible for the game clock, and the game clock was running between downs, the side judge could have determined that it had not been 40 seconds since the end of the last play. Failing that, any official who checks the clock at the conclusion of the play can also assist.

If the crew cannot resolve the issue but believe there was some sort of malfunction, the back judge or referee can call the play clock operator booth from a dedicated sideline phone. If the play clock operator explains the error, the crew may also put the correct time on the play clock.

The crew is not permitted to consult with the replay official or a game supervisor to make the clock correction. If the crew cannot rectify it amongst themselves, with the lone exception of consulting the play-clock operator, the delay-of-game penalty must stand. Ultimately in the Eagles–Cowboys game, the crew did not determine any correctable action, other than assessing the 5-yard penalty against the Cowboys.

9. In a divisional playoff game on January 10, 2009, the Baltimore Ravens were driving for their eventual game-winning score in the fourth quarter against the Tennessee Titans. Prior to the snap, the play clock counted down to zero. ESPN.com reporter Tim Graham wrote that the snap came two seconds after the expiration of the play clock. Why wasn't a delay-of-game penalty called with the play blown dead before the snap?

For a species that has two eyes, humans have not been able to observe two independent objects at the same time. Had we evolved as such, this play may have been ruled differently. In this case, the back judge, the late Bob Lawing, observed the play clock counting to zero, then looked down to see if the ball was snapped. At LP Field in Nashville, the play clocks are positioned up on the scoreboards, not along the wall at the back of the end zone. Referee Terry McAulay defended Lawing's call after the game: "So there is going to be a natural delay from zero to getting to the ball," McAulay said. "And when he gets to the ball, if it is being snapped, we don't call it."

What is the minimum height of the numbers on the play clock? Twenty-eight inches.

TEN-SECOND RUNOFF

A 10-second runoff is assessed when an action that conserves time occurs in the final minute of either half. When a 10-second runoff is assessed, the clock is adjusted while time is still out and runs when the referee winds the play clock.

10. Which of the following situations with the clock running under one minute in the half would result in a 10-second runoff?

A. Intentional grounding
B. Delay of game by spiking the ball in the field of play after the play is over
C. Fourth charged timeout for injury on the offense
D. Fifth charged timeout for injury on the offense
E. Fifth charged timeout for injury on the defense, if the defense is trailing in score
F. Illegal substitution by the offense between downs
G. Encroachment, if the defense is trailing in score
H. False start
I. Offensive holding
J. Illegal forward pass beyond the line of scrimmage
K. Illegal forward pass for a second forward pass during the down from behind the line of scrimmage
L. Illegal forward pass from behind the line of scrimmage by an offensive lineman who picks up a loose ball
M. Pass interference on either team
N. Backward pass out of bounds
O. Intentional forward fumble out of bounds
P. Twelve players in the offensive formation for more than three seconds

Even though the offense may benefit from a clock stoppage due to a foul against the team, the 10-second runoff is intended to counter deliberate actions to stop the clock. Penalties such as pass interference and holding are not considered to be deliberate acts, so they are not subject to a runoff. However, if an offensive player spikes the ball (except after a touchdown) or commits a substitution violation between downs, these are considered acts that warrant a 10-second runoff in addition to the penalty.

Addressing some of the other choices in the list, an illegal forward pass depends on where the foul occurs before a 10-second runoff can be determined. Only illegal passes beyond the line of scrimmage are considered to be desperation acts aimed at stopping the clock by penalty. Any other illegal forward pass does not result in a 10-second runoff. An official who observes an intentional forward fumble out of bounds will rule this act an illegal forward pass if it is beyond the line of scrimmage or intentional grounding (presuming all parameters are met for that penalty) if it is behind the line of scrimmage; both cases are 10-second runoffs. A backward pass or intentional backward fumble out of bounds is not ordinarily a foul, but in an effort to conserve time, this is a 5-yard penalty and a 10-second runoff.

The defense cannot be assessed a 10-second runoff under any circumstances. In most cases, fouls aimed at stopping the clock intentionally or injuries on the defense with less than one minute in the period will result in the play clock being reset to 40 seconds instead of 25, and the game clock running when the ball is made ready for play.

Injury timeouts by the offense will result in a 10-second runoff if they have already used all three timeouts in the half, unless the clock was stopped for some other reason, such as a penalty, an incomplete pass, or a running play that goes out of bounds. This is the one runoff provision that applies to any point after the two-minute warning, not just the final minute of the half.

The score of the game is not a factor in determining whether a 10-second runoff will apply. Injury stoppages beyond a team's three allotted timeouts were once subject to a possible runoff only if the offense was trailing or tied in the score; that provision was removed in 2007.

As to when a 10-second runoff is assessed, the correct answers are A, B, C, D, F, H, J, N, O, and P.

11. If the defense is in a situation where they are forcing the offense to punt, can the defense do anything to avoid a 10-second runoff being assessed on the offense to save more time after the punt?

Whenever a 10-second runoff is warranted against the offense, the defense has the option of declining it. They are also able to accept any applicable penalty yardage against the offense while declining the corresponding 10-second runoff. The defense cannot, however, accept the 10-second runoff and decline the penalty yardage.

12. If the defense accepts a runoff, can the offense do anything to prevent it?

If the offense has a timeout remaining, they may use it to counter the 10-second runoff. The referee will always ask the defensive team's head coach first if he would like to force a runoff, then ask the offense's head coach if he wants to use a timeout to avoid the runoff. Of course, if the offense does not have a timeout, that coach would not be consulted.

13. If there are 11 seconds remaining in the half and a 10-second runoff is assessed on an offensive penalty, when does the clock start and how does it affect the next play?

Usually the clock at the end of the half will remain stopped after all penalty stoppages, even if the penalty is declined. However, when a 10-second runoff is assessed, the game clock starts when the referee signals the ball is ready for play. The referee should clearly explain this to the quarterback, because as soon as the whistle blows, the one remaining second will tick off the clock. The offense must be ready in formation in order to put the ball in play in time.

14. Minnesota Vikings running back Jerick McKinnon appeared to score a touchdown against the Atlanta Falcons with 22 seconds remaining in the second quarter in a game on September 28, 2014. The replay review determined that McKinnon was down in bounds, just short of the goal line. The play was reversed to take away the touchdown, and gave the Vikings the ball at the 1-yard line. How does this ruling from replay affect the game clock?

In addition to having a 10-second runoff due to specific offensive penalties, some replay reversals can also incur a runoff. If replay reverses a play where the clock is stopped to a situation where the clock is running, the 10-second runoff rules would apply. Also, as with all the examples illustrated in this section, there must be less than one minute remaining in either half.

In this example, McKinnon is initially ruled to have scored, which stops the clock. The reversal spots the ball short of the end zone in the field of play. Had this initially been ruled correctly, the clock would have continued to run. To account for some of the time that would have ticked off the clock, a 10-second runoff is applied. This seems like it is penalizing the offense for correcting the ruling on the field, but it is intended to take away a clock advantage that the offense ordinarily would not have had.

Just as with any other 10-second runoff, the defense may decline runoff, and the offense may use a timeout prior to the time coming off the clock. In this case, the Vikings opted to not use one of their timeouts; they eventually kicked a field goal instead, but, inexplicably, they still had one timeout remaining as the half ended.

15. If, on the previous play, McKinnon was running along the sideline, and in replay it is determined that he stepped out of bounds prior to scoring the touchdown, does this alter the situation?

In this case, there is no 10-second runoff, because both the ruling on the field and the replay reversal have the clock stopped. As described in this hypothetical example, if the field official had ruled out of bounds, the offense does not get a clock advantage when the play is reversed. Also, since the out-of-bounds ruling precedes the time when the touchdown call stopped the clock, the referee will *add* time to the clock to correct it to the instant the foot landed out of bounds.

Except for the 10-second runoff, the referee cannot subtract time off of the clock in replay, even if there is an obvious correction to be made.

16. During a Monday night game on December 1, 2003, the New York Jets were running out the clock in the fourth quarter with a couple of short runs by running back Curtis Martin. On third down, with less than 40 seconds remaining, the Tennessee Titans committed an encroachment penalty, which stopped the clock. Does this give the Titans a chance to possibly get the ball back after stopping the Jets on fourth down with a few seconds on the clock?

The Titans foul on third down would reset the play clock to 25 seconds, and when the clock is under five minutes in the fourth quarter, the game clock stops when there is a penalty, even if it is declined.

The encroachment foul can give the Titans an additional 15 seconds that ordinarily would have ticked off the clock without the stoppage. To offset this advantage, there is a conserving-time rule that applies to the defense. Just as the runoff rule against the offense is triggered at the one-minute mark of the half, a defensive foul at that time causes the play clock to reset to 40 seconds and the game clock to start when the ball is ready for play. This provision restores the clock to where it would be if there was not a foul in the first place; however, it is not invoked if the game clock is stopped for any other purpose. (This also includes a situation where there are offsetting fouls, because the defense is not solely responsible for stopping the clock.)

There are a few additional criteria to the defensive conserving-time rule that correlate to the offense's 10-second runoff. The offense is given the option to start the game clock at the snap instead of when the ball is ready for play. Also, if the defense opts to use one of its timeouts, it offsets the conserving-time rule: the play clock is reset to 25, and the game clock starts at the snap.

In the Titans' case, the team did not have any timeouts left, and the game clock was under 40 seconds, running. Therefore, by rule, referee Walt Anderson declared the game over in what amounted to a 40-second runoff against the defense.

Similarly, if a defensive player is injured in the final 40 seconds of the half with the clock running and the defense has no timeouts remaining, the offense may opt to end the half at that point.

UNTIMED DOWN

On the last play of the fourth quarter between the Detroit Lions and the Cleveland Browns on November 22, 2009, Lions quarterback Matthew Stafford threw a long pass to the end zone. The ball was intercepted, and all zeros showed on the game clock. During the play, the Browns committed a defensive pass interference penalty in the end zone.

17. What happens as a result of the penalty?

The penalty, first, nullifies the interception. Anytime the defense commits a foul as time expires, the offense is given the ability to extend the quarter by one untimed down. This provision can be used repeatedly, so if there is a defensive foul on the untimed down, the offense can keep extending the quarter until there is one down free of a defensive penalty.

This provision is allowed at the expiration of any quarter. Generally, untimed downs are only strategically favorable for the end of the half, but the offense may opt to extend the first or third quarter on a defensive penalty before switching sides of the field to start the next quarter.

18. On November 5, 2006, Dallas and Washington were battling another tightly contested game in their storied rivalry, down to the final six seconds in regulation. Dallas kicker Mike Vanderjagt attempted a 35-yard field goal to break the 19–19 tie. Troy Vincent, the future NFL executive vice president of football operations, blocked the kick and Sean Taylor recovered the ball and began to run it toward his end zone. Dallas lineman Kyle Kosier grabbed Taylor's face mask and pulled it, drawing a penalty flag. Taylor was able to advance to the Cowboys' 44-yard line before being tackled. Time in the fourth quarter expired during the play. What happens to the foul on this play?

The option to extend the quarter is allowed when there is a defensive penalty. The Cowboys were on offense at the start of the play, but the recovery by Washington effectively reversed the roles of the two teams.

The Dallas penalty was enforced as if it was a normal defensive penalty on a running play, and the 15-yard face mask foul was tacked on to the end of the return. This brought the ball from the 44-yard line to the Cowboys' 29.

With the clock showing zeroes, Nick Novak kicked the game-winning field goal, giving Washington a 22–19 victory. It was a bitter pill for the Cowboys in the two teams' ongoing rivalry.

Vanderjagt, the veteran Colts kicker the Cowboys picked up that season, was perhaps jinxed by a graphic that flashed on the screen prior to the blocked kick, indicating he had 11 career game-winning field goals. Three weeks after the loss to Washington, Vanderjagt was released by the Cowboys, never to kick in the NFL again. He retired from football after playing one final season with the Toronto Argonauts of the Canadian Football League.

19. Would the option to run an untimed down exist if the face mask foul came before the loose-ball recovery by Washington?

As we posed earlier, only a foul by the defense can extend the quarter, and the premise that the offense and defense changed in the middle of the down gave Washington an untimed-down option. Theoretically, since the ball has not yet changed hands, Washington is still on defense and Dallas is the offense in this hypothetical scenario, and thus the ability to have an untimed down has not switched to the other team.

However, there is an exception that closes this loophole. Rule 4–8–2b allows for an untimed down when there is "a foul by the kicking team prior to a player of the receiving team securing possession of the ball during a down in which there is a safety kick, a scrimmage kick, or a free kick." In rulebook parlance, a field goal kick, blocked or not, is a scrimmage kick. The rationale behind this exception is that the offense is surrendering possession by kicking, and that, as long as the receiving team takes possession, that untimed-down option is still available for the receiving team.

Other offensive-team fouls that can result in an extension of the quarter include an illegal touching of a kick, a palpably unfair act (explained in chapter 13), and a personal foul or unsportsmanlike conduct foul that occurs before a turnover or when the offense fails to convert a fourth down.

20. Cincinnati Bengals quarterback Boomer Esiason was intercepted by safety Nate Odomes in a November 26, 1989, game against the Buffalo Bills. Prior to the interception, linebacker Bruce Smith committed a face mask penalty, which wiped out the interception. Since time had expired in the second quarter, the Bengals were able to extend the half by an untimed down. The Bengals were going to attempt a field goal on the untimed down, but a false-start penalty on the Bengals prevented the snap. Referee Red Cashion ruled that, since there was an offensive penalty, the provision for an untimed down was rescinded. Was this the correct ruling?

If there is an accepted offensive penalty on an untimed down at the end of the half, the result of the play is nullified and the half is over. Since there was no snap for the untimed down, NFL supervisor of officials Art McNally determined that the false start foul does not revoke the opportunity for an untimed down. The Bengals should have been given an opportunity to have the snap for the untimed down after the 5-yard penalty was assessed.

21. In the late game of the 2012 opening weekend Monday night double-header, the Oakland Raiders were hosting the San Diego Chargers. With four seconds remaining, the Chargers were leading 22–14, and Mike Scifres was punting on fourth down. The Raiders attempted to block the kick as their only way to get the ball for a potential miracle touchdown. The punt was not blocked, and the ball rolled down to the 5-yard line, where the Chargers downed the ball. Time has expired, but is the game over?

Technically, the Raiders have an option to run an untimed down to attempt a 95-yard touchdown play and two-point conversion. When the kicking team touches the ball before the receiving team on a punt that has crossed the line of scrimmage, that touch is, by rule, a first-touch violation. It is not the same as illegal touching of a kick—for example, a kicking team player who goes out of bounds and is the first to touch the ball—which is a 5-yard penalty. The first-touch violation is tied to any illegal touch foul for the purposes of the untimed down rule.

The Raiders did not realize they had the option and thus did not run a play. They were down by eight points and facing what amounted to a fourth-and-95 play with an extraordinarily low chance of being converted.

A few other notes about the untimed down: If there is a dead-ball foul at the end of the half (and no foul other than another dead-ball foul), then the half is over. If it is the end of the first half, the dead-ball foul carries over to the second-half kickoff. If the game is tied at the end of regulation, the dead-ball foul is assessed on the overtime kickoff. Fouls by both the offense and the defense as time expires also give the opportunity for an untimed down, as long as there is a live-ball foul on the play. However, if the enforcement rules vacate certain penalties, leaving only the dead-ball fouls or no defensive fouls, then there is no untimed down.

INJURY TIMEOUTS

Returning to the aforementioned 2009 Browns–Lions game, Detroit quarterback Matthew Stafford was injured as a result of a legal hit on the play when time expired. The Lions did not have any timeouts remaining, but the defensive penalty was going to give the Lions an untimed down.

22. How is the injury timeout properly assessed? Do the Lions lose the untimed down?

Any injury after the two-minute warning for either team results in a charged team timeout, unless there was a change of possession, a successful field goal, or a point-after-touchdown attempt on the play. However, if an injury is the result of a foul by the opponent, there is no charged timeout. The hit on Stafford was not illegal, so there is no timeout exception for the Lions.

It is irrelevant whether the clock is running; timeouts are automatically assessed unless one of the exceptions is met. It also does not matter that the game is being extended for an untimed down; the same rules apply.

In this case, the Lions had no timeouts to give, so the rules allow for a "fourth" timeout to be granted for the injury without a yardage penalty. If a team must take a fifth timeout, the offending team is assessed a 5-yard delay-of-game penalty between downs.

Stafford is also required to sit out for the next play, a rule that applies throughout the game to any stoppage due to injury. A team may avoid this provision if it takes a charged timeout, but since the Lions did not have a timeout to give, he must leave the field for the next play.

23. During the injury timeout, Lions backup quarterback Daunte Culpepper entered the field. In order to assess their options, the Browns took a timeout. Does this change the situation?

This does change the situation completely and, in fact, the Lions were able to get a major advantage because of the Browns' timeout. An injured player must leave the game for at least one play, unless one of the following situations happens:

A. The injury was caused by a foul by the opponent.
B. The quarter ends before the next snap.
C. The two-minute warning occurs before the next snap.
D. Either team takes a timeout before the next snap.

Even though there was no time remaining on the clock, the next play is an untimed down, so the quarter is not over. But, since the Browns took a timeout, Stafford was able to return for the final play.

24. If the Lions were charged for a fifth timeout on this play instead, does that offset the defensive pass interference and change the extension of the quarter by an untimed down?

The delay-of-game penalty for a second excess timeout for injury is assessed as a between-downs foul. In this situation, the ball would be placed at the 1-yard line for the pass interference, then the ball would move to the 6 for the delay of game. The untimed down would still be allowed under the rules.

25. What if a Browns player was also injured on the same play?

As long as the Browns player is not injured due to a foul by the Lions, both teams are assessed a timeout. In this case, the Lions would be given an excess timeout, and the Browns would be docked one of their remaining timeouts. It does not matter that the Browns' timeout was involuntarily surrendered, and that the Lions have no timeouts to give—the fact that either team uses one of the three allotted timeouts gives Stafford the ability to return to the game.

26. The Tampa Bay Buccaneers were on a last-minute drive, trailing the St. Louis Rams 19–17 during a game on September 14, 2014. Quarter-

back Josh McCown completed a pass over the middle to receiver Mike Evans, who hit the turf and was slow to get up. The play was dead with 15 seconds remaining, but the clock was still running. McCown and the offense were rushing to line up and quickly spike the ball to stop the clock, but Evans was staggering to get to his feet. The officials stopped the clock with eight seconds remaining. The Buccaneers were out of timeouts, so this would be their fourth timeout. How is this injury stoppage properly assessed, and how much time should remain on the clock?

The injury timeout is in effect when a signal is given to have the clock stopped, although it may be adjusted if any of the officials observes that there was more time on the clock when the official's timeout signal was given. That was not the case here, so the clock stayed at eight seconds, and the timeout was not retroactive to the 15 seconds at the end of the previous play.

The offense is given a fourth timeout without a yardage penalty, but when an offensive player's injury occurs with a running clock that is stopped with less than one minute to go, 10 seconds are taken off the clock. The defense does have the option to decline the 10-second runoff as usual, but obviously this is not an option the Rams would request. In this case, the game was over immediately.

If Evans's catch had been incomplete, the clock would have stopped with 15 seconds remaining. The Buccaneers would have been assessed the additional timeout, but not hit with a 10-second runoff. If the play results in a stopped clock, there is no runoff.

The officials could not allow the Buccaneers to run a play with a player who was obviously injured. While it would have been beneficial to allow the Buccaneers to get Evans in a position to spike the ball and stop the clock, a player who cannot move around on his own power must have the intervention of the medical staff before another play is run. Player safety trumps the team's clock-management needs.

27. What happens if Evans' injury stops the clock with 1:15 remaining in the fourth quarter and the Buccaneers do not have any timeouts? 2:15 remaining?

While there is no 10-second runoff in the rules for penalties that occur between the two-minute warning and the one-minute mark, excess injury timeouts are potential runoffs immediately following the two-minute warning. The fourth timeout is granted without any penalty, but the 10 seconds would be taken off the clock, and the clock starts on the referee's ready-for-play signal.

Any injury that occurs before the two-minute warning is not charged as a team timeout, so there can be an unlimited number of injury stoppages at that time.

The restart procedure coming out of all injury stoppages is to handle the clocks as if there was no interruption. The game clock will run if it was already running, and the play clock will resume from the point at which it was paused when the injury timeout occurred. In the case where a team is forced to use one of its three timeouts, the normal timeout restart applies: the play clock resets to 25, and the game clock starts on the snap. Excess timeouts are not treated this way, because a team did not expend a timeout, and the clock will be run or remained stopped depending on its state when the injury timeout was called by the referee.

CALLING TIMEOUT

An unusual sequence of events played out as Houston Texans kicker Randy Bullock attempted to kick a 51-yard field goal with five seconds remaining, tied with the Tennessee Titans, 24–24.

His first kick did not count because the Titans called timeout prior to the snap.

His second attempt was blocked, but since the Titans committed an offside penalty, the Texans had another shot. Time had expired on the play, but the Titans got one untimed down by rule.

The third attempt was from 46 yards. The Titans, again, called timeout just before the snap.

28. Is the second timeout by the Titans legal?

A team cannot call consecutive timeouts between plays, but the Titans were able to take the second timeout because there was a play that intervened, even though the penalty wiped out the result. The offside foul allows the play to continue, but the situation would be different if the Titans were assessed an encroachment foul. If the intervening foul kills the snap, it means there is no play. Without that play, the timeouts are considered consecutive. Other snap-killing fouls include a false start, 12 men in formation, and delay of game.

A timeout can also be called by the opposing team in the same between-play period. Before the second kick attempt, the Texans may also call a time-out, but a play must be carried out before the next timeout by either team.

If a team requests a consecutive timeout, the request is ignored and a legal snap can still occur. Calling timeout when you don't have the ability to call one is not a penalty, unless it occurs to "ice" a kicker (the practice of the defense calling timeout to interrupt and psych out the kicker). Just as in any other situation, play will continue, but the offense will have the option of accepting a 15-yard unsportsmanlike conduct penalty. The same procedure applies to a team that requests a timeout when they have used all of them: no foul is assessed unless it is an attempt to ice the kicker.

Since the timeouts are not consecutive, both timeouts to ice the kicker are legal.

The fourth kick counted. It bounced off the left upright.

FOUR

BASICS OF OFFENSE

C'mon, Lenny, pump it in there, baby. Just keep matriculating the ball down the field, boys.

—*Chiefs coach Hank Stram, referring to quarterback Len Dawson in his legendary malapropism recorded by NFL Films, Super Bowl IV, Minnesota Vikings vs. Kansas City Chiefs, January 11, 1970*

Every play from scrimmage starts with a snap. This very basic element of the game is carried out more than 30,000 times in a season, and, unlike its counterpart in baseball, the pitch, the snap from scrimmage is carried out with little variation.

Deriving from the game's rugby origins, a play originally started with the ball being kicked backwards or rolled with the foot to a player who was roughly a quarter of the distance back in the offensive backfield, or the quarterback. In 1890 the rules were changed to allow the ball to be tossed to the quarterback. After the turn of the century, the use of the modern snap became more prevalent, and the kick method was soon written out of the rules.

1. Which of the following applies to snaps?

A. A snap is considered a backward pass.
B. A legal snap must go through the snapper's legs.
C. A snap must have the nose of the ball pointing in a line parallel to the sidelines.
D. Only a player behind the line of scrimmage may receive a snap.

Rule 3, Section 32 defines what constitutes a snap, and Rule 7, Section 6 governs the conditions of a legal snap. By rule, the snap is considered a backward pass, regardless if it is a hand-to-hand exchange, to a quarterback in shotgun formation, or to a punter or holder in a kicking formation.

The ball does not have to go through the snapper's legs; any toss back or handoff is a legal snap, as long as it is "one quick and continuous motion," as stated in the rulebook. The ball must immediately leave the snapper's hands in this motion.

Rule 7–6–3 states that the "snap must start with the ball on the ground, with its long axis horizontal and at right angles to the line [of scrimmage]." Turning the ball sideways is prohibited.

Choices A and C are correct. In reference to choice D, consider this scenario from college football in the context of an NFL play: The Nebraska Cornhuskers and the Miami Hurricanes were playing for the national championship in the 1984 Orange Bowl. Early in the second quarter, a deliberate trick play was called by Nebraska coach Tom Osbourne. Quarterback Turner Gill intentionally fumbled the snap from center, but continued to fade back as if he had the ball. The ball landed on the ground and offensive guard Dean Steinkuhler picked it up. While the cameras and the Miami defense were following Gill's roll out to the right, Steinkuhler ran to the left and scored a 19-yard touchdown.

2. Is this a legal play in the NFL?

This play is commonly known as the "fumblerooskie" play, and it was created by the legendary college coach John Heisman, but its most prominent use by far was during the Orange Bowl. The fumblerooskie allows the center to exchange the snap to another offensive lineman through a snap that has been intentionally fumbled. No player on the offensive line is eligible to receive a snap, but the fumblerooskie converts the snap into a fumble, making all offensive players eligible to pick up the ball, subject to other rules regarding fumbles.

The touchdown in the Orange Bowl was legal, and it is a legal play in the NFL. Eight years later, the NCAA effectively abolished the fumblerooskie, and the National Federation of State High School Associations followed suit in 2006, by ruling that all intentional fumbles are illegal.

Steinkuhler, the Nebraska offensive lineman, was drafted with the second overall pick in the next NFL draft by the Houston Oilers. Steinkuhler played exactly 100 games for the Oilers in the next eight seasons. In that time, he recovered four of his team's fumbles but never gained a single yard, much less scored a touchdown.

Returning to the original multiple-choice list, answer D is true, with the exception of a fumble recovery off of the snap.

3. Philadelphia Eagles center Jason Kelce was attempting to snap the ball to quarterback Michael Vick in a September 19, 2013, Thursday night game against the Kansas City Chiefs. Kelce assumed Vick was right behind him, and not in shotgun formation. The ball caromed off of the back of Kelce's leg and hit the arm of his teammate, right guard Todd Herremans. The ball was recovered by the Chiefs. How is this play ruled?

Even when viewing the play in slow motion, it is hard to imagine how Kelce was able to snap the ball through his legs and have the ball touch the arm of the player right next to him. As unusual as this occurrence is, the rules state that Herremans is not an eligible snap receiver because he is on the line of scrimmage. However, there is no foul, as Herremans did not take the snap, and the Chiefs' recovery stood.

But, if Herremans had reacted quickly and caught the ball out of mid-air—or, for that matter, made any attempt to gain possession of the ball—this would have been a penalty on the Eagles. An illegal snap in any situation is not a legal play, so the play is whistled dead immediately and assessed a 5-yard penalty. In this case, the subsequent recovery by the Chiefs could not occur, because there was no play.

Herremans can play the ball only if the ball touches the ground first or is muffed by an eligible snap receiver. Although Herremans touched the ball first, he did not muff the snap, according to the rules. A muff is defined as "the touching of a loose ball by a player in an unsuccessful attempt to obtain possession of it . . . Touching the Ball refers to any contact with the ball." As long as Herremans did not attempt to obtain possession of the snap before it hit the ground, he may pick up the ball off the ground as an impromptu fumblerooskie play.

A snap that caroms off of a quarterback may be caught out of the air by a lineman, because in this case the quarterback is attempting to secure possession of the ball. There is no requirement in that case for the ball to touch the ground before being possessed by an offensive lineman.

Because the ball must either touch the ground or be muffed, this is a highly risky play, and is probably the reason there has not been a planned fumblerooskie play in the NFL.

4. In the fourth quarter of a game in Philadelphia between the Eagles and the Chicago Bears on October 21, 2007, Bears quarterback Brian Griese was lined up under center for the team's first possession of the fourth quarter. The snap went through Griese's legs, and Eagles safety Sean Considine recovered the ball for a first-and-goal. The officials conferred and decided that the snap going through the quarterback's legs was a false start, which means the play had to be shut down immediately. That means there was no fumble recovery, and the Bears keep the ball after the 5-yard penalty was assessed. Were the rules properly applied?

Officiating supervisor Art McNally explained the ruling to a pool reporter after the game: "If the ball is snapped in between the quarterback's legs, he has to be the one to get the ball. Under these circumstances, it has to be ruled a false start. If he's in shotgun and the pass is snapped over his head, clean play, pick it up, go ahead and go the other way, everything's fine. The fact that he's taking the snap direct from the center, goes through his legs, he's got to kill it right away, false start."

The rule at hand was added to the rulebook in 1945, but it did not survive the off-season after this play, which would now be ruled a fumble and a recovery by the Eagles. Although the Griese play was not a deliberate act, there is nothing that precludes the center from deliberately snapping the ball through the quarterback's legs to a halfback or fullback.

OFFENSIVE FORMATIONS

The Chicago Bears were lined up for a punt during a *Monday Night Football* game against the New Orleans Saints on December 15, 2014. Facing a fourth-and-3 from their own 39-yard line, the Bears attempted to fake the punt and go for the first down. The Saints were able to stop the Bears easily, because they had only 10 players on the field for the play. A penalty flag was thrown for illegal formation on the Bears.

5. Is it legal to have 10 players in formation?

A legal offensive formation has four basic criteria that must always be met, which apply no matter what alignment or play occurs.

First, there must be at least seven players lined up on the line of scrimmage. There can be more, but there cannot be any fewer than seven. These players must have their shoulders square to the line of scrimmage.

Second, the two players on the ends of the line must have the uniform number of an eligible receiver (see Table 4.1). If one of these players is wearing a number outside of that range, he must report as eligible to the referee. Between the two eligibles on the line, there can be only ineligible interior linemen. Similarly, an interior lineman may report ineligible to the referee if his number does not correspond to his position.

Third, no player may be out of bounds.

Fourth, no player may have any part of his body at the snap in the neutral zone (the width of the ball point to point), except the snapper, who cannot have a part of his body *beyond* the neutral zone.

For linemen to be considered on the line of scrimmage, the helmets of the linemen must break the vertical plane from the snapper's belt. This is not to say this measure is *exactly* followed, but as long as the player reasonably exhibits himself as a lineman, it is legal. If he starts to cheat that a little, a head linesman or line judge will give him a warning during a stoppage in play. Receivers who are on or off the line will often look to a line official who can give them a quick signal if they are in compliance or are too close.

Table 4.1. Eligible and Ineligible Receivers by Uniform Number

Eligible Numbers		Ineligible Numbers	
1–19	Quarterbacks, punters, kickers	50–59	(Linebackers)
10–19	Wide receivers	50–79	Centers, (defensive linemen)
20–49	Running backs, (defensive backs)	60–79	Offensive guards and tackles
		90–99	(Defensive linemen,
40–49	Tight ends, H-backs, (linebackers)		linebackers)
80–89	Wide receivers, tight ends, H-backs		

Defensive players are listed in parentheses, as they are permitted to substitute on offense, but their eligibility is determined by their number.

Note: A player lined up under center to receive the snap is considered an ineligible receiver for that play; this is typically the quarterback, but it can be any player who would ordinarily be eligible.

A quarterback in a shotgun formation remains eligible.

The violation that most often occurs is the eligible receiver at the end of the line: either there are two eligibles at the end of the line (which creates a situation where one is "covering" the other) or an ineligible who is uncovered, which is illustrated in Figure 4.1.

For the Bears, their play was a violation not because they had only 10 players in formation, but because the missing player was a key part of making the formation legal. The Bears had number 72, offensive tackle Charles Leno Jr., at the end of the line, with tight end Dante Rosario set 1 yard off the line of scrimmage. A player with an eligible number should have covered Leno at the end of the line.

6. With the 10 players on the field, is there any way that the Bears' formation could come into compliance?

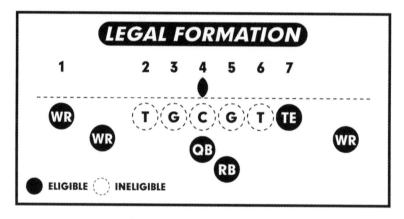

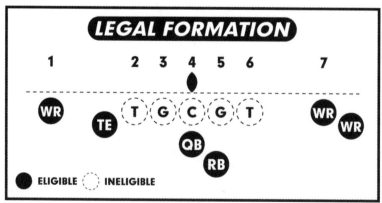

Figure 4.1.

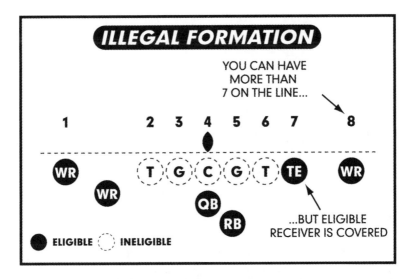

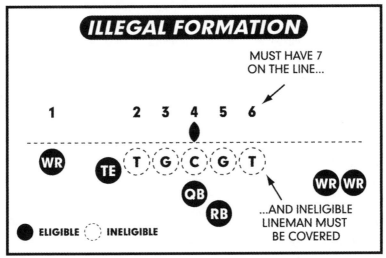

Figure 4.1. (*continued*)

The Bears could have made that formation become compliant, even with 10 players. Any eligible player (including the punter) could have moved to the outside and covered Leno. This could have simply been accomplished if Rosario lined up on the line of scrimmage. The other way to make the formation compliant is if Leno reports to the referee that he is lining up in an eligible position, but he must either report immediately upon entering the game or have done so on a previous play and remained in the game since. Once in formation, the ability to declare oneself eligible is lost.

This means the minimum number of players that the offense can have legally in formation is eight: seven players on the line, and one non-lineman to receive the snap. However, following a timeout or change of possession, the offense must have a huddle of 11 players inside the hash marks so that the referee may declare the ball ready for play. (The team will be warned once if they do not leave the sideline for the restart, and it is a 15-yard unsportsmanlike conduct foul for the second violation.)

7. *On the final play of a December 14, 2014, game, the Tennessee Titans were trailing the New York Jets and were going to attempt to score by lateralling the ball several times to get a touchdown. When the Titans lined up, their interior linemen had the numbers 20, 86, 60, 44, and 29. Can these players with eligible numbers line up in an ineligible position?*

Just as an offensive lineman can report to the referee that he is lining up in an eligible position, a player wearing an eligible number can declare he is ineligible. For the lateral play, the Titans wanted to get more skill players on the field to increase their chance at scoring the touchdown. For this play, 20, 86, 44, and 29 are considered interior linemen and still have to be covered on either end of the line by an eligible receiver. They are not allowed to catch a forward pass, but once the ball is caught it is a running play. They can take possession of a lateral (backward pass, as it is in the rulebook) just as any oversize lineman would be allowed. If there was more than one play remaining, their ineligibility would remain as long as they were continuously in the game.

8. *In a 2007 AFC Wild Card game against the San Diego Chargers, Titans coach Jeff Fisher pulled out an unusual formation at the start of the game. After initially lining up in a standard set, the entire line shifted, leaving quarterback Vince Young in the middle of the field with tight end Ben Hartsock and a running back. Two receivers were behind the line of scrimmage to the right, and six players were on the line far to the left (see Figure 4.2). Can the tight end legally snap the ball?*

This very unorthodox play is known as the "swinging gate," which essentially leaves a minimal amount of personnel in the immediate proximity of where the ball is spotted, and stretches the offensive formation as far as

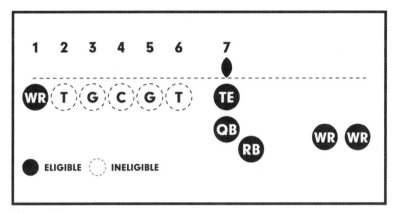

Figure 4.2.

the opposite sidelines. As far as the snap goes, this is a legal play, as the only requirement is that the snap be made by a player who is on the line of scrimmage. Legally, this includes the two eligible receivers who are on either end of the offensive line. Therefore, an offensive guard, a tackle, or even a tight end can snap the ball. A receiver set back from the line or an H-back cannot initiate a snap, because they are not on the line of scrimmage.

In this formation, the intent is to draw the defense to unbalance its attack, allowing the offense either to run uncontested up the middle of the field or to have a receiver unmatched by the defense. However, Chargers linebacker Shaun Phillips revealed the key as to how his team defended the play.

"I hadn't seen anything like that from anything I had seen on [game film of] Tennessee," Phillips told reporter Kevin Acee of the *San Diego Union-Tribune*. "But if they've got eight over there, we need to have eight over there. We just went with assignments. The rules of football are simple, even for a play like that. It was crazy, but we knew it was just a one-play thing."

9. When the tight end snaps the ball, can he catch a pass?

The player who snaps the ball has no restrictions on him for the duration of the play. Even though Hartsock snapped the ball, he can immediately do anything that any eligible receiver can do and is not pinned with the restrictions that the interior linemen have. In fact, Hartsock told a reporter that he was supposed to catch the pass on that play, but Young threw instead to receiver Justin Gage. The pass was incomplete.

SHIFTS, STANCES, AND FALSE STARTS

The Houston Texans were on the defense when the Carolina Panthers lined up in an unusual formation against them on December 18, 2011. Six of the seven players on the line of scrimmage stood up in a two-point stance with the center in a standard position to snap the ball. Quarterback Cam Newton had fullback Richie Brockel right next to him in a half-squatting posture, and two others in a fullback position behind him. Newton took the snap and handed the ball to Brockel through his legs, which the defense could not see with the offensive linemen standing up and blocking the view. Once Brockel had the ball, the entire offense simulated a quarterback run to the right, while Brockel ran to the left for an uncontested touchdown.

10. Is this play legal?

There is no rule that expresses the number of players that must be in a three-point stance on the line of scrimmage or mandates that lineman must start in a low posture. The only restriction on a lineman is that once he assumes a set position, he may not move in a way that simulates the snap. If any of the interior linemen were set in a three-point stance and then moved to a two-point stance, it would be a false-start penalty, regardless of whether the defense was drawn offside. Conversely, an interior lineman in a two-point stance is allowed to shift to a new position or go into a three-point stance without penalty, as long as he is set for a full second prior to the snap.

Compare these two plays:

The first play is from a Thursday night game at Lincoln Financial Field in Philadelphia. On December 13, 2012, the Cincinnati Bengals were attempting a long field goal when penalty markers started to fly. A Bengals lineman jumped out of his stance early when he heard a player in the Eagles defense mimic the cadence of the holder, who was calling the count for the snap.

Earlier that season on October 23 in Tampa, Florida, the New Orleans Saints were lining up for a field goal attempt. The Buccaneers' entire defensive line simultaneously rose out of their stance and shifted over, but in an exaggerated manner. The shift was enough to cause someone on the Saints line to believe the ball was snapped, and he moved prematurely. The play was whistled dead prior to the snap, and penalty flags flew.

11. What is the proper call in these two situations?

In both of these cases, the offense was absolved of the false-start penalty. While the offensive line is expected to remain essentially motionless until the ball is snapped, they are not expected to remain in place if the defense starts to simulate a charge or if the defense has fooled them with a fake snap count.

Not only is it not a penalty for the offense, but it is a huge penalty on the defense. The Eagles were guilty of "disconcerting signals" and the Buccaneers were charged with a "disconcerting act." It is not often called, but Rule 12–3–1 states that the defense is assessed an unsportsmanlike conduct foul for "using acts or words . . . that are designed to disconcert an offensive team at the snap. An official must blow his whistle immediately to stop play."

Rather than pushing the offense back 5 yards on a false-start penalty, the unsportsmanlike conduct foul gives the offense 15 yards and an automatic first down.

The disconcerting signals foul is a difficult one to pin down by the officials because it is so unusual. The defense is allowed to call out its own play signals as well, so any sound coming from a lineman or a linebacker is not, by itself, disconcerting. But a defender who utters a "hut hut!" signal, for example, is not communicating with the defense, but trying to draw the center into an errant snap. Generally, a player on the offense will bring this to the attention of an official during a break in the game, and the crew will be aware of a potential infraction. On the two plays illustrated here, the field goal formation has the umpire and side judge right behind the defense. This provides ample opportunity for one of them to isolate the signals coming from the defense compared to their standard positions at other points in the game.

Quarterback Matt Hasselbeck, while playing for the Tennessee Titans in 2011, also complained after a game that Broncos defensive lineman Kevin Vickerson was simulating the snap count. There may have been merit to that complaint. Vickerson and Hasselbeck were teammates with the Titans and previously with the Seattle Seahawks.

SUBSTITUTIONS

In the early days of the game, teams were limited in the number of substitutions they could make in a game. When the NFL established its own set of rules separate from college in 1932, substitutions could be made only during a timeout or other stoppage, and a player could not return to the game in the same quarter in which he was withdrawn. In addition, teams did not have enough players for separate offensive and defensive squads, which required many players to play both sides of the ball for a full 60 minutes. (See Table 4.2 for player limits through the league's history.)

From 1943 to 1945, teams were allowed free substitution due to player shortages caused by men of that age and physical ability serving in World War II. In 1946 the league restricted substitutions to three players between downs, and the present unlimited substitution rule was adopted in 1950.

The New England Patriots led the Denver Broncos 43–21 with 6:32 remaining in the fourth quarter. While in punt formation on fourth-and-1,

Table 4.2. NFL player limits

Years	Players (active roster)
1921–24	No limit*
1925	16
1926–29	18
1930–34	20
1935	24
1936–37	25
1938–39	30
1940–42	33 (min. 22)
1943–44	28**
1945–46	33 (min. 22)
1947–49	34 (for first 3 games, 35)
1950	32†
1951–56	33†
1957–58	33
1959	36
1960	38
1961–62	36
1963	37
1964–73	40
1974	47
1975	43
1978	45
1982‡–84	49
1985–present	45

* Players were initially subject to territorial limits for each franchise.
** Reduction due to player shortages around World War II.
† Minimum 25 players must be dressed for a championship game.
‡ After the second game of the 1982 season.

the Patriots executed a planned substitution of all 11 players to attempt to cause a mismatch on the Broncos.

12. Is this a legal substitution?

The offense may make as many substitutions as they want, even as they line up in formation. The caveat is that the defense is permitted time to make an equal number of substitutions, and the offense cannot immediately attempt to catch the defense with too many players on the field.

A similar tactic was employed in the NFL by the 1988 Cincinnati Bengals, whereby the offense would get a play call at the line of scrimmage. If the opponent tried to substitute, the Bengals would snap the ball, and the defense would be penalized for 12 men. The Bengals could not do a quick swap in this situation, but they could keep going with the same 11 personnel to freeze up the defense's ability to send in situational specialists.

Various teams have tried different methods of no-huddle and hurry-up offenses to leverage an advantage against the defense, most recently noted with Eagles coach Chip Kelly decreasing the whistle-to-snap time. This is nothing new, as legendary college coach John Heisman used the hurry-up offense effectively at Auburn University—in 1899!

In the Patriots' substitution, umpire Jeff Rice ran from his normal punt position in the backfield to stand over the ball. The Patriots could not snap the ball while the umpire was there. Referee Walt Anderson held his fists out at arm's length, to signal the substitution period for both teams. Once Anderson saw that the Broncos had matched up, he lowered the signal, indicating to Rice that he was to return to his position.

13. If the play clock runs out during the Broncos' substitution, can the Patriots have the clock reset?

The Patriots executed the late substitution at their own peril. If the Broncos cannot reasonably substitute in time, the Patriots are charged with a delay-of-game penalty (or they may take a timeout, if they have one). This does not mean that the Broncos can drag their feet. The Patriots change-out was quick, and the Broncos must exhibit an equivalent amount of urgency in their substitution.

That's also not to say that the Patriots do not get an advantage. If there is a miscommunication on the Broncos sideline, where a substitute misses his assignment, the play would continue with 10 men in the defensive formation, which is not a foul, but a disadvantage. If too many come in on a blown assignment, the Broncos can be charged with a 12th man on the field.

After all of the excitement, the Patriots committed a false start and wound up lining up for a punt after the 5-yard penalty.

14. On November 19, 1989, in the final seconds of the game, the Phila-delphia Eagles were leading the Minnesota Vikings, 10–9, with a fourth down at their own 24-yard line. The Eagles had 14 players in punt formation when they kicked. How is this penalty assessed?

Setting aside the fact that the officials missed an extra three players in the offensive formation—with 12 on the line, a punt protector, and the punter—this was an exploitable loophole that remained on the books for almost 23 years after this play.

Coach Buddy Ryan's corrupt play, further compounded by an ethnic epithet that implied the punt formation originated in Warsaw, actually backfired when the officials did not throw a flag. The intent was to draw an intentional live-ball foul that, if the Vikings accepted the penalty, would allow the Eagles to run additional time off the clock. On the flip side, being massively outnumbered, the Vikings were unable to block the punt.

The play largely passed into obscurity when Vikings quarterback Wade Wilson threw an interception on the next play, which became the focal point of the last-second attempt. However, in ironic timing, the *Philadelphia Daily News* noted the next day that Polish union organizer Lech Walesa happened to be in the City of Brotherly Love, but not to root on the punt team.

This formation, under the current rules, would kill the snap, either on offense or defense. If the offense has more than 11 players in formation for three seconds or if the defense has too many players in formation when the snap is imminent, the officials are to shut the play down before the snap.

Either side may have a player leaving the field, and the play will continue even if the 12th player does not make it to the bench in time. The 12-men foul, in that case, is enforced as a live-ball foul.

LINING UP NEAR THE SIDELINE

Compare these two plays.

Play No. 1: The ball is at the 39-yard line. Cleveland Browns quarterback Johnny Manziel was swapped in for Brian Hoyer on a first-down play during the middle of a second-quarter drive against the Baltimore Ravens on September 21, 2014. After handing off for a negative 1-yard run, Hoyer returned to take the snap under center. Manziel appeared to leave, but he remained in the field of play as an 11th player and was the required eligible receiver on the line of scrimmage. Manziel pretended to be arguing with offensive coordinator Kyle Shanahan near the bench. While facing the sideline, Shanahan gave Manziel a quick "Go, go go!" cue, and Manziel sprinted downfield uncontested for a 39-yard touchdown before he was caught.

Play No. 2: The ball is at the 27-yard line. The St. Louis Rams were hosting a Monday night game with the San Francisco 49ers. Rams quarterback Austin Davis was leaving the field after a third-down play as the punt team entered the field. Davis was 2 yards behind the line of scrimmage with his back to the sideline. The 49ers saw this and immediately covered Davis, so the Rams called timeout with their trick play exposed. For purposes of example, let's say Davis also caught a 39-yard pass.

15. Are these plays legal?

Manziel was too crafty for his own good, as his attempt to deceive the defense was an illegal hideout play. An offensive player is prohibited from lining up within 5 yards of his bench area. This rule was a reaction to a play when the Rams faced Baltimore on September 26, 1954—except the Rams were located in Los Angeles, and the Baltimore team was the Colts. On the first play of the season, no less, Rams quarterback Norm Van Brocklin connected with halfback Skeet Quinlan for an 80-yard touchdown on a hideout play. Commissioner Bert Bell halted the practice, saying, "This thing never should have happened in the first place. No matter how many good rules we have, somebody also comes up with something that we have to correct."

A memo was issued to the 12 NFL teams the next day, making a hideout an unsportsmanlike conduct foul.

Austin may have been the first Rams player since Quinlan to attempt a hideout play, but he was actually in a legal position. The deceptive act is not being near the sideline, but being near the bench area. Austin can't be confused as a player on the sideline, because he is not in front of his team's designated bench area, which is centered between opposing 32-yard lines. Not only is the zone from either goal line to the nearest 31-yard line acceptable, but also the entire 100 yards of the opposite sideline can be used for a legal hideout.

Once Austin is matched up by a defender, as he is on this play, he cannot be flagged for an illegal hideout, even if he is 5 yards from his own bench area.

Manziel is also guilty of an illegal formation foul. As an eligible receiver on the line of scrimmage, Manziel is required to have his shoulders square to the line of scrimmage. The head linesman was also fooled, apparently, as the Browns were flagged for an illegal shift, rather than the hideout or the illegal formation.

16. Why aren't Manziel and Austin guilty of a substitution foul for lining up outside of the yard numbers on the field?

Both quarterbacks are allowed to line up outside of the numerals, which are 12 yards from the sidelines, because they participated in the previous play. Manziel had to come in on the first-down play in order to line up outside the numerals in the second-down play. Similarly, Austin never left the field on third down, despite the fact that 10 players came in from the punt team.

If either player is an incoming substitute, he must reach the *inside* of the numerals (which are 2 yards in height) before retreating to a position outside of the numerals. Failure to do so is a 5-yard illegal substitution penalty. The penalty is off, though, if the defense matches up with the incoming player.

17. On a Monday night against Dallas on October 27, 2014, an incoming substitute for Washington entered the huddle and then returned to the bench after the huddle broke. Another player substituted for him. Assuming Dallas has the ability to make a personnel change, is this a foul?

In this situation, this is an illegal simulated substitution, and it rises to the level of unsportsmanlike conduct, much the same as the hideout play, because there is an intent to deceive. Once a player enters the field as a substitute, he must participate in the following down.

This is not to say that this is an absolute hard line. Discretion is given to the officials, as is detailed in Rule 5–2–5:

> **Note:** The intent of the rule is to prevent teams from using simulated substitutions to confuse an opponent, while still permitting a player (or players) to enter and leave without participating in a play in certain situations, such as a change in a coaching decision on fourth down, even though he has approached the huddle and communicated with a teammate. Similarly, if a player who participated in the previous play leaves the playing field by mistake, and returns to the playing field prior to the snap, he is not required to reach the inside of the field numerals, provided that the defense has the opportunity to match up with him. However, a substitute (i.e., someone who did not participate in the previous play) is required to reach the inside of the field numerals.

SUBSTITUTIONS IN THE HUDDLE

Compare these three huddle situations.

Huddle No. 1: During a 2011 NFC Wild Card game against the New York Giants, the Atlanta Falcons had 12 players in their offensive huddle. Before the penalty flag was thrown, the Falcons called a timeout.

Huddle No. 2: In an October 6, 2013, game against the Indianapolis Colts, the Seattle Seahawks had one player leave the huddle after the ready-for-play signal. After the huddle broke, there were 11 players, but referee Ron Winter threw a flag.

Huddle No. 3: In a 2013 NFC Divisional Playoff game against the Carolina Panthers, the San Francisco 49ers had 12 men in the huddle when an incoming player reported as an eligible receiver. The player reported to the referee after a penalty enforcement but before the ready-for-play signal. On the ready-for-play, one player exited the huddle immediately and ran to the sideline.

18. What is the proper call in these situations?

The 12-in-the-huddle penalty can be retroactively applied in the between-downs time before a legal snap. When the referee has ascertained there are too many occupants in the huddle, the whistle is blown and the penalty assessed. Although the Falcons attempted to head off the count by calling a timeout, the referee is still to complete the count, because the huddle was noncompliant at some point between downs. The Falcons were assessed a 5-yard penalty but were not charged the timeout.

In the Seahawks' situation, there was confusion from the television commentators when a replay showed 11 players breaking a huddle. Winter was accused of failing to count properly. What was not shown was that one player had exited earlier, so the count must include him. The counting was delayed, as the huddle was tight, so Winter is seen stepping in closer, with one hand on his flag and the other on his whistle. Once the huddle breaks, he is able to get a clear count, including the player who had already reached the sideline.

The 49ers were not charged with a huddle foul because the play clock was not running. A player who reports as an eligible position is handled on the fly when the play clock is running—the referee makes an announcement, and crew members mirror a signal with two hands sweeping up and down to indicate recognition. But when there is a stoppage, the announcement and

Table 4.3. Illegal Substitution Penalties

Foul	Penalty
Twelve players in offensive huddle	5 yards*
Substitute enters during live ball (without interfering with play)	5 yards
Incoming substitute does not come inside numerals	15 yards
Illegal simulated substitution (in-and-out player)	15 yards
Player subs out by exiting through opponent's sideline or the end line	5 yards
Illegal return of a suspended player (equipment violation)	5 yards
Illegal return of an ejected player	15 yards
Player reports ineligible, but does not line up in the "core" of the formation (new rule in 2015)	15 yards

*Whistled dead immediately and enforced between downs.

crew signals are handled before running the play clock. This extends the time that the huddle can be noncompliant but still legal. Once the whistle is blown, there is an immediate effort to return the huddle to 11 players, so no foul was called.

While a replay review is allowed to challenge the number of players on the field during a play, the number of players in the huddle is not reviewable.

DOWNS

One of the most basic components of game administration is the down. It is such a routine part of the game that it mostly runs effortlessly throughout the game. Fans watching the game on television are further assisted by the on-screen graphics to inform them of the current down. But it is human nature to get distracted and get mixed up counting something. In those situations, one just stops counting and starts again.

An official does not have the luxury to stop and count downs in the middle of the game as if counting golf strokes. Every official must be in perfect synchronicity with the rest of the crew throughout the game, and low-level bookkeeping such as the number of the down cannot slow the game down.

In 1968 the Los Angeles Rams, with a 10–1–1 record, were just behind the 11–1 Baltimore Colts in the Western Conference Coastal Division. On

December 8 the Rams hosted the Chicago Bears at Los Angeles Coliseum for the game before the season finale against the Colts.

The referee was Norm Schachter, the venerable official who had two years previous been the referee in the first Super Bowl. Schachter was one of the great officials, not because he was first; he was first because he was great.

Schachter and his crew lost track of the correct down on the Rams' last-chance drive in the fourth quarter, trailing 17–16. There were six-member crews then, as the side judge would be added in 1978. An offensive holding penalty—which at the time was a whopping 15-yard penalty *from the spot of the foul*—was assessed on first down, but the crew failed to repeat the first down. The Rams were out of field goal range and faced a second-and-31, instead of first-and-31.

19. Who is ultimately responsible for the number of the down, and when can a correction be made?

Today, the standard equipment for all officials is a finger band that serves as a down counter. It is quite simply a loop of elastic that connects to a wristband. Upon the completion of a down, the referee will signal to the crew the upcoming down. The official will advance the loop one finger on his hand for every down.

All crew members are responsible for ensuring the down is correct. In the unlikely event that the loop and the down marker or referee's signal do not match up, the referee will take a timeout to make the correction. If, for some reason, the crew cannot come to a consensus as to the number of the down, the referee is to make the decision. However, once a snap takes place, there cannot be a correction to the down. If a snap occurs as second-and-31 instead of first-and-31, there cannot be a decision by the crew to make the next play second down.

Oddly, the error in the Bears–Rams game was not caught immediately. Elroy Hirsch—the Hall of Fame running back of the 1940s and '50s who earned the nickname "Crazylegs" for his running style—was the general manager of the Rams. After the game, he asked Art McNally, the game's officiating observer, if the Rams were denied a fourth down. McNally was not sure, as his job was to observe the officials' mechanics, not to log individual plays. Mark Duncan, the director of officials, whom McNally would eventually replace, was able to ascertain the down was dropped when he contacted the cameraman who was developing the game film. Judgment was entered swiftly on Tuesday when NFL commissioner Pete Rozelle issued a statement:

> National Football League game officials erred in not permitting Los Angeles one more down near the end of the Rams game with the Chicago Bears Sunday.
>
> A penalty against Los Angeles on the first down of its final series nullified an incomplete pass play. Following three additional incomplete passes by Los Angeles, the ball was turned over to Chicago, thus depriving Los Angeles of a fourth down play to which it was entitled.
>
> Los Angeles would have started the fourth down from its own 47-yard line with five seconds to play and 31 yards needed for a first down.
>
> All six game officials are equally responsible for keeping track of the downs.
>
> The crew which officiated the Los Angeles-Chicago game is considered among the most competent in pro football. However, because all six must bear responsibility for the error, the entire crew will receive no further assignments for the remainder of the 1968 NFL season, including post-season games.

There was only one more regular-season game, so the entire crew was suspended for one game, but they were also shut out of any playoff games. All six returned to good standing for the 1969 season.

At the time, the replay official wasn't even a figment of the imagination, but now the replay official is not permitted to intervene. In fact, the rules specifically list "proper down" as an example of a nonreviewable call.

Compare these two situations that oddly have head coach Mike Shanahan in common.

Game No. 1: On December 12, 2010, Washington was driving for a touchdown against Tampa Bay with less than a minute left in regulation, trailing 17–10. After a completed pass on first down to the 3-yard line, the down marker showed a 2, leading the television graphics and the scoreboard to show second-and-1. After three incomplete passes, the announcers stated that the ball would go to Tampa Bay, but instead Washington lined up for one more play and scored a touchdown.

Game No. 2: During a *Sunday Night Football* game on December 1, 2013, Washington was trailing the New York Giants at the two-minute warning, 24–17, with the ball and no timeouts, second-and-5 at their own 41. Quarterback Robert Griffin III completed a pass to wide receiver Pierre

Garçon for approximately 5 yards. The first-down chains began to move to mark the new set of downs, but then they halted. Shortly thereafter, Washington snapped the ball, and Griffin threw an incomplete. Referee Jeff Triplette got on the microphone and clarified the number of the next down: "It's fourth down." Griffin was upset because he would not have thrown a deep pass if he had known it was third-and-short.

20. How are these situations properly handled?

At the end of every play, the referee will signal the number of the up-coming down: if the team has made a first down, it is the referee—and not the spotting official—that signals first down. The first-down signal is the obvious open-palm point in the direction of the offense's charge. The other downs are signaled over the referee's head: two fingers, three fingers, and finally a fist for fourth down.

The official down and distance markers are on the sideline with the head linesman; an auxiliary first-down marker and down indicator are on the opposite sideline for information only, as these markers are approximations for the official markers.

In the Tampa Bay game, the auxiliary down box was stuck on 2, leading to confusion in the press box. Referee Pete Morelli clearly indicated each down, and when the auxiliary box was corrected one down later, it was as-sumed by the media and the scoreboard operator to be in error. In all cases, the referee's down signal between plays is the official indication of the down, even if either of the down markers is incorrect. In this case, Morelli prob-ably should have made an announcement of the correct down, but he might not have known there was an incorrect number on one sideline, because the down markers are the line officials' responsibilities.

When Washington was playing the Giants, the chain crew gave a false impression that it was a first-down play upcoming. Because Triplette sig-naled third down at an outward angle, it seems to have been misconstrued as a first-down point without the arm motion. Triplette recognized the game situation—running clock under two minutes with no timeouts—and did not reset the chains. This would have given Washington a brief free timeout to assess their play and get in formation. In this case, the game has to be shut down while everyone is apprised of the correct down. While there is no hard-and-fast rule, it would seem Triplette's logic would be applicable with only a few seconds on the clock, where the number of the down is no longer relevant, but rather beating the clock is.

FIVE

IN THE END ZONE

The game's final play. As Wilson lofts for the end zone which is—brought down by Tate with Jennings, simultaneous. Who has it? Who will they give it to?

> —*ESPN announcer Mike Tirico, calling the*
> *controversial catch by Golden Tate from Russell Wilson known*
> *as the "Fail Mary," Green Bay Packers at*
> *Seattle Seahawks, September 24, 2012*

When the ball is dead in the end zone (or out of bounds through the end zone), one of three results is possible: a touchdown, a safety, or a touchback. While it is fairly easy to determine a touchdown, the determination of a safety versus a touchback rests on which team provided the impetus to put the ball in the end zone.

THE RULE OF IMPETUS

When a mover sets a body in motion he implants into it a certain impetus, that is, a certain force enabling a body to move in the direction in which the mover starts it. . . . It is because of this impetus that a stone moves on after the thrower has ceased moving it. But because of the resistance of the air (and also because of the gravity of the stone) which strives to move it in the opposite direction to the motion caused by the impetus, the latter will weaken all the time.

—Jean Buridan, 14th-century philosopher and scientist,
who first defined the concept of impetus

Impetus is the action of a player who carries the ball or provides the force (i.e., a pass, kick, snap, or fumble) that causes a ball in the field of play to touch or cross a goal line. If a Loose Ball touches or crosses a goal line, the impetus is attributed to the team whose player passed, kicked, snapped, or fumbled the ball, unless an opponent (a) muffs a ball that is at rest, or nearly at rest; or (b) bats a ball that has been kicked or fumbled; or (c) bats a backward pass after it has struck the ground; or (d) illegally kicks any ball.

—NFL definition of impetus, Rule 3-17

The NFL's definition of *impetus* will frustrate physics scholars, because it disregards the principles of force and acceleration, but that is another conversation for another day at your favorite sports bar.

In short, the rule attributes the impetus to the offense, unless one of the enumerated items occurs when the ball is loose as it enters the end zone. On any kicking play, the kickers are treated as the offense. If there is a change of possession during a play, the team that is on "offense" also changes with respect to this definition, but if the ball is already in the end zone, the team charged with providing the impetus does not change. It is important to note that impetus—in the football context—is not automatically determined by the player who physically propelled or caused the ball to move into the end zone.

Following the 1992 season, in Super Bowl XXVII at the Rose Bowl in Pasadena, California, the Dallas Cowboys had the title well in hand in the fourth quarter. Leading the Buffalo Bills by the score of 52–17 with about five minutes remaining, the Cowboys were able to force a fumble by quarterback Frank Reich. Defensive lineman Leon Lett scooped up the loose ball at the Cowboys' 35-yard line and raced to the opposite end of the field.

During the fumble return, Lett's eyes gazed upward toward the scoreboard, where a live video feed showed his 65-yard dash to increase the Cowboys' tally to a Super Bowl record 58 points. Lett began to celebrate early by holding the ball out and slowing down. While he was showboating, Bills wide receiver Don Beebe raced behind Lett and swiped the ball out of his hand at the 1-yard line. The loose ball rolled through the end zone and out of bounds over the sideline.

1. The play was a fourth down. What is the ruling and where does the ball get spotted?

The first thing to remove from consideration during this play is the number of the down. Once the ball was turned over to the Cowboys without any penalty flags at that part of the play, the original down, distance, and line of scrimmage are ignored. (In rare cases, multiple fouls combined with multiple changes of possession on the same play can cause the down to be replayed.) Once the turnover has taken place, whichever team has possession at the end of the down will have a first-and-10.

Lett's fumble is a forward fumble into the opponent's end zone and out of bounds, which is ruled a touchback. Rule 8–1–7 states, "If a ball is fumbled in the field of play, and goes forward into the opponent's end zone and over the end line or sideline, a touchback is awarded to the defensive

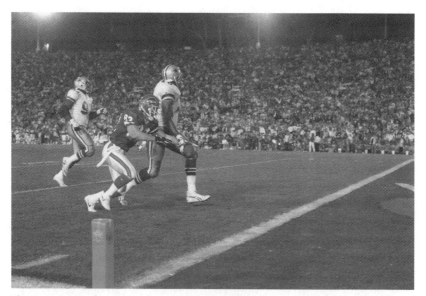

Figure 5.1. Defensive end Leon Lett was this close to giving the Cowboys a Super Bowl record, but Bills receiver Don Beebe stripped the ball away at the last minute.

Photo by John Biever/Sports Illustrated/Getty Images

team." Even though the defensive squad of the Cowboys is on the field, they are designated the offense because there was a change of possession. Lett provided the impetus under the rule, because it was his loss of possession that put the ball in the end zone, that determines if this is a safety or a touchback.

Therefore, the ball is next put in play at the 20-yard line and, even though the Bills did not regain physical possession of the ball on the play, they are awarded possession on the touchback, with a new first-and-10.

Referee Dick Hantak discussed the play with line judge Dick McKenzie and head linesman Ron Phares before ruling the play a touchback. One of the elements that had to be considered was whether Lett broke the plane of the goal line with the ball prior to fumbling the ball. Because it was an abrupt change in direction, the officials did not catch up to have a look down the goal line as Lett approached. They did not have the benefit of a replay review, because the owners had scrapped the replay system after the previous Super Bowl. (A vote of 21 of the 28 teams' owners was required to keep replay, but only 17 owners voted in favor of it.) A revamped replay system would be instituted in 1999, but Hantak and his crew would get no help from anyone watching a television screen on a play that was partially caused by a player watching himself on the screen.

On January 11, 2014, the New England Patriots were facing a punting situation against the Indianapolis Colts in the second quarter of an AFC Divisional Playoff game. The play started at the Patriots' 44-yard line. The snap from center sailed over the head of punter Ryan Allen and rolled all the way to the 3-yard line. Allen gained possession but was not able to hold the ball while being tackled. It appeared that Allen was attempting to throw a shovel pass, but he never initiated a throwing motion. The force of the tackle made him lose his grip on the wet football, causing the fumble to go forward. Colts nose tackle Jeris Pendleton was rushing in to make a tackle, and the ball immediately bounced off of his hands in midair, redirecting the ball to go through the end zone and over the end line.

2. What is the proper call?

A. Incomplete pass, since it was a forward fumble, regardless of whether it was a deliberate forward fumble. The Colts get the ball at the 44-yard line, because it was fourth down.

B. Intentional grounding penalty on Allen. Because of the loss of down with the penalty, the Colts get the ball at the 3.

C. Illegal bat penalty on Pendleton, giving the Patriots an automatic first down.

D. Touchback. Patriots ball first-and-10 on the 20.

E. Safety. Two points for the Colts, and the Patriots kick off.

There are many considerations that have to be made on this play, and referee Pete Morelli was able to get in position on the goal line to judge the actions near the goal line. He correctly determined that there was no shovel pass, even though the ball was fumbled forward. Although Allen showed an intent to attempt a shovel pass, he did not actually propel the ball forward, so this is a fumble instead of a pass. This means that it cannot be ruled incomplete or intentional grounding.

Even though Pendleton touched the ball in the field of play and redirected the ball toward his opponent's end zone, he is not automatically charged with an illegal bat. Because the errant snap sent the play 40 yards backwards, Pendleton was rushing to make a tackle or a recovery, and not to push the ball in the end zone. Therefore, Pendleton cannot be charged with an illegal bat penalty. It also means that under the definition of the football rule (and not of physics), the defense did not give new impetus to the ball by way of batting or kicking a ball or adding a new force to a ball at or nearly at rest.

By elimination, the answer is E. The offense placed the ball loose by fumbling, and the ensuing scramble does not give a bailout for the offense by attributing new impetus to the defense. Even though the offense was not responsible for the direction the ball took, they caused the ball to be loose and thus are pegged with the impetus to put the ball into the end zone. It was correctly ruled a safety by referee Pete Morelli and his crew.

3. How does that play change if the ball goes out of bounds in the end zone because Pendleton deliberately swatted at the loose ball or if he tried to pick up the ball after it slowed to a near rest?

If Pendleton had enough time to react to make a deliberate swipe at the ball without trying to recover, then it is an illegal bat penalty. As long as the loose ball has not come to a rest on the field, the impetus is still charged to the Patriots. Under current rules, when the dead-ball spot and the defensive foul are behind the line of scrimmage, the penalty is enforced from the line of scrimmage. (This is known as a "behind/behind enforcement.") Even though the foul occurs near the 2, the ball returns to the line of scrimmage at the 44-yard line and is enforced 10 yards into Colts territory.

4. In a Monday night game at AT&T Stadium in Dallas on October 27, 2014, Cowboys defensive back J. J. Wilcox intercepted a pass from Washington quarterback Colt McCoy in the end zone. Shortly after catching the interception, Wilcox fumbled the ball out of the back of the end zone. Assuming Wilcox had control of the ball in the end zone prior to the fumble, what is the correct call?

Again, the call is going to center on the impetus that put the ball into the end zone, not the action that placed the ball out of bounds. Since the McCoy pass placed the ball into the end zone, the charging of impetus is on McCoy. Dallas is not suddenly disadvantaged once it has fumbled. If Wilcox runs around in the end zone, the Cowboys are not charged with impetus unless the ball exits the end zone and reenters through the Cowboys' impetus.

That is not to say that there isn't any risk by running around in your own end zone. Even though the impetus is provided by the opponent, if your teammate commits a post-possession penalty in the end zone and you are unsuccessful in running out of the end zone, the penalty is enforced from the end zone, resulting in a safety. This applies *only* if a runback attempt occurs *and* the foul happens in the end zone on the runback. If both criteria are not met, it is not a safety. If the player does not attempt to get out of the end zone, the touchback is deemed to have occurred first, and it is a "20/10 enforcement" of the penalty (spot at the 20 and penalize half the distance to the 10). On the other hand, if the ball has left the end zone, the foul is enforced from the dead-ball spot as usual.

If Wilcox, rather than fumbling, attempted to lateral the ball to a teammate in the end zone but instead was ruled to have thrown an illegal forward pass, Wilcox would be charged with a safety. The pass attempt would be an attempt to advance the ball out of the end zone, rather than just taking a knee and the touchback. Since the illegal forward pass is a spot foul enforced in the end zone, the rule of impetus does not prevent the standard penalty assessment of a safety.

Returning to the original play, the officials correctly awarded the Cowboys a touchback.

KICKOFFS AND THE END ZONE

The Dallas Cowboys and the New York Giants tested the officials early in a September 18, 1988, matchup in Texas Stadium. Giants kicker Raul

Allegre sent the opening kickoff to Cowboys returner Darryl Clack. Clack bobbled the catch at the 2-yard line, and the muffed catch rolled into the end zone. Clack picked up the ball, but he wasn't able to get out of the end zone before he was tackled by the Giants. Referee Pat Haggerty ruled it a safety.

5. Was this call correct?

Since Clack never took possession of the ball at the 2-yard line, the impetus behind the ball is still attributed to the kickers. Even though Clack touched the ball in the field of play, the Cowboys were still entitled to a touchback when the ball was ruled dead in the end zone. Once a ball enters the end zone, the run by Clack is irrelevant to the determination of touchback versus safety.

The two points from the safety wound up being the decisive margin in the game, as the Giants won 12–10.

Replay judge Armen Terzian was responsible for correcting this error under the NFL rules of the first system of replay review. He admitted at halftime that the call was in error. Commissioner Pete Rozelle then suspended Terzian for two games, but Terzian opted to retire rather than serve a suspension.

6. On the opening kickoff of the 2013 season, Shaun Suisham of the Pittsburgh Steelers kicked to Tennessee Titans returner Darius Reynaud. Reynaud stood on the goal line, reached out into the field of play to catch the bouncing ball, took a step back, and kneeled to take an apparent touchback. Referee Jerome Boger huddled his entire crew and determined that it was a safety. Was this the correct call?

In this scenario, it is correctly ruled a safety, and the replay review upheld the ruling on the field. The impetus from the kick stopped when Reynaud had possession of the ball inside the 1-yard line. Reynaud then imparted new impetus on the ball by tucking the ball in and stepping back to take a knee. It was Reynaud's action that put the ball in the end zone; therefore he is charged with the impetus.

The rule attributes the impetus to the offense unless the defense invokes one of the aforementioned exceptions. When the ball was kicked, the Steelers were deemed to be the offense. When possession switches teams during the play, the designation of offense and defense also changes. The instant Reynaud secured the ball, the Titans were put on offense.

Reynaud does not get any benefit from the fact that he was standing on the goal line. On a punt, the kicking team can create a touchback by touching the goal line and the ball simultaneously, but this rule does not apply to a kickoff.

Reynaud also ended the play immediately when he kneeled, because he indicated that he was "giving up" as a runner and not intending to advance the ball. Even if he had realized his error when he kneeled, he could not start running, because the ball was dead.

7. On November 16, 2014, a kickoff by the Patriots was muffed by the Colts at the 3-yard line and rolled to the middle of the field at the 2-yard line. It was muffed again as the Colts tried to jump on the ball but drove the ball into the end zone, where they were tackled with possession. Is this a safety against the Colts?

As mentioned in chapter 4, a muff is defined as "the touching of a loose ball by a player in an unsuccessful attempt to obtain possession of it." This means that possession is not yet established when the ball is muffed.

The key judgement on this play is whether the ball was considered "nearly at rest" at the 2-yard line. To be clear, the ball would not have gone into the end zone without that second muff at the 2; however, the definition of impetus (the NFL version) does not account for force or acceleration. Therefore, this is still a judgement call.

The applicable standard from the rule is that impetus switches from the Patriots (the kicking team or the offense) to the Colts (receiving team or the defense) when that team "muffs a ball that is at rest, or nearly at rest." In this case, there was still active handling of the ball in proximity to the players, so the ball is continuing to be a muffed kick. This would be contrasted to a ball that enters unoccupied space on the field of play and rolls to a near stop; a muffed ball in that situation would clearly be muffing a ball at rest.

Also, as long as an attempt at a recovery is made, the Colts are not going to be charged with batting the ball, unless there is an overt swipe at the ball to move it to a more favorable position or to prevent a recovery by the Patriots.

All of these considerations are leading the covering official to formulate a judgement call that favors the Colts. Absent a really pronounced effort by the receiving team or the defense to impart a new force on the ball, the impetus will remain charged to the offense. If it is close enough that it could go either way, then the official would have to go with the touchback over the safety call, simply because the touchback does not cost the defense two points.

8. In an AFC Divisional Playoff game on January 12, 2013, Denver Broncos kicker Matt Prater kicked the opening kickoff, which hit the crossbar of the goalpost and rebounded into the field. Is this a live ball?

No. Once the ball hits the goalpost, it is a dead ball. (The single exception is on a field goal attempt, where the ball may bounce off the goalposts on its way through and count as a successful field goal.) The goalposts are out of bounds with the outside face on the vertical plane of the end line. This was ruled a touchback.

Incidentally, a kickoff that goes through the goalpost does not score any points, because it is not a field goal attempt. Oddly, a safety kick was allowed to score a field goal for the kicking team until that rule was dropped in 1954.

PLAY AT THE PYLON

The four corners of each end zone are marked with orange pylons, a foam pillar no more than 18 inches in height and about 4 inches wide on all sides. The NFL required the use of pylons in 1974 over the hazardous flexible-shaft flags that were used in the past.

The two pylons on the goal line have their front faces aligned with the plane of the goal line and the inside edges on the limit of the sideline. The pylons on the end line match one corner of the pylon to the corner formed by the sideline and end line. The entirety of the pylon is in the white border surrounding the field.

On October 19, 2014, Broncos quarterback Peyton Manning had already thrown one first-quarter touchdown pass against the 49ers to bring him one touchdown away from the NFL career record, held at the time by quarterback Brett Favre. Near the end of the first quarter, a catch by Wes Welker was initially ruled the record-tying 508th touchdown. In replay, Welker is seen diving for the pylon with the ball. While in the air, his forearm where the ball is tucked touches the pylon.

9. Is this a confirmed touchdown or not?

All Welker needs to do is break the plane of the goal line with the ball in his possession. Even though the pylon is located fully on the white sideline paint, this does not put Welker out of bounds. As soon as Welker knocks down the pylon with the ball and establishes possession, this is confirmed as touchdown 508 for Manning.

10. On November 28, 1993, the Phoenix Cardinals were playing the New York Giants at Giants Stadium. The Cardinals punted in the second quarter, and special teamer Anthony Edwards tried to down the ball at the 1-yard line. Edwards brushed the pylon as he went out of bounds. Assuming he does not carry the ball or touch in the end zone, how is this ruled?

Under the rules of the time, this was ruled a touchback, because the pylon was considered an out-of-bounds object. The rules were revised in 2002 to allow a player to touch the pylon and not be ruled out of bounds. The current rules would allow Edwards to continue out of bounds, and if he can touch out of bounds at a point before the plane of the goal, Edwards successfully has downed the ball at the 1-yard line.

11. On November 17, 2002, the Falcons were leading the Saints 7-0 in the third quarter when the Falcons had a third-and-goal on the 7. Quarterback Michael Vick ran along the sideline, with the Saints squeezing him out of room, to make a touchdown play. Vick switched the ball to his left hand, stepped with his right foot at the 2, and lunged for the goal line. The airborne Vick was entirely out of bounds, except for a fraction of his hand, maybe, as the ball traveled over the pylon. Is this a touchdown, or is Vick ruled short of the goal and out of bounds?

Vick's spectacular effort was a touchdown, although continued replays just made viewers shake their heads in disbelief that Vick was able to convert such a play.

In order to get the touchdown, an airborne player must have any part of the ball pass inside, over, or into the pylon. By switching the ball to his left hand, Vick was able to get the ball in position to score the touchdown. Had the ball remained in his right hand, the ball would have been spotted at the point where the ball crossed the sideline, which would likely have been near the 2-yard line.

If Vick is able to make this play running, as opposed to diving, he is generally not required to ensure the ball crosses over or is inside the pylon. Therefore, he can keep the ball in his right hand over the sideline, as long as his body is in bounds in the end zone when the ball crosses the goal line extended. A running player who steps in the end zone does not have to mind the pylon on the touchdown; only a player who is airborne has to.

A running player who does not step in the end zone or on the goal line, but steps from the field of play to an out-of-bounds spot over the goal line, is considered an airborne player by rule. Even though the player is still standing, he must be in bounds in some part of the end zone for the pylon to not be a consideration as the ball crosses the plane of the goal.

PUNT COVERAGE

When a punt is kicked past the line of scrimmage, the kicking team always has the ability to down the ball near the goal line to pin their opponent deep in their territory. This action makes the ball dead at that point. These are the overriding principles on every kick, whether it is a kickoff, a punt, a blocked punt, or a missed field goal: (1) a kick remains a kick until possessed, and (2) if the kicking team is the first to possess, the ball is dead immediately (in the case of a punt or field goal, it would be live only if the ball did not cross the line of scrimmage).

On November 16, 2014, while hosting the Detroit Lions, the Arizona Cardinals punt early in the fourth quarter. Cardinals special teamer Justin Bethel grabs the ball before it goes into the end zone and tosses it back into the field of play. If Bethel carries it into the end zone, this is obviously a touchback. With the ball still bouncing around, Lions punt returner Jeremy Ross picks up the ball and runs 46 yards into Cardinals territory.

12. Obviously, the Lions will take the spot that gives them the best field position, but what are the options on the spot?

There actually is only one spot for the ball, and it is not inherently obvious. When the kicking team touches a punt, it becomes a first-touch violation. The kicking team may commit multiple "first touches" prior to the receiving team taking possession of the ball or the ball being declared dead. Each first-touch point by a different player becomes a potential spot for the receiving team to be awarded possession.

However, Bethel has established possession by completing the same elements that make up the process of a catch: firm control of the ball, two feet down in bounds, and having the ability to perform an act common to the game. Bethel's pitching motion prior to releasing the ball is a deliberate act, and it is undeniably an act common to the game, as this is a typical action when a player is attempting to keep the punt out of the end zone. It did seem ironic that Bethel secured possession by beginning an action to release possession of the ball.

Whenever a kick is first possessed by the kicking team, the ball is dead. In this case, the Lions have not yet touched the ball, so the Cardinals do not get possession on their recovery. Everything that happens after Bethel's toss is all null and void, because the ball is already dead. (Bethel's possession was determined in a replay review, which is why the play was able to continue.)

There is only one spot option on the play: Lions ball inside the 1-yard line.

13. Since the ball is dead upon Bethel's possession, couldn't he just carry the ball into the end zone?

For the downing of a punt, there is an exception to the rule to avoid just this scenario being converted into an unearned attempt to pin the receiving team deep in their territory. When Bethel gains possession, he still must prevent himself and the ball from going into the end zone. If he sets one toe on the goal line or if he drops the ball in the end zone, the Lions are awarded a touchback at the 20-yard line. Under this scenario, a return by the Lions still would not be counted.

All Bethel has to ensure is that the ball lands in the field of play or touches another player or an official who is in the field of play. Although the play occurred at the middle of the field, if he was near the sideline, Bethel could have also thrown the ball out of bounds, as long as it did not go out, of course, through the end zone.

14. If the ball lands fully in the field of play but bounces back into the end zone after Bethel's toss, where is the ball spotted?

Once Bethel begins the pitching motion with the ball still in his hand, the ball is dead. It is still Lions ball at the 1-yard line.

A similar play to save a touchback occurred on September 15, 2013, when the Houston Texans faced the Tennessee Titans. On a fourth-quarter punt by the Texans, long snapper Jon Weeks zipped downfield and caught the ball in midstride and came to a near stop at the 1-yard line. Sensing his impending step into the end zone, Weeks tossed the ball behind him. The same principle applied: he did not carry the ball into the end zone, so the play is killed retroactively to the point where he gained possession at the 1. If he did not establish possession but batted the ball backwards, the Texans would still need to down the ball.

15. The play by Weeks occurred near the sideline. Assume he steps out at the 10-yard line and then reestablishes in bounds at the 5-yard line. Then, Weeks makes the play at the 1. Where is the ball spotted?

A player on the kicking team who goes out of bounds (either on his own or if he is forced out by the receiving team) may not be the first player to touch the kick beyond the line of scrimmage. In the hypothetical case where Weeks steps out of bounds, there is a 5-yard penalty assessed against the Texans. This would ordinarily place the ball at the 6-yard line, which is still beneficial to the Texans, so there is an exception to offset the advantage. If there is an illegal touching foul inside the 5-yard line, the receiving team may opt to be awarded a touchback and the penalty, which would spot the ball for the Titans at the 25-yard line for first-and-10.

If the ball is not possessed but batted by the player committing the illegal touch foul inside the 5, it is still a live ball. The receiving team can still recover the ball and advance it to try to attain a better field position than the 25-yard line.

16. If Weeks steps out of bounds inadvertently at the 1 and fields the punt before he gets two feet down in bounds, where is the ball spotted?

In this case, Weeks would continue to be out of bounds until his second foot steps in bounds. Once a loose ball touches an out-of-bounds player, it is a dead ball immediately. The provision that Weeks must keep the ball out of the end zone does not apply, nor does he have to establish possession, because the ball would be out of bounds even though it may never cross the sideline. Titans ball at the 1.

INTERCEPTING MOMENTUM

On September 11, 2011, the Tampa Bay Buccaneers were hosting the Detroit Lions at Raymond James Stadium. On a second-quarter pass, quarterback Josh Freeman was intercepted by Lions cornerback Chris Houston, who caught the ball on the 1-yard line in the air, but his second foot came down on the goal line. Houston made a move to try to run with the ball, but he was tackled in the end zone.

17. Is this a safety or a touchback?

Possession is established when the process of the catch is completed: (1) secure control of the ball, (2) touch the ground with two feet or any part of the body other than hands or arms, and (3) have the ability "to perform an act common to the game." In this case, Houston attempted to run with the ball, fulfilling the common act criteria; just having the ability to run is enough to complete the process of the catch.

Because Houston completed the process of the catch when his second foot was in the end zone, this is ruled a touchback.

18. If Houston completes the process of the catch at the 1-yard line instead of in the end zone, and his momentum takes him into the end zone, where is the ball spotted?

In this case, the Lions technically put the ball in the end zone, because Houston would have possession in the field of play and then cross the goal line with the ball in his possession. However, to avoid a cheap safety for the Buccaneers or a deliberate attempt to draw a touchback by the Lions, there is an exception in the rules for intercepting momentum. Under this exception, the Lions would get the ball at the spot where Houston's second foot (or other body part) touched the ground to establish possession.

MOMENTUM ON CHANGE OF POSSESSION

The Seattle Seahawks hosted the Oakland Raiders for a rainy Saturday afternoon game on December 16, 2000. The Seahawks were finishing their first season at Husky Stadium, their temporary home since the Kingdome was imploded and before CenturyLink Field was built in its place. In the fourth quarter, Seahawks running back Ricky Watters was churning off a long run along the sideline when he lost his grip on the football at the 23-yard line. Raiders defensive back Marquez Pope was able to pounce on the loose ball at the 2-yard line, and he slid on the wet grass into the end zone.

Also, on September 17 in that same season in Charlotte, the Carolina Panthers were hosting the Atlanta Falcons. Running back Jamal Anderson was peeling off a long run for the Falcons when he fumbled the ball in full stride at the 16-yard line. Panthers cornerback Doug Evans dove for the ball at the 3-yard line, and his momentum took him into the end zone and out of bounds.

19. What is the proper call in these two situations?

These plays are both legal recoveries with the change of possession being awarded at the spot of recovery.

However, under the rules in effect for the 2000 season, the rule on momentum on a change of possession applied only to a ball that was intercepted. One official signaled the Panthers' play a touchback, but another official indicated this was a safety. Panthers coach George Seifert challenged the ruling, but the safety call was upheld. The replay official that day was the future vice president of officiating, Dean Blandino.

After the Falcons–Panthers game, the NFL released a statement on the ruling:

> If a player brings the ball into the end zone on a fumble recovery, he must bring it out or it is ruled a safety. On an interception, if a player's momentum carries him into the end zone, the ball is spotted at the point where the interception occurred.
>
> In this case, however, there was no intercepting momentum. Therefore, Evans' recovery and subsequent return into the end zone was correctly ruled a safety because there is no consideration for momentum on a fumble recovery.

Bernie Kukar was the referee in Seattle, and it is very likely the Doug Evans play was on a training tape for all of the officials to see. It was a clear call to make, even if it was inequitable.

The Competition Committee revised the rule to include the momentum exception for the recovery of a fumble, kick, or other loose ball. Under the current rules, the ball on both of these plays would be returned to the spot of the recovery.

20. On the recovery by Marquez Pope, what would the ruling be if Pope was able to get on his feet before being touched by a defender and was able to run to the 10-yard line? What if he ran to the 1-yard line and was stopped there?

Assuming there is no penalty in both cases, once the defensive player leaves the end zone with the ball, any momentum exception that would apply is ignored. The defense will get the ball wherever the play ends, even if it is behind the spot where the momentum exception would be enforced.

POINT-AFTER-TOUCHDOWN CONVERSION

The point-after-touchdown conversion is a vestigial rule from football's rugby origins that emphasized kicking the ball through the goal when the ball crossed the goal line. For decades, the NFL only allowed one point to be scored on a conversion try: a successful kick scored the same as a run or pass into the end zone. The rulebook simply refers to this play as a Try (with a capital T), as a further linkage to the rugby try. This term is rarely encountered by itself outside of the rulebook and referee announcements.

The point-after-touchdown kick has become nearly automatic, as kickers set an NFL record in 2013 with a 99.6 percent rate of success. It was down slightly in 2014, to 99.3 percent. Recently, the NFL has considered modifications to the extra-point kick in order to increase its difficulty or to remove it from the game entirely. In the first half of the 2014 preseason, the league initiated a trial run to move the snap for extra-point kicks from the 2-yard line to the 15; this rule will be in effect for the 2015 season only, and may be extended or made permanent in 2016.

In 1960 the upstart American Football League implemented a two-point conversion for runs and passes, making the rule disparity the equivalent of Major League Baseball's designated hitter rule. In baseball, interleague games allow a designated hitter in games played in American League ballparks, just as is the case for games between American League teams.

21. The AFL and NFL played the first four Super Bowls as separate leagues before they merged in 1970 and also scheduled several interleague preseason games. What was the rule on two-point conversions?

Football fans were reminded of this rule disparity when the NFL Network replayed the broadcast of Super Bowl III between the New York Jets and the Baltimore Colts from January 12, 1969. NBC's venerable sportscaster Curt Gowdy noted before the kickoff that the two-point conversion rule was not in effect, as it was for all of the interleague championship games.

The merged NFL did not implement the AFL's two-point rule, but all AFL records were subsumed into the NFL record book. For another 24 years, the two-point conversion remained in the record book uncontested. The NFL finally instituted the two-point conversion rule for the 1994 season. Bill Belichick, then the head coach of the Cleveland Browns, faked a first-quarter conversion kick and had punter Tom Tupa (who was lined up as the holder) run the ball for the first two-point play under the new rule. At the conclusion of the season, the Chargers scored a pair of two-pointers in Super Bowl XXIX—the first such conversions in Super Bowl history.

As for interleague preseason games, the two-point conversion rule was occasionally in effect, with the Bears scoring the only premerger NFL two-pointer. The two leagues also experimented in 1968 interleague games with a one-point conversion without the option to kick.

22. If a one-point kick is blocked, can either team score?

The longstanding rule in the NFL has always been that, on a conversion kick, once the kick is made, the ball is no longer playable: either it will continue in the air until it scores or it is a dead ball when it fails. The offense would not be able to pick up a failed kick for a scramble to make two points. However, the NFL changed that rule in 2015, allowing the play to continue until the ball is declared dead.

Also introduced in the 2015 rule change, the play is no longer dead when the defense takes possession of the ball during a conversion attempt. Matching the college team rule, the defense can score two points on their opponent's conversion attempt by returning the ball 98 yards on defense.

With that in mind, consider the following four conversion attempts.

Play No. 1: The Minnesota Vikings had a 3–10 record when they faced the New Orleans Saints on December 15, 2002. The Vikings scored a touchdown with five seconds remaining and, trailing by one point, went for the win instead of defaulting to overtime. Quarterback Daunte Culpepper fumbled the snap, recovered the ball, and lunged over the goal line.

Play No. 2: Vikings quarterback Teddy Bridgewater was attempting a two-point run on December 21, 2014, against the Miami Dolphins. Bridgewater fumbled and the ball was recovered in the end zone by the Vikings. There was 4:46 on the clock in the fourth quarter.

Play No. 3: On November 12, 2014, Steelers punter Brad Wing was the holder for an extra-point kick against the Ravens. He had a problem with the placement and picked up the ball just before Shaun Suisham kicked it. Wing lobbed a pass to tight end Matt Spaeth in the end zone.

Play No. 4: On a hypothetical two-point conversion attempt, the offense fumbles the ball. In order to prevent the offense from recovering, a defensive player intentionally kicks the ball, which hits the pylon.

23. What is the ruling on these four conversion attempts?

On the first conversion play, while the rule at the time prevented an advance of a failed kick, Culpepper is allowed to advance his own fumble on the two-point try. The Vikings get the two points and the one-point lead.

Bridgewater's attempt in the second example does not score for the Vikings. This will be discussed in further detail in chapter 7, but basically the fourth-down fumble rules apply to the two-point conversion. Bridgewater must recover and advance his own fumble, just as Culpepper did. If a teammate recovers the ball or if the fumble goes into a pile and Bridgewater is not in the pile, the conversion attempt is over and does not score.

The Steelers in the third conversion play are successful in scoring two points. Under the rules in effect at the time, since there was no kick, there is no failed kick, which would kill the play. Wing is able to keep the play alive by aborting the kick attempt, and Spaeth makes a heads-up decision to get open immediately on the broken play.

The fourth example is a total anomaly that has not been seen in the NFL. To explain it better, assume this is a regular scrimmage down and not a conversion attempt. The ball is out of bounds in the end zone once it strikes the pylon. The action that provided the impetus is the deliberate kick by the defense. It is a safety charged against the defense if it provided the impetus to put the ball dead in its own end zone.

Moving back to the original scenario, a "touchdown" on a conversion attempt is two points, and a "field goal" is one point. To align this play into the scoring structure of the conversion attempt, the offense scores a one-point safety. There is no safety kick on the ensuing kickoff, however.

The defense also would be flagged for an illegal kicking foul. The offense would have the option of (1) assessing the 10-yard penalty on the kickoff, or (2) taking the one-point safety off the board and trying to convert a run or pass from the 1-yard line.

Since possession by the defense is allowed with the 2015 rule revision, there are more possibilities for the defense to be charged with the impetus that would create a one-point safety. Even so, there are only two occurrences of a one-point safety in Division I college football, with the most recent being in the Fiesta Bowl on January 3, 2013, when Kansas State gave Oregon one point on a blocked kick. Texas scored a point on November 26, 2004, when Texas A&M was charged with a safety. In both cases, it involved the defense taking possession of a blocked conversion kick and retreating into their own end zone, thus providing the impetus needed for the safety call.

In the Fiesta Bowl, referee Ron Cherry prefaced his explanation of the call with these words: "On the previous play, we have an unusual ruling." It certainly was unusual, compounded by the extraordinary coincidence that Brad Nessler, the television announcer for the Fiesta Bowl, was the play-by-play announcer for the 2004 Texas–Texas A&M game.

24. What is the call if the result of the play on a conversion attempt is a touchback?

The ball is dead and the conversion fails. The team that scored the touchdown kicks off.

25. On November 29, 1998, the Patriots scored a touchdown on an un-timed down at the end of the game against the Bills. On the previous play, the Bills were penalized for defensive pass interference, a call that Jerry Seeman, the senior director of officiating, later stated should not have been made. In-censed by the ruling that set up the winning score and a controversial fourth-down spot earlier in the drive, the Bills protested by leaving the field before the extra-point conversion was attempted. Given that the score was 23–21 and there was no time left on the clock, can the conversion attempt be bypassed?

The rules state that the conversion attempt is always made following every touchdown, even if there is no time remaining on the clock and even if the victor is already determined. The lone exception is overtime, where the rules specifically exclude a conversion attempt and the touchdown scores six points.

The Bills still refused to put 11 players on the field, so the ball was made ready for play. The Patriots snapped the ball and kicker Adam Vinatieri walked into the end zone uncontested for two points. The Patriots coach was Pete Carroll, who would oddly be on the winning end of another game-ending controversy that also had complications on a meaningless extra-point kick.

As coach of the Seahawks on September 24, 2012, Carroll and his team won on a disputed catch—referred to as the "Fail Mary," a pun on the Hail Mary play—at the end of the game against the Packers. The game was offici-ated by replacement officials, with the regular staff off the field due to a labor dispute. Once the replacements realized that the extra-point kick following the questionable game-winning touchdown was required, it took time to assemble 11 Packers players, as the team had already retired to the locker room in disgust. Eventually the kick was performed. It wound up being the last play officiated by replacement officials, spurring intense negotiation that resolved the labor impasse before the next week's games.

26. Say a team scores a touchdown as the clock expires in the fourth quarter with the score 6–0. The team lines up for the extra-point conversion and the quarterback takes the snap and sprints with the live ball to the locker room, taking him out of bounds over his own end line 108 yards away. Does the defense score a one-point safety on the play, making the final score 6–1?

This was considered a dead ball with no points scored on the conversion attempt through the 2014 season. Since the defense is allowed to score on a conversion attempt, the one point is awarded to the defense, making this the only way a team can score a single point in an NFL game. A one-point safety can also be awarded to the defense if the defense fumbles its return of a recovered conversion attempt, and then the offense is charged with the impetus that creates a dead ball in the end zone.

SIX

SCRIMMAGE KICKS

Back up a bit farther. We're back and just kick the hell out of it.

—Holder Joe Scarpati as told by kicker Tom Dempsey
during a post-game interview after kicking a record-breaking
field goal to win the game, Detroit Lions at
New Orleans Saints, November 8, 1970

A scrimmage kick is defined in the rulebook in its typical clunky language as "a punt, dropkick, or placekick from on or behind the line of scrimmage." Rule 9 is designated for all scrimmage kicks, whether they are punts or field goal attempts. As a practical matter, punts and field goals are generally adjudicated the same and differ in the execution of the kick and the ability to score points.

PUNTS

A gusty wind swept in off of Lake Michigan as the New York Giants met the Chicago Bears at Soldier Field for an NFC Divisional Playoff game for the 1985 season. With the ball snapped at the 12-yard line, Giants punter

Sean Landeta took three steps to the 2-yard line when he suffered just about one of the most embarrassing blunders in any postseason game. A gust of wind blew the ball enough that Landeta connected with the ball only on the side of his foot—a very small part of the side of his foot. The shanked kick sputtered out to the 5-yard line, still 7 yards behind the line of scrimmage. Appropriately named for the conditions that day, Bears cornerback Shaun Gayle picked up the ball and ran it in for a score. Officially, the punt was negative 7 yards (since the distance is measured from the line of scrimmage), and Gayle set an NFL-record shortest punt-return touchdown of 5 yards.

1. While this was clearly a touchdown for the Bears, if one of the Giants players recovered the ball at the 5-yard line, which of these could he do?

 A. Run for a first down
 B. Pass it
 C. Punt it again
 D. None of the above; the ball is dead immediately.

A punt that has not crossed the line of scrimmage is a live ball for either team to recover. This applies equally to blocked punts and the very, very short variety that Landeta and few others have accomplished. The Giants would be able to recover the ball and run for the first down. Interestingly, the Giants have not forfeited the ability to pass the ball or punt it again as long as the ball remains behind the line of scrimmage.

In a case where the ball crosses the line of scrimmage but there is enough backspin on the ball to return it behind the line of scrimmage, the kicking team may recover and advance. However, once the ball has crossed the line of scrimmage, the options to kick a second time or to pass are no longer available. The penalties in this case are 5 yards for the pass and 10 yards for the kick, although neither is a loss-of-down penalty. (The loss of down only applies for a pass that is beyond the line at the time of the pass, and a punt under these circumstances is not grouped with other illegal kicks that are losses of down.)

2. In the second quarter of a game on October 13, 2013, the Baltimore Ravens had a fourth-and-13 from their own 30-yard line. A punt by Sam Koch was blocked and then touched by Packers special teamer John Kuhn at the 37. The ball was recovered by the Ravens at the 41-yard line, 2 yards short of the first-down line. Where is the ball spotted and who has possession?

The fact that the punt is blocked is essentially irrelevant; when a scrimmage kick crosses the line of scrimmage, the kicking team has essentially surrendered possession. In this situation, a short punt and a partially blocked punt are in the same category as long as the ball crosses the line.

When Kuhn touches the ball at the 37, he is just like a receiver that touches a deep punt—the ball is made live for either team to recover. Because the Ravens had surrendered possession by punting (and the ball crosses the line of scrimmage), they start a brand-new possession on the recovery of the loose ball. Even though they are 2 yards short of the first-down marker, the Ravens get a new first-and-10 to start the new possession.

MISSED FIELD GOALS

It was Thanksgiving Day in 1993, and the Miami Dolphins departed from the Sunshine State that week with temperatures in the low 80s to a kickoff in Dallas at 32 degrees with a mix of freezing rain and sleet. The field at Texas Stadium was covered in about one-third of an inch of the icy precipitation, and it was a struggle to maintain footing on the slippery surface throughout the game.

In the fourth quarter, the Dolphins trailed the Cowboys 14–13 with 15 seconds to go. Dolphins kicker Pete Stoyanovich lined up to kick a 41-yard field goal, and holder Doug Pederson cleared a bull's-eye in the ice pellets to spot the ball. Stoyanovich's kick was blocked by Jimmie Jones, virtually ensuring the win for the Cowboys.

As the NBC cameras panned to the celebratory Cowboys sideline and a dejected Dolphins coach Don Shula, the clock continued to run. The play was still live. It wasn't readily apparent as to what happened, until they checked the videotape. As the replay rolled on television, the ball spun in place after the block, and commentator Bob Trumpy narrated the action: "Now someone touches the football here . . . It's Leon Lett! Nooooooooo!" Lett, the Cowboys' defensive lineman, had already earned infamy (and another discussion in chapter 5) on a fumble return in Super Bowl XXVII in January that year. The Dolphins' center, Jeff Dellenbach, recovered the ball.

3. The previous line of scrimmage was the 24-yard line, the kick was from the 31, the block occurred near the 23, Lett touched the ball at the 7, and the

Dolphins recovered the ball at the 1 and slid into the end zone. Who has the ball, and where do you spot it?

A missed or blocked field goal behaves just like a punt once the ball has cleared the neutral zone. If the block occurs at the defensive side of the line of scrimmage, it is considered to be "behind" the line of scrimmage for purposes of the rule. This means that the initial touch by the Dolphins (the kick block) occurs before the ball crosses the neutral zone.

As the ball is spinning, the Cowboys players stay away from the ball. Just as on a punt, the Cowboys are considered the "receiving" team on the field goal attempt, and if they touch the ball first, it is a live ball. The Dolphins' block is not considered to be the first touch of the ball, because for kick purposes that is only after the ball crosses the line of scrimmage.

While the ball is live and may be recovered by either team, the Dolphins may not advance the ball. As with the punt rules, a kick remains a kick until it is possessed. Since Lett did not possess the ball, the officials are still enforcing the kick rules when Dellenbach jumps on the ball. Even though he slides into the end zone as part of the recovery, he is only entitled to the point of recovery, which is the 1-yard line.

Referee Ed Hochuli had to gather his crew (which included future referee and CBS Sports rules analyst Mike Carey at side judge) and determine the spot of recovery. They were handicapped by ice covering all the yard markings on the field with the exception of the goal line. The crew also did not have the benefit of a replay review, as the owners had abolished the original replay system a year previous, and would not reinstate it for another six years. After a short delay, the Dolphins had the ball, first-and-10 at the 1-yard line with three seconds left. The second field goal attempt was successful, and the Dolphins won, 16–14.

4. What would have happened if the Dolphins recovered in the end zone instead of at the 1-yard line?

Even though the Dolphins could not advance the ball, if the recovery occurs in the end zone, it is a touchdown. As the play occurred, the slide into the end zone does not count. If Lett had secured possession of the ball and then lost it, it would be under the rules of a fumble, rather than the rules of a kick. As a fumble play, the Dolphins would be able to advance the ball.

5. If Lett did not touch the ball first, how would this affect the play?

Lett's actions were solely responsible for making the ball a free ball for either team to recover, just as John Kuhn had done on the aforementioned

Ravens punt in 2013. If, for instance, the ball deflects off a Dolphins line-backer who was not on the line of scrimmage after the block, then the Dolphins have committed a "first touch" beyond the line. This means that the Cowboys will keep the ball (save for a highly unusual exception to the rule), and the Cowboys can negate any adverse result by reverting back to the spot of the first touch. It is the same as a punt, in which, as was discussed, the only scenario that could not be reversed by a first-touch violation is a sequence where the Cowboys take possession, then lose it on a fumble and commit a post-possession penalty.

Unlike punts, however, the Cowboys are also entitled to get the missed field goal at the spot of the kick as long as they do not touch or take possession of the loose ball until it is dead.

6. With the score tied 6–6 in overtime on September 7, 1980, a field goal attempt by Packers kicker Chester Marcol was blocked by the Bears at the line of scrimmage (the 18-yard line) and deflected right back to Marcol. He caught the ball at the 24 and ran to the end zone untouched. The kick was attempted from the 25-yard line. Who has possession, and where is the ball spotted?

Marcol's recovery is behind the line of scrimmage and, unlike the Dolphins' kick, the ball never crosses the neutral zone. This allows him (or any kicking team member, for that matter) to attempt to advance the ball without restriction. Marcol, however, must at least gain a first down, contrasted to the Dolphins' kick (a muffed kick beyond the line of scrimmage), where a new first-and-10 is awarded to the Dolphins on the recovery. Marcol's run gave the Packers the game-winning touchdown, and he had previously kicked two field goals—making him responsible for all 12 points scored by the Packers on the day. The game ended immediately.

WHEN IT'S NOT FOURTH DOWN

The Steelers were tied 13–13 with the Browns in overtime with the ball on the third possession of the extra period. With a second-and-goal from the 6, Steelers coach Bill Cowher opted to kick the chip-shot field goal. Todd Peterson's attempt was spotted at the 14 and was blocked at the line. Peterson recovered at the 12 and ran to the 9, where he fumbled. Steelers special teams lineman John Fiala recovered Peterson's fumble at the 13.

7. What happens as a result of the play?

With a goal-to-go situation, Peterson won't be able to get a first down without scoring a touchdown, but it is irrelevant here. When Marcol recovered the blocked kick, he was compelled to achieve the first down because it was a fourth-down play. Peterson's recovery behind the line of scrimmage is just like a standard second-down running play. Even the fumble and the re-recovery of the ball by the Steelers does not affect the Steelers' possession.

The ball goes to the dead-ball spot. The Steelers are not starting a new possession, because the ball never crossed the line of scrimmage. Therefore, the Steelers have a third-and-goal at the 13-yard line.

The Steelers, with a second chance at redemption, kicked the game-winning field goal on third down.

With a commanding lead late in the fourth quarter of the AFC Divisional Playoff game on January 14, 2012, the New England Patriots had the ball on a third-and-10 against the Denver Broncos. Rather than face a punt rush on fourth down, Patriots coach Bill Belichick instructed quarterback Tom Brady to punt the ball from the standard shotgun formation. The punt rolled out of bounds for a 48-yard kick, since there was no deep player for the Broncos.

8. Is this a legal kick by the Patriots?

A team may punt on any down it chooses. Belichick said he was avoiding a play that could cause potential injury, since his team's advancement to the conference championship was essentially cinched, although the play call stirred up a lot of grumblings out of the Mile High City that he was showing their team up.

The Patriots also do not need to line up in a standard punt formation. By doing so, a defensive player may line up across from the center; this is a player-safety rule, but the only way to fairly apply it is if the offense presents a standard kicking formation.

FAIR CATCHES

The fair catch is a player-safety measure to allow receivers to catch high kicks where contact might be imminent. To encourage more kick returns, the fair catch was removed from the college football rulebook in 1950. It was quickly restored a year later due to an increase in injuries. The fair catch allows the kick returner to forfeit his right to return the ball in exchange for an unimpeded attempt to catch the ball without the risk of contact. The ball is dead immediately upon the successful completion of a fair catch.

The fair-catch signal is one hand over the helmet and waved side to side. Evaluate these four plays for a potential fair-catch signal.

> Play No. 1: On a punt during the season-opening game on September 10, 2009, Titans punt returner Cortland Finnegan signaled for a fair catch as soon as the ball was kicked by Steelers punter Daniel Sepulveda.
>
> Play No. 2: A punt returner is attempting to catch a punt without calling for a fair catch. To block the sun, he puts his hand up in front of his face.
>
> Play No. 3: A punt is kicked high, and a gust of wind blows the ball back behind the line of scrimmage, where a player on the receiving team signals for a fair catch.
>
> Play No. 4: During the NFC Championship game against the 49ers on January 22, 2012, Giants punt returner Will Blackmon put his hand over his shoulder pads but not over his helmet, and he did not wave his hand side to side.

9. Which of these is considered a fair-catch signal?

On the first play, there is no one Finnegan can be signaling to if the ball has just been kicked. This could set up a potentially dangerous situation after the catch, because the signal has not been properly communicated to the kicking team. The rules specifically state that the ball must be in flight, which means some sort of trajectory must be established.

For the second play, the rules allow for the receiver to shield his eyes from the sun with one or both hands. However, he must keep his hands below the top of the helmet, or it would be construed as a fair-catch signal.

There cannot be a fair catch behind the line of scrimmage on the third play.

Blackmon's hand on the fourth play is misleading his opponent into easing up in their pursuit. A valid fair-catch signal is above the helmet with a waving motion, but any gesture where a player raises a hand above the shoulder pads must be considered a fair-catch signal (either valid or invalid). Upon Blackmon's catch, the ball is dead, and a 5-yard penalty is assessed. Even though the ball is dead, it is not a fair catch.

The first three actions are neither valid nor invalid fair-catch signals, and they are simply ignored. The fourth is considered to be an invalid fair-catch signal.

FAIR-CATCH INTERFERENCE

On October 19, 2009, Buccaneers kick returner Clifton Smith attempted to make a fair catch at the 20-yard line on a punt by Panthers punter Jason Baker. Well before the ball reached Smith, Panthers safety Dante Wesley applied a full-speed-locomotive hit on Smith. The ball rolled out of bounds at the 18 while Smith lay flat at the 20, apparently unconscious.

10. Obviously this is a foul, but how is this enforced?

Referee John Parry summed up the infraction best in his penalty announcement: "Fair-catch interference, which was also a personal foul, number 21 of the kicking team. That player, by virtue of his actions, is disqualified from further participation. Fifteen-yard penalty."

The fair-catch interference and the personal foul cannot be combined into a 30-yard penalty, although if there was ever a case for a 30-yard unnecessary roughness penalty, this would be the play. The fair catch is awarded at the 20 and 15 yards added on from there. Even though there is a double foul and one must be declined, the Wesley ejection is not offset.

This play would not be enforced much differently if Smith had not signaled for a fair catch. The receiver is still entitled to make a catch, but the instant he does, he may be tackled immediately absent the fair-catch signal. The foul in that case would be kick-catch interference, and the difference would be that the fair catch is not awarded.

The punishment for the hit continued for Wesley on Monday afternoon, as the league announced that Wesley was suspended one game for the hit—a disciplinary action infrequently levied by the league at that time for a live-ball hit. Smith returned after a few weeks off, then was placed on injured reserve after a second concussion that season.

11. On September 9, 2009, Jacoby Jones, the kick returner for the Houston Texans, signaled for a fair catch of a punt by Craig Hentrich of the Tennessee Titans. Jones muffed the catch at the 9-yard line, and the ball bounced directly into the hands of Titans cornerback Jason McCourty at the 10-yard line, just off the fingertips of Jones. McCourty had given Jones a clear path to catch the ball before it was muffed. Which team gets the ball and where?

Because Jones calls for the fair catch, he is entitled to "an unhindered catch of an airborne kick." The term *airborne kick* includes an airborne muffed catch, because the ball has not touched the ground and, without being possessed, it is still considered a kick. Jones is entitled to make good on his muffed catch and finish the fair catch while the ball remains airborne.

Despite the fact that McCourty caught a ball that fortuitously bounced right to him, he still is committing "interference with the opportunity to make a fair catch," as it is specifically stated in the rulebook. Because Mc-Courty snatched the ball out of midair and Jones was still able to make a play on the ball (as it was just about an arm's length away), McCourty was hit with a 15-yard fair-catch interference foul. The interference by McCourty was completely innocuous, but it was still lumped into the category with Dante Welsey's hit on Clifton Smith mentioned earlier.

This play spurred a rule change that took effect in the following season. McCourty's action was still considered fair-catch interference, but when the ball is muffed by the receiver, it essentially becomes a zero-yard penalty, with the fair catch awarded. The caveat is that the receiver must still have a reasonable ability to make the catch; otherwise the defense cannot be ruled to interfere if the receiver cannot complete the catch under any circumstances.

Case in point: When the Giants were playing the Eagles on October 12, 2014, Giants receiver Odell Beckham Jr. muffed a punt at the 9-yard line. The ball bounced off his knee and just outside his reach. The ball then hit the knee of incoming Eagles defender Josh Huff in midair, which abruptly propelled the ball over the end line. Side judge Rick Patterson and back judge Steve Patrick discussed it at the goal line before ruling a touchback and no foul. Because the ball was at knee level and out of Beckham's reach, he was not being restricted from a reasonable path to the ball. Had Beckham been lunging for the loose ball, this would be a judgment call if there still was a reasonable opportunity to complete the catch.

Back to the Jason McCourty play, under current rules, the fair-catch interference penalty would still be called, which negates the recovery by the Titans. The Texans would get possession of the ball, and the fair catch would be awarded at the 10-yard line. It would be a spot foul, so no yardage would be assessed, and the Texans would have the ball first-and-10 at their own 10. This enforcement applies only if the catch is muffed. If it is not muffed, the fair-catch interference remains a 15-yard penalty.

FAIR-CATCH KICK

If football has an equivalent to baseball's rare feat of an unassisted triple play, it has to be the fair-catch kick. On November 21, 1976, at Rich Stadium in Buffalo (now known as Ralph Wilson Stadium), this obscurity was buried in further layers of obscurity for several years.

The league does not track fair-catch kicks, and so the yeoman of the aptly named *Quirky Research* blog took on the task. They admit that they haven't covered the full history of the NFL, but they have uncovered many of the lost instances of the fair-catch kick. *Quirky Research* found that San Diego Chargers kicker Ray Wersching, noted more for his All-Pro career with the San Francisco 49ers, is the last kicker to successfully convert a fair catch into three points; he did it in the 1976 game in Buffalo.

In the late 1980s, more detailed play descriptions were kept by teams and the league, allowing for a more thorough examination of these elusive plays. Since 1988, when the league began to standardize the written play-by-play practice, only five confirmed fair-catch kicks have been attempted, including one by Wersching's successor on the 49ers squad, Mike Cofer. Cofer's attempt in a divisional playoff game on New Year's Day 1989 is the only known postseason attempt at a fair-catch kick.

Most of the rarity of the play has to do with a set of conditions strategically occurring at the right time. The most likely scenario begins with a punt from deep in a team's own territory. The receiver of the punt must call for a fair catch and make the catch. Then, the team who made the fair catch has the option to either perform a fair-catch kick or run a regular play from scrimmage as normal. If the field position is right and there is a time constraint at the end of the half, the fair-catch kick is a wise option. This is why these attempts tend to happen near the end of the half.

The fair-catch kick is also in unique territory, as it extends the quarter if time has expired. The team who makes a fair catch at the conclusion of the quarter is allowed to attempt a fair-catch kick, but they may not take a snap on offense unless a foul by the opposing team allows a snap to occur.

The key elements of the fair-catch kick are that the team does not snap the ball and there is no chance of the kick being blocked. In a standard field goal attempt, the kick takes place about 7 yards behind the line of scrimmage. For a fair-catch kick, the ball is placed on the yard line of the catch, but is moved in to the nearest hash if it is caught outside of the hash marks. Also, the defense cannot charge the kicker; in fact, the defense must line up 10 yards away from the kick, just as if it is a kickoff.

12. On October 12, 1986, the New York Jets traveled to Sullivan Stadium for a game against the New England Patriots. With a 31–24 lead, the Jets punted with seconds remaining in the fourth quarter. Patriots receiver Irving Fryar made a fair catch on the punt at the Patriots' 25-yard line as time expired. Not only was an 85-yard field goal attempt downright impossible, the three points would not be enough to win. Since the teams are in kickoff formation, could the Patriots have attempted an onside kick?

The fair-catch kick was once referred to in the rulebook as a "free kick after a fair catch." That language was removed to avoid confusion with other uses of the term *free kick*, which is commonly any kickoff. While the fair-catch kick looks like a kickoff, the similarities end at their appearances.

The kick is still a field goal attempt, and the only modification to standard field goal rules is that there is no line of scrimmage. Therefore, once the kick is not going to be a successful field goal, all of the provisions for a missed field goal apply.

(As a technical matter, this means that a fair-catch kick is neither a scrimmage kick nor a free kick, but it is included here because it most closely adheres to the rules for a scrimmage kick. As unorthodox as this play may be, it does not merit its own chapter.)

The Patriots may recover a ball that is touched or possessed by the Jets. If the ball is only touched, the Patriots cannot advance the ball, meaning they can only recover a touched ball in the end zone. The Patriots can advance a fumble.

The only real option for the Patriots was having Fryar attempt a runback of the punt rather than call for a fair catch, but apparently he believed that the Patriots would have time for a play from scrimmage.

And, no, the Patriots cannot kick the ball backwards to keep it behind the "line of scrimmage."

13. On a fair-catch kick, which of the following is true?

A. The clock runs as soon as the ball is touched by a player on the defense.

B. The kicking team must follow the formation rules of an ordinary kickoff.

C. The kicker has the option of using a tee for the kick.

D. The kicker may drop-kick the fair-catch kick.

Since this is a field goal attempt, the kicking team may not recover the kick unless the opposing team has touched the ball first. Also, following the field goal rules, the clock will start when the ball is kicked, as opposed to a kickoff, which starts when the receiving team has touched the ball in the field of play. The kicker cannot use a tee for the kick; the ball must be held, or it can be drop-kicked, as long as any part of the kicker's body is behind the fair-catch kick line.

With the two restraining lines 10 yards apart, it has all of the appearances of a kickoff. Because of player-safety issues, the rules pertaining to legal kickoff formations still apply to the fair-catch kick, even though it is not a free kick. This means that the kicking team cannot have fewer than four players on either side of the kicker. (The holder, by rule, will count as the fourth player on either side, no matter which side of the ball he is on.)

Of the options presented, B and D are true for a fair-catch kick.

14. If the kick is missed, does the kicking team keep the ball? Where is it spotted next?

Assuming there is time left on the clock, the kicking team has surrendered the ball to their opponents on the fair-catch kick. If the ball goes out of bounds, or if it is recovered by the kicking team without touching a receiving-team player, it is spotted as a missed field goal: the receiving team has the ball at the spot of the kick. If the missed kick was inside the 20-yard line, it is a touchback.

However, just as with any other missed field goal, if the receiving team catches the kick and runs with it, they do not get the ball at the spot of the kick, but at the dead-ball spot instead.

15. On November 18, 1984, at the Hoosier Dome in Indianapolis, the New England Patriots were leading the Colts 26–10 with three seconds remaining in the second quarter. Patriots kicker Tony Franklin pops a squib kick up in the air, and the Colts signal for a fair catch, which makes it a dead ball as soon as the Colts catch the ball at their 49-yard line. Is this legally a fair catch, and are the Colts entitled to a fair-catch kick?

A fair catch on a kickoff is legal, but it is not generally advantageous to the receiving team, because kicking-team players cannot outrun a deep kickoff. For this reason, it is rare for a fair catch to be made on a kickoff, let alone made at a time when a fair-catch kick was even a remote possibility.

Colts kicker Raul Allegre did, in fact, line up for a 61-yard field goal attempt, but he came up about 5 yards short.

16. A fair-catch kick may be attempted after which of the following?

A. A failed fair catch due to fair-catch interference
B. Kick-catch interference
C. Catch by a player whose teammate signaled fair catch
D. Catch after an invalid fair-catch signal

As illustrated with the Jason McCourty play in the previous section, a fair catch is awarded when there is fair-catch interference, so the spot of a kick would be either at the spot of the foul or 15 yards from the spot of the foul, depending on the enforcement. Kick-catch interference would allow a team to run an untimed scrimmage down, but not a fair-catch kick. The other two scenarios create a dead ball immediately, but a fair catch is not made, so there is no kick option.

The only one of the above scenarios that will permit a fair-catch kick is A.

THE KICK IS UP . . . AND IT'S —?

17. A field goal kick that goes above the height of the goalposts is good, as long as the entire ball does not cross beyond the ___ plane of the post. Inside or outside?

The field judge and back judge are stationed underneath the goalposts. In the NFL, they will look up the outside edge of the goalpost, and it is an unsuccessful field goal if any part of the ball protrudes outside of the outside plane when the ball travels over the post. In the NCAA, the inner plane is used.

Browns kicker Phil Dawson was attempting to equalize the score at 30–30 at the end of regulation against the Browns' AFC North nemesis, the Baltimore Ravens, on November 18, 2007. The 51-yard attempt deflected off the left upright at an odd angle and bounced into the end zone. Rather than signal "no good" immediately, back judge Keith Washington and field judge Jim Saracino conferred with each other, then declared the kick did not score. However, the ball also hit the curved support leg of the post—the technical term is the *stanchion*—when it bounced out.

18. Is this a successful or unsuccessful field goal?

If you picture the goalpost as four distinct pieces—two uprights, a cross-bar, and the stanchion—the "goal" itself comprises all but the stanchion. Once the ball clears the mouth of the goal, the field goal is *still* not counted until the ball strikes another object, such as the net, the ground, a camera. Since the stanchion is not part of the goal, the field goal counts once the ball hits the stanchion after going through the uprights.

This was not a reviewable call in 2007, and referee Pete Morelli, Washington, and Saracino had to sort this out through discussion. The field goal was eventually declared good, and the game went into overtime.

It is now reviewable to see if a field goal is good or no good, provided that the ball is lower than the top of the uprights (45 feet from the ground) when it crosses the end line. There is no review allowed for kicks over the goalposts.

It is possible, on a very windy day, that a strong wind gust could blow the ball back through the goal opening to "block" a field goal. As long as it does not touch any object beyond the goalposts, such a kick is no good.

BLOCK THE KICK, LEGALLY

In the cavernous Los Angeles Memorial Coliseum, the Rams unveiled a unique field goal blocking tactic when the Bears visited on October 30, 1955. As George Blanda was about to attempt a field goal, Blanda saw Rams safety Don "the Blade" Burroughs looming much taller than the 6-foot-4 in the game program. Burroughs was standing on defensive tackle Eugene "Big Daddy" Lipscomb, listed as 6-foot-7, as Lipscomb held Burroughs's feet at waist level. Blanda's kick was unaffected by the wobbling tower of Burroughs and Lipscomb, and the field goal was good.

19. Is this a legal play?

At the time, the play was legal, despite being outlawed in the college game after Oregon State University attempted a self-illustratively named pyramid play in 1933. It is now prohibited under multiple provisions of the unsportsmanlike conduct rule, which include jumping or standing on a team-mate or opponent and picking up a teammate in order to block a kick.

20. On October 20, 2013, Steelers safety Troy Polamalu did his best to keep the Ravens' tying extra-point kick off the board with two minutes remaining in regulation. Standing about 4 yards deep in the end zone, Polamalu ran forward and leaped over the center in an attempt to have a near-automatic block. Is this an unsportsmanlike conduct foul?

Polamalu may run and leap the line, but he had better get enough elevation. Running and leaping is a 15-yard unsportsmanlike conduct foul if the defender lands on a player—either his opponent or his teammate. If the hurdle is clean, as in Polamalu's case, then there is no foul. This leaping foul does not apply to defensive players who are on the line of scrimmage or are a yard off the line, as their leap would be part of standard kick-blocking procedures, and it would not be as much of a safety hazard if the leaping player landed on another player.

Although Polamalu's vertical move was legal, his horizontal one was not, as he crossed the line of scrimmage just before the snap. The play was whistled dead immediately, as Polamalu had an unabated path to the holder and kicker, just as it would be called on an ill-timed quarterback blitz.

The Ravens were allowed to choose to accept the offside penalty on the extra-point attempt or on the ensuing kickoff. Enforcing on the extra-point would move the ball only half the distance to the 1-yard line, but a team might attempt a two-point conversion after accepting a defensive penalty.

21. Houston Texans linebacker Connor Barwin was assessed an unsportsmanlike conduct foul in a Sunday night game against the Green Bay Packers on October 14, 2012. On a field goal attempt, Barwin put his hands on an offensive lineman and jumped over him. Although he wound up contacting his opponent in the back with his feet, Barwin was lined up a yard from the line of scrimmage, giving him the exemption of landing on a player. Was the foul correct?

An additional provision related to the kick-blocking package of unsportsmanlike conduct fouls is leverage. A player cannot gain leverage, or increase his height in the jump, by putting his hand on an opponent or a teammate. There can be an incidental contact with the hand without a foul being called, but if there is a push, then it will be flagged.

On December 8, 1962, the Baltimore Colts hosted Washington at Memorial Stadium. Bob Khayat was attempting a 40-yard field goal, but it was blocked by Colts receiver R. C. Owens. However, Owens was not lined up near the line of scrimmage, and he did not break through the line to get his block. The 6-foot-3 Owens was blessed with an outstanding leaping ability and, while with the San Francisco 49ers, popularized the alley-oop play, in which he jumped much higher than the defender to catch the ball, much like the similarly named play in basketball. Owens was standing under the crossbar (at the time, the goalposts were on the goal line), timed his leap, and batted the ball away. This was a legal play at the time.

22. What is the penalty if this occurs today, and where does the ball get spotted, if the line of scrimmage was the 32-yard line?

As Owens is known for a play that shares a term in basketball, it is fitting that the penalty for blocking a field goal also shares a basketball term: goaltending. In basketball, a ball that is on its descent toward the basket cannot be blocked from going in; otherwise the basket (they call it a field goal, too) counts. The football goaltending foul does the same: a block at the goalpost (deemed a palpably unfair act) gives the offense the option of being awarded the three points for the field goal. The kicking team has a second option to accept an unsportsmanlike conduct foul, which is 15 yards from the spot of the snap and an automatic first down.

The offense can select only one of the two options. By accepting the 15-yard penalty, they continue the possession to increase the potential score to a touchdown. But if they opt to be awarded the three points, they cannot use the 15-yarder on the kickoff, because the penalty was "used up" to create the score. If the Owens play happened today, it would either be a first-and-10 for Washington at the 17, or a kickoff from the 35-yard line after the awarded field goal.

After Owens's legal goaltending maneuver, Dolphins tight end Morris Stroud attempted a few unsuccessful blocks of his own in the early 1970s before the practice was abolished outright. On September 9, 2012, Packers receiver Randall Cobb attempted to goaltend a 63-yard field goal by 49ers kicker David Akers right before halftime. Cobb missed the ball, but not by much. Akers's kick skipped off the top of the crossbar on the way in for the field goal, which was then a record-tying score. Cobb was not assessed a penalty for the attempt; he can draw a flag only if he makes contact with the ball above the level of the crossbar.

It would have been interesting to see the first goaltending foul be called on a kick that was to tie a record.

23. During the first preseason game played at AT&T Stadium in Arling-
ton, Texas, on August 21, 2009, a punt by A. J. Trapasso of the Titans hit
the underside of the large video screen installed above the field. What is the
procedure for handling this situation?

There was no precedent for this type of situation, but the crew called for
a do-over. This was actually provided for in the rules, but it was not clearly
stated how to carry out the rule. Walt Anderson's crew was working the
game and interpreted the rule to mean that the clock is reset to where it was
at the time of the snap.

"The only thing we've talked about really is the do-over of the play,"
said Mike Pereira, who was the vice president of officiating. "We've never
talked about resetting the clock back to where it was. That's obviously something we're going to have to talk about. And that may be what we arrive at."

What Pereira needed to talk about was a more detailed rule on how
to handle a situation such as this and codify it. Since this happened in the
first game at the stadium the Cowboys had just opened, there was concern
that the next issue would occur again soon. The Competition Committee
reviewed a quickly drafted proposal that affirmed the decision of Anderson's
crew to reset the clock to the time of the snap and give the punter a do-over.
It also empowered the replay official or the coach to call for a review if the
officials on the field did not see the ball hit the overhead object. The rule
pertained equally to any overhead object, which included aerial cameras and
support cables.

This was an unconventional situation, passing a rule outside of the normal off-season review and approval process. Rule 3-1 states, "An Official
Ruling (O.R.) is a ruling made in the interim between the annual rules meetings and is official only during the current season." Once the Competition
Committee resolved the proposed rule, it was sent to the owners for their
consent, putting it in effect for the 2009 season. In March 2010 the Competition Committee resubmitted the rule, as required, at the owners' annual
meeting, at which time it was made permanent.

One additional provision added to this do-over rule: most penalties
that occur during the play are erased along with the play; however, 15-yard
penalties for personal fouls and unsportsmanlike conduct would continue
to be enforced.

SEVEN

PASSING AND POSSESSION

After reviewing the play, the quarterback's arm was going forward. It is an incomplete pass.

> —*Referee Walt Coleman, announcing the replay*
> *reversal that was known as the Tuck Rule,*
> *2001 AFC Divisional Playoff Game, Oakland Raiders at*
> *New England Patriots, January 19, 2002*

1. Fill in the blanks from Rule 8-1-1: "A ball that is intentionally fumbled and goes forward is a _____. A ball that is intentionally muffed, and goes forward or backward, is a _____."

An intentional forward fumble is considered a forward pass. A muff, as discussed in chapter 4, is when the ball is touched in an unsuccessful attempt to secure possession of the ball. An intentional muffed ball is an effort to deliberately propel the ball, and less of an attempt to secure possession. An intentionally muffed ball is considered a *batted ball*, just as if the player punched a loose ball downfield to prevent the opponent from recovering the ball. Depending on the circumstances that pertain to the batted ball, this could be an illegal bat.

CHAPTER SEVEN

UNUSUAL PASSES

On September 13, 1992, Green Bay Packers coach Mike Holmgren benched starting quarterback Don Majkowski after halftime, bringing in future legend Brett Favre. On Favre's first NFL snap, he was lined up under center with the ball at the Packers' 17-yard line. He attempted a pass from the 10-yard line, but it was batted down by Tampa Bay Buccaneers defensive end Ray Seals. Favre caught the deflected pass at the 8, ran it forward to the 10, and was tackled there.

2. Is this a legal play? Where does the ball get spotted?

Favre wore an eligible number, but a quarterback who lines up under center to receive the snap is not considered an eligible receiver for that down. (See Table 4.1 in chapter 4 for the eligible and ineligible numbers.) Once the ball is tipped by an eligible player, Favre becomes eligible again. This allowed Favre to run with the ball without penalty after he caught his own pass, although he wound up registering a 7-yard loss. The ball is spotted for second-and-17 from the Packers 10.

Of course, after this play, the receiver of Brett Favre's first NFL pass went on to a prolific, record-setting football career, not as a receiver, but as a quarterback.

3. In Super Bowl IX on January 12, 1975, Minnesota Vikings quarterback Fran Tarkenton threw a pass that was deflected behind the line of scrimmage by Pittsburgh Steelers defensive lineman L. C. Greenwood. Tarkenton caught the deflection and threw the ball 41 yards to receiver John Gilliam. Is this a legal play?

Tarkenton is allowed to run with the ball, but there cannot be a second forward pass. It is irrelevant if the quarterback catches the ball behind where he threw it, because the pass was going in a forward trajectory when it first left the quarterback's arm.

At the time, the penalty for a second pass behind the line of scrimmage was to count it as if it was an incomplete pass: the ball is returned to the previous spot and a loss of down. Today, that foul is a 5-yard penalty from the line of scrimmage but no loss of down.

Future Vikings quarterback Brad Johnson might have seen film of this play, judging by this entry in the box score of a game between the Vikings and Panthers on October 12, 1997: *Vikings—Brad Johnson 3-yard touchdown pass from Brad Johnson (Eddie Murray kick).*

Johnson caught the ball behind the line of scrimmage and ran in for the score. It was the first time a player caught his own pass to score a touchdown.

4. Let's say Tarkenton's first pass was a backward pass, tipped by a defender and caught by either Tarkenton or his intended receiver. Can the Vikings throw a forward pass?

Yes, legally, they can. A team can have any number of backward passes during a down, but the offense is limited to just one forward pass, as long as that forward pass is behind the line of scrimmage.

A basic trick play in the back of every team's playbook is a backward pass to a receiver. The receiver can still throw a pass himself, because there was no forward pass during the down. This can deceive the defense, thinking the quarterback's initial throw was the only allowable pass. There are numerous examples of this being successful over the years.

In the hypothetical tipped backward pass presented, the head linesman or the line judge must make a judgement call on the flight of the pass to determine if it is a forward pass. A defensive player who bats the ball behind the quarterback has not made the pass backward. Similarly, if the passer's hand is going forward and his arm is grabbed by a defender, causing the pass to go backward, it is still a forward pass by rule. The throwing motion of the quarterback determines the direction when there is a batted ball or if he is materially affected in throwing the ball.

Also, when a defender contacts the passer's arm, the ball must already have begun a forward motion in order for it to be counted as a forward pass. If the ball goes forward without the hand moving it, this is a fumble under the "empty hand" rule. This rule clarifies the pass versus fumble determination: if the quarterback's hand does not have control of the ball when the forward movement of the hand begins, it is a fumble.

5. What if the backward pass is caught by a defender who then fumbles the ball. Can the quarterback pick up the fumble and throw a forward pass?

No. Once the ball is in the possession of the defense, the line of scrimmage is irrelevant for the remainder of the down (except penalties might still be enforced back to the previous spot). This would be a double change of possession, and without a line of scrimmage, any forward pass is illegal. In this case, there is a 5-yard penalty from the spot of the pass. The offense would get a new first-and-10 from that spot—because of the change of possession—regardless of where the ball ends up or the previous down and distance.

6. Is the ball dead immediately when there is an illegal forward pass? What happens if the defense intercepts the illegal pass or if it lands incomplete?

The down runs to its completion despite the illegal forward pass. If the defense intercepts any illegal pass, they can decline the foul and keep the ball. It just creates a headache for the official statistician.

Also, the defense may decline an illegal forward pass that falls incomplete, since the down will count, but the penalty would replay the down.

7. In an NFC Divisional Playoff game against the Seattle Seahawks on January 11, 2014, New Orleans Saints receiver Marques Colston attempted to keep a game-ending play alive by throwing a lateral beyond the line of scrimmage. Instead, he threw the ball forward, and it bounced once on the ground and then into the hands of a teammate. The officials immediately killed the play rather than allowing it to continue. Were they correct to stop the play?

Since Colston's pass is a forward pass, it is ruled an incomplete pass, so the play ends immediately. Only a backward pass may strike the ground and the play continues. The illegal forward pass incurred a 10-second runoff on the clock as well, which took the remaining time off the clock.

Had there been enough time on the clock, Colston's foul would have been assessed a 5-yard penalty from the spot of the pass and also would have incurred a loss of down. Since it is essentially a running play when the foul occurs, it takes the enforcement spot of any other foul on a running play. The loss of down, though, closes a loophole that would allow the offense to advance the ball downfield without incrementing the down.

Conversely, a second forward pass from behind the line of scrimmage is not a loss of down, even if the ball crosses the line of scrimmage and returns behind the line for the second pass.

8. Let's say that Colston's pass was not at the end of the game. It was a third-and-2 play, and Colston gained 13 yards before the pass. What is the down and distance of the next play?

Although it is rare that a distinction has to be made, the term *loss of down* is slightly misleading. In reality, this means that the down number is counted, rather than being repeated. If there was time for another play, the Saints would actually have the ball with a first-and-10, 8 yards downfield from the previous play. The third down counts up to the point of the illegal pass, and the subsequent penalty still gives the Saints the first down. The loss of down essentially does not affect the penalty enforcement in this circumstance; it would never be enforced as a second-and-10.

If the Saints were facing a third-and-10 play instead, then Colston's pass would have occurred 3 yards past the first-down marker. The penalty would move the ball back 2 yards from the first-down line, and the loss of down would count the third down. Even though Colston goes beyond the first-down line, the number of the next down is determined after the penalty enforcement. This means the third-and-10 play would be followed by a fourth-and-2.

9. On a recovery of an Eagles fumble on November 1, 2009, Giants defensive tackle Fred Robbins lateralled to linebacker Osi Umenyiora. Both players were running parallel, with Umenyiora trailing behind Robbins by a couple of yards. When viewed on replay, Robbins released the ball at the Eagles 37-yard line. Even though the pitch was basically backward, the fact that both players were running caused Umenyiora to first touch the ball at the 35—2 yards in front of where Robbins released the ball. Does this count as a forward or backward pass?

Without any other complications of whether a passer's arm was materially affected by an opponent, the ruling of a forward/backward pass hinges on the point of the ball when it was released to when it is first touched. It then becomes basic geometry of a line: if the line shows it forward, it is a forward pass; if the line is parallel to the goal line or behind, it is a backward pass.

Even though Robbins threw backward, the line connecting the points goes toward his opponent's goal line. Therefore, the illegal forward pass is assessed from the point where Robbins released the ball. In this case, since there is no line of scrimmage, it is a 5-yard penalty from there, but the Giants keep the ball on the turnover.

ILLEGAL TOUCHING OF A PASS

During an NFC Wild Card Playoff game on January 9, 2011, in Green Bay, the Philadelphia Eagles were preparing for a two-point conversion after scoring a touchdown in the fourth quarter against the Packers. Quarterback Michael Vick threw a pass to tight end Brent Celek that was complete in the back of the end zone. Just before the ball arrived, field judge Jon Lucivansky dropped his hat on the end line, and he threw a penalty flag after the catch.

Celek had stepped out of bounds and then reestablished himself in bounds. Referee Pete Morelli announced that there was a foul for illegally touching a forward pass.

10. How is the illegal touching of a forward pass enforced on the two-point conversion?

Because Celek caught the pass, the Packers must accept the illegal touching penalty to nullify the score. Because an illegal touching foul is not a loss-of-down penalty, the Eagles are entitled to retry the touchdown conversion after the 5-yard penalty is enforced. The Eagles were unsuccessful on their pass attempt from the 7-yard line. The Packers could decline the penalty only if Celek did not catch the pass in bounds; otherwise Celek's illegal action would be ignored and the catch would stand. The foul cannot carry forward to the kickoff.

11. The Dolphins were hosting a Monday Night Football game from Miami's Orange Bowl against the Dallas Cowboys on December 17, 1984. Just after the two-minute warning in the fourth quarter, the Cowboys had the ball at their own 34-yard line, trailing 21–14. On a pass route, wide receiver Tony Hill stepped out of bounds, and side judge Dick Creed dropped his hat to indicate Hill was an ineligible receiver. Quarterback Danny White threw a pass to running back James Jones, but the ball was deflected by Dolphins cornerback Don McNeal. Hill, who was back in bounds, caught the deflected ball just above his shoelaces at the 50-yard line and ran to the end zone. Where is the ball spotted for the next play?

At the beginning of the play, any of the offensive interior lineman are ineligible to catch a pass, as discussed in chapter 4. All players on the defense are eligible. As the play progresses, any eligible receiver, including a defensive player, who steps out of bounds loses his eligibility.

Once the ball is tipped by an eligible player, all 22 players on the field become eligible to catch the ball. The tip by McNeal makes Hill an eligible receiver once again. His catch is legal, and the touchdown counts. The ball is spotted at the 2-yard line for the point-after-touchdown attempt, which enabled Dallas to even the score at 21–21. The tied score did not last long, as Dolphins quarterback Dan Marino would find receiver Mark Clayton for a 63-yard touchdown pass, completing Marino's fifth game-winning drive in the fourth quarter. There would be many more to come.

INTENTIONAL GROUNDING

When the New York Jets and the Miami Dolphins square off, chances are something exciting, perhaps miraculous, is about to happen.

On November 27, 1994, quarterback Dan Marino was attempting the 39th fourth-quarter game-winning drive of his career when he marched the Dolphins 76 yards downfield in the closing minutes of the game. After a completion to the 8-yard line and with less than 30 seconds left, Marino shouted, "Clock! Clock! Clock!"—a signal that he would immediately spike the ball as an incomplete pass. Spiking the ball was added as an exception to the intentional grounding rules in 1987 as a clock-stopping strategy, and the resulting incomplete pass means the offense sacrifices a down in the process.

The Jets, however, didn't realize they were about to be duped. Marino took the snap and began an immediate throwing motion to spike, but he did not let go of the ball. Marino even stood still as if the play was over before quickly recocking his arm for a pass. Jets cornerback Aaron Glenn bought the fake, allowing a moment's hesitation for receiver Mark Ingram to sprint to the end zone to catch a game-winning touchdown.

12. Was Marino's fake spike permitted under the rules, or should the ball be ruled dead since he initiated a spiking motion?

There is nothing in the rules that prohibited Marino from faking the spike. However, he did risk an official blowing his whistle inadvertently, killing the play. This happened to quarterback Peyton Manning when he played for the Indianapolis Colts in a November 25, 2001, game against the New Orleans Saints. The referee was tricked by the fake spike, and he blew the play dead.

Generally, if a team has a trick play that has the potential to catch the officials off guard, the coach or a player will make the referee aware before the game or during a timeout.

13. On the same day as Marino's fake, 17 years later in Oakland, the Bears were trailing the Raiders by five points with seconds to go and the clock running. Bears quarterback Caleb Hanie took the snap, pumped his arm once to fake a spike, hesitated briefly, and then spiked the ball. He was not under the threat of being sacked. Is this legal?

By rule, the clock-stopping spike must happen immediately after receiving the snap. By pausing to consider his strategic options, Hanie actually lost the option to spike the ball. Hanie was charged with intentional grounding. Also, since the penalty carries a ten-second runoff, the remaining four seconds were taken off the clock, ending the game right there.

Referee Ron Winter briefly checked with his head linesman to make certain the elements for intentional grounding were there, as is standard practice on any such call. It was the correct call, even though Hanie was not under imminent threat of a sack.

The spike rule also requires a quarterback to be under center in order to stop the clock. If a quarterback receives the snap in a shotgun formation, it is an intentional grounding penalty if he spikes the ball.

14. At the end of the 2011 season, the Patriots had a rematch with the Giants in Super Bowl XLVI, three years after they had faced off in the title game. In the first quarter from his own 6-yard line, Patriots quarterback Tom Brady retreated to his own end zone to pass. In order to avoid a sack, he rolled slightly to his right to a spot roughly behind where his right tackle was lined up before the snap. With no one open, Brady heaved a pass about 30 yards downfield where there was no chance of completion or interception. What is the call?

- A. Because Brady wasn't in the pocket, his pass only had to get to the line of scrimmage. No foul.
- B. Brady was actually in the pocket, but since the pass was far downfield, it could have been caught by a receiver running his route correctly. It's a judgment call if it is a foul.
- C. Brady intentionally grounded the ball, which results in a loss of down and the ball is placed at the 3-yard line (half the distance to the goal from the previous spot).
- D. Brady intentionally grounded the ball, which results in a safety.

The correct answer is D. Even though he was aligned to the edge of the tackle box, Brady was still considered to be inside the pocket. (The tackle box is established at the snap as an imaginary boundary extending backward from the outside shoulder of the offensive tackles.) Because the pass had no realistic chance of completion, this is intentional grounding; the downfield distance is not a consideration, nor is a receiver who is out of position (unless he is fouled in the process). Usually, the referee will confer with the head linesman or the line judge to determine if there was a receiver in the area.

Because the pass was so deep, it was back judge Tony Steratore who had to truck in to conference with referee John Parry on the grounding call. Parry ruled intentional grounding on Brady. Since it was a penalty enforced from a spot in the end zone, it was a safety, giving the Giants an early 2–0 lead. It was a set of unusual circumstances, but the proper call was made.

15. If Brady was pursued outside of the pocket and heaved a similar un-catchable ball, what is the ruling?

Incomplete pass. In order to protect the quarterback from injury, the intentional grounding rule does not apply to a quarterback who has left the pocket and has thrown a pass to the line of scrimmage or beyond.

16. If Brady ran outside of the pocket, reentered the pocket area, and then threw the same pass, what is the call?

Incomplete pass. Once a quarterback leaves the pocket, that area no longer exists.

17. In a game against the St. Louis Rams on December 2, 2012, San Francisco 49ers quarterback Colin Kaepernick avoided a sack in the end zone and left the pocket area. He threw the ball toward the sideline. It crossed the sideline short of the line of scrimmage, but landed out of bounds at the line of scrimmage. The referee ruled intentional grounding in the end zone and awarded the Rams a safety. Was this the correct call?

No. The pass has to reach the line of scrimmage, which it did when it contacted the ground out of bounds. The point in which the ball goes over the boundary line in the air is irrelevant to the call. Unfortunately for the head linesman, the ball landed behind him before he could turn around. Since the ball was in his zone, the head linesman must report to the referee if the ball reached the line of scrimmage, even though in this case it happened out of his field of view.

PASS INTERFERENCE

A few surprises were in store on opening day of the 2009 season at Cleveland Browns Stadium when the Minnesota Vikings came to town. Vikings coach Brad Childress opted to open the season with an onside kick. Despite having the entire off-season to prepare for this play, the surprise was that the Browns recovered the onside kick at midfield.

In the middle of the second quarter, Browns quarterback Brady Quinn connected with receiver Braylon Edwards at the 3-yard line, and Edwards walked in for a score. Cornerback Cedric Griffin committed a defensive pass interference foul, and in doing so, pushed Edwards out of bounds at the 6. Edwards came back in bounds to catch the ball.

18. Is Edwards an eligible receiver, and where is the ball spotted?

This was ruled on the field as a complete pass to an eligible receiver, even though Edwards stepped out of bounds. If an eligible receiver is forced out of bounds due to a foul, that player keeps his eligibility to catch or touch a pass. The only requirement is that the out-of-bounds player must make an immediate attempt to return in bounds, and he must reestablish himself with two feet down in bounds, without any part of the body being out of bounds.

In Braylon Edwards's case, field judge Scott Edwards (obviously, no relation) ruled that the receiver was able to reestablish himself in bounds prior to the catch. Even though the defensive pass interference foul is key to maintaining Braylon Edwards's eligibility, the Browns are allowed to decline that penalty and still take the score.

This play would be subject to a replay official confirmation today, but at that time scoring plays were not automatically reviewed, so Childress challenged the call. Referee John Parry saw on replay that, although Edwards's body was completely in bounds, his second foot did not come down in bounds before the catch. This means Edwards is still considered out of bounds when he touches the ball, making it an incomplete pass.

Because of the reversal, the Browns were able to accept the pass interference penalty, which at least gave the Browns the ball at the 6-yard line—the spot where the foul occurred, not where Edwards caught it. This was a pivotal challenge for the Vikings, as they were able to stop the Browns and force them to kick a field goal.

19. In the AFC Championship game between the Denver Broncos and the New England Patriots on January 19, 2014, Broncos quarterback Peyton Manning completed a 10-yard pass to Eric Decker. The play was negated by pass interference penalties on the Broncos and the Patriots. Is offsetting pass interference a correct call?

Typically, if there is mutual hand fighting between the receiver and the defender on the play, this will not draw a flag, as neither player is gaining an advantage on the reception. To call offsetting pass interference in this situation would give the offense an unfair opportunity to replay the down.

In this case, the two interference fouls came from opposite sides of the field, so the fouls were independent of each other. It is also technically possible for a defender to draw a pass interference near the line of scrimmage and the receiver to commit the foul when the ball is in the air; these would be offsetting fouls as long as the two illegal acts are separate.

Pass interference is perhaps one of the most controversial penalties that can be called in the game. Although there are some objective criteria, it remains a subjective call on the actions of both players. Because it is a subjective call, it has not been allowed to be reviewed under the replay rules, which means the on-the-spot call will always stand. Pass interference will, in effect, grant a reception for a defensive foul and can take away one on an offensive foul. There are indications that the Competition Committee is reviewing proposals to reduce the defensive pass interference on a deep pass to 10 or 15 yards or to allow a coach to challenge a pass interference call. So far, the needle has not moved on fundamentally modifying pass interference rules, but it may be a tight call in a huge game that becomes the tipping point for the Competition Committee to take action.

20. On November 9, 2014, the Saints were tied 24–24 with the 49ers with only four seconds remaining in regulation. Saints quarterback Drew Brees threw a deep desperation pass that was caught by receiver Jimmy Graham for a touchdown. Graham pushed off a player in the scramble for the ball and was penalized for offensive pass interference, nullifying the game-winning touchdown. Is this the correct call?

Pass interference is rarely called on the Hail Mary–type passes. The quarterback is throwing to an area as opposed to a specific receiver, hoping for a lucky break. At the receiving end, there are multiple players who all have equal right to catch the ball, resulting in the inevitable collision of bodies at the endpoint of the pass arc. This is considered legal action, as each player, regardless of uniform, is making a play on the ball and not on a receiver.

In Graham's case, he pushed a 49ers defender to the ground to gain a position on the pass prior to the arrival of the ball. By making an action to restrict the defender, this is a pass interference call on any pass play, Hail Mary or otherwise. Had Graham established a position downfield after the pass reached its apex, he could generally have protected his position, as long as he did not deliberately disrupt the defender's right to the ball. The touchdown did not count, and the game went to overtime.

If the roles were reversed and the 49ers defender pushed Graham out of the way, the ball would be placed on the 1-yard line for the foul, and the Saints would get one untimed down, since the half cannot end on a defensive penalty.

Another desperation play occurred with eight seconds to go and the Lions trailing the Browns 37–31 on November 22, 2009—the same play we explained at great length in chapter 3. Lions quarterback Matthew Stafford was under pressure in the backfield and rolled out to the left to heave a pass for the end zone. The ball was intercepted by safety Brodney Pool. Browns defensive back Hank Poteat pushed a Lions receiver while the ball was in the air and drew a penalty flag.

Following the game, Pool said he thought the call against Poteat was incorrect: "I thought by rules once a quarterback is out of pocket, everything is live and if you have a receiver running on the end line I thought you could push him out so he can't come back in and catch the ball."

Poteat also defended his actions, saying, "My understanding is, once the quarterback's out of the pocket you can force the receiver out of bounds, and that's what I was trying to do. That's what I was always coached to do."

21. Were Pool and Poteat correct, and was the flag in error?

Poteat is correct that the action he speaks of is a legal action when the quarterback is scrambling to avoid a sack. When the quarterback carries the ball outside of the pocket, it is not a pass play anymore, but a running play, and typical run blocking is allowed. This gives the defense an advantage to put a potential receiver out of bounds, and thus ineligible to catch a pass. As soon as Stafford leaves the pocket, illegal contact fouls cannot be called, but defensive holding can be called as usual for a run or a pass play. However, both Pool and Poteat omit a very crucial aspect of the rule.

When Stafford eventually sets and throws the pass, the play has reverted back to a pass play, meaning all of the blocking that was allowed is now considered pass interference once the ball is in the air. Poteat's block came after the ball left Stafford's hand, so the defensive pass interference call wiped out the interception, and the Lions had the ball for an untimed down at the 1-yard line. Had the block come earlier, while Stafford was still a runner, it would be a legal block as long as it did not cross the line into a defensive holding foul.

PROCESS OF THE CATCH

There once was an item in the rulebook known as the "tuck rule." An apparent fumble by Patriots quarterback Tom Brady in a 2001 AFC Divisional Playoff game against the Raiders was overturned to an incomplete pass only because he had not finished tucking the ball back to his body. Although there were several other instances of the tuck rule, that play became indelibly linked with the rule as it continued to remain in the NFL rulebook. Fans protested the rule; even Rich Eisen, who cashed a paycheck from the league as the top banana on the NFL Network's signature show, lobbied the vice president of officiating on-air repeatedly to repeal the tuck rule.

In 2013 the league owners voted nearly unanimously to kill the tuck rule. (Patriots owner Robert Kraft abstained.) And so a different rule assumed the mantle of the rulebook's most infamous entry, and it, too, has a signature play that frequently evokes one player's name almost every time it comes up.

It was opening day, September 12, 2010. The Lions were traveling a road of despair, having only three wins in the last 37 games played, including a winless 2008 season. On a last-minute drive against the Chicago Bears, it seemed that the fortunes of the franchise were about to change. The Lions found out that every silver lining has a dark cloud, to reverse a metaphor, when an official signaled a go-ahead touchdown for the Lions, only to be overruled by another. Much like Brady's play was *the* tuck rule, this has been repeated in the years since as *the* Calvin Johnson play without any elaboration necessary.

Johnson was in the end zone and grabbed the pass in midair. As his second foot comes down in the end zone, Johnson continues to fall to the ground. After one elbow hits in the end zone, Johnson's hand holding the ball comes to the ground, and the ball comes out. As the replays flashed across the enormous screens in sports bars across this country, the fans' consensus was that Johnson had control of the ball long enough in the end zone to merit a touchdown.

The incomplete ruling was confirmed in replay, and a nation of football fans felt the Lions were robbed. After being unable to score again on the next two plays, the Lions added this game to their unlucky streak, winning only 2 of the next 11 games, before finishing the season 6–10.

For a player going to the ground, the process of the catch must involve these three items in order for the catch to be ruled complete:

1. The receiver must have firm control of the ball.
2. He must get two feet down in bounds.
3. He must be able to perform an "act common to the game," sometimes referred to as a "football move," using old terminology from the catch rule. An act common to the game includes taking another step, turning, stretching for the end zone—basically an action that establishes the receiver as a runner. This gives a moment to transition from the catch to the run. The caveat is that if a player is falling to the ground before he has the ability to perform an act common to the game, he must maintain control of the ball all the way to the ground.

In Johnson's case, by putting the second hand down and having the ball pop out of his hand, he did not fulfill this requirement.

The process of the catch applies equally to plays in the middle of the field, at the sideline when a player falls out of bounds, and in the end zone. Therefore, being out of bounds or in the end zone does not absolve the player of completing the third catch requirement.

Johnson may have a partner in karma after Cowboys receiver Dez Bryant had a fourth-down catch near the goal line reversed in an NFC Divisional Playoff game against the Packers on January 11, 2015. As Bryant made the catch, he was going to the ground as his second foot touched in bounds. Bryant landed with the ball touching the ground and momentarily lost control of the ball. The play was ruled complete on the field and overturned in replay.

22. Was the incomplete ruling correct, and is there anything on this play that could be open to interpretation?

In order to better understand this process of a catch, take Calvin Johnson's catch and put it in the field of play at the 50-yard line. Without the third step in the process of the catch, Johnson's play would be ruled a catch and a fumble as he goes to the ground. Just as in the end zone play, Johnson was not contacted by a Bears defender after he caught the ball, so Johnson would not be ruled down by contact when he hits the ground. The Competition Committee saw many plays like this hypothetical catch at the 50, and they felt that this created a cheap fumble. Similarly, if the receiver is not going to the ground at the 50-yard line but instead is hit immediately by a defender, the ball might pop out immediately. This was also looked upon as a cheap fumble, because the receiver would have had control of the ball for such a short period of time.

These two hypothetical catches at midfield become the baseline for the rule. But, in order to be consistent, a catch in the end zone must be ruled the same as a catch in the field of play. There cannot be a two-step process for the end zone catch and a three-step process everywhere else. Even though it may feel as though Johnson was cheated from a sure touchdown, the tight rules that define a professional football catch mean that his catch can only be fairly ruled as incomplete.

Dez Bryant was sure that his catch would be upheld in the replay review. "I had possession," a shell-shocked Bryant said in a postgame interview. "I *had* possession of the ball coming down. That's possession, right? One, two [steps], reach?" Asked if he attempted to stretch to the end zone, Bryant said, "Did you see my hand? I tried to stretch for it. I wasn't off balance. I'm trying to stretch for it, trying to get in the end zone."

As much as Bryant was sure he stretched, he did little more than what a falling player would do. After the two steps, he was not under his own power. Another foot touched down, but, again, it was incidental to him falling. Had the third step planted firmly, Bryant would have a much clearer case of a completed pass, because he would have performed an act common to the game.

Bryant was able to reestablish control of the ball. To see if this effort counts for something, consider a similar come-from-behind situation from the 1999 NFC Championship game.

It was three weeks after Y2K, and a bug was discovered in the rulebook during the fourth quarter of the NFC title game. The Tampa Bay Buccaneers were successful in shutting down the St. Louis Rams' high-scoring offense, known as the "Greatest Show on Turf." The Bucs were holding on to a tenuous 6–5 lead into the fourth quarter when the Rams finally scored the first touchdown of the game with less than five minutes to go. After a failed two-point conversion, the Rams led 11–6, giving the Buccaneers a chance to retake the lead.

With less than a minute to go, Buccaneers quarterback Shaun King threw a 10-yard completion to Bert Emanuel on a second-and-23 play. This gave the Bucs the ball on third down from the Rams' 22-yard line. Referee Bill Carollo was then called to review the catch by the replay official.

The replays showed that Emanuel controlled the ball, and as he contacted the ground, the point of the ball did as well. However, Emanuel had a firm grip on the ball, and it did not move as it hit the turf.

23. Is this a catch?

The result of the catch was the so-called Bert Emanuel Rule, passed before the 2000 season, but the replay review on that day obviously could not use that rule. Emanuel's catch was ruled incomplete because the ball had contacted the ground, despite being in the receiver's possession. The rule added in the off-season allowed the ball in a receiver's hands to touch the ground as long as the receiver maintained control of the ball and did not use the ground to trap or assist the securing of the catch.

In Bryant's catch, once the ball touches the ground and he loses control of the ball, it is an incomplete pass, just as any other pass that bounces off the ground. Therefore, he could not get relief from Emanuel's test-case catch. Bryant was given a small margin for error when the ball touched the ground: the ball could move slightly in his hand when he contacted the ground and still be ruled a completion, as long as he demonstrated full and continuous control of the ball.

The rule change was little consolation to the Buccaneers, as King threw two incomplete passes following the Emanuel play to seal their fate and send the Rams to Super Bowl XXXIV.

FORWARD FUMBLES

One typical cold and snowy day at Chicago's Soldier Field, the Bears and Packers were squaring off to determine the 2013 NFC North champion in the final game of the regular season on December 29. With 3:34 remaining in the second quarter, the Packers had the ball first-and-10 on the Bears' 17-yard line. Quarterback Aaron Rodgers appeared to have thrown a pass, but was ruled to have fumbled the ball at the 23-yard line as Bears defensive end Julius Peppers hit Rodgers. Receiver Jarrett Boykin recovered the ball at the 15-yard line, but, convinced the ruling was an incomplete pass, stood around as if the play was over. After getting frantic signals from the sideline, Boykin hastily ran the 15 yards to the end zone untouched.

24. What is the correct spot on this forward fumble?

Since Rodgers was attempting to pass, this is not a case where the ball is intentionally fumbled forward. The hit by Peppers jarred the ball loose before Rodgers could begin any forward motion of his arm. This was a fumble under the empty hand rule.

The recovery by Boykin is legal, and the play remains live. Field judge Greg Meyer immediately signaled touchdown. Referee Clete Blakeman conferenced on the conclusion of the play with Meyer and head linesman Tony Veteri. Blakeman has responsibility for the quarterback but checked with Meyer on the pass ruling, much like a home-plate umpire will get assistance from a crewmate on a checked swing in baseball. Also, Blakeman had to confirm that neither official whistled the play dead prior to the ball crossing the goal line.

The offense is entitled to advance a forward fumble at this point in the game, as long as that fumble is not ruled an incomplete forward pass. If the offense fumbles forward out of bounds, the ball returns to the spot of the fumble, rather than to the out-of-bounds spot. Consequently, the clock continues to run, because the dead-ball spot is moved to a point where the ball was in bounds, negating the fact that it actually went out of bounds unpossessed.

Compare these two plays involving forward fumbles.

Play No. 1: During a Christmas Eve game in 2011, the Philadelphia Eagles were leading the Dallas Cowboys 7–0 in the second quarter when the Eagles were at the Cowboys' 9-yard line, threatening to increase the lead. Quarterback Michael Vick connected with receiver Jason Avant at the 6-yard line, and Avant stretched the ball out and dove for the end zone. As Avant landed on the ground, the ball was out of his possession, but it was ruled that he broke the plane of the goal before losing the ball. This was reviewed in replay, which showed that Avant lost control of the ball inside the 1-yard line. The loose ball touched the pylon on the corner of the end zone.

Play No. 2: Approaching the two-minute warning in the second quarter, the Houston Texans were trailing the Indianapolis Colts and had the ball at the 9-yard line. Quarterback Matt Schaub found running back Ryan Moats on a short pass, which he took to the 1-yard line. The Colts challenged the call, and the replays showed that Moats fumbled the ball near the sideline prior to being down by contact. Moats did not touch the ball while he was on the sideline. Colts cornerback Jerraud Powers, who got one foot down in bounds after being out of bounds, picked up the ball as it lay on the goal line.

25. What is the correct spot for these forward fumbles out of bounds?

Since both of these plays went to replay, they are subject to the additional requirements under the replay rules. If a play is not ruled a fumble, then a reversal can be considered only if the fumble *and* possession can be determined through video evidence. Rule 15–2–4 goes one additional step: "If the Referee does not have indisputable visual evidence as to which player recovered the loose ball, or that the ball went out of bounds, the ruling on the field will stand." In lieu of a recovery, a fumble out of bounds is also reviewable.

Both of these fumbles were clearly out of bounds when reviewed in replay. But, unlike a fumble out of bounds in the field of play, fumbles in the end zone are treated differently. When a ball is dead behind a goal line, there are only three options: touchdown, touchback, or safety. (There is one exception to this involving the momentum rule, which does not apply here but is discussed in chapter 5.) If the offense fumbles the ball out of bounds in the opponent's end zone, it is ruled a touchback, giving the opponent the ball at the 20-yard line.

In the play by Avant, the pylon has some unique properties that vary depending on how it becomes involved in the play. If a player touches the pylon, he is not considered to be out of bounds. However, when a loose ball touches the pylon, the ball is deemed to be out of bounds in the end zone. Avant fumbling into the pylon gave the Cowboys the ball at the 20-yard line.

The recovery by Powers was a little more complicated, but the same principles apply. With the ball lying on the goal line, it has penetrated the Colts' end zone, even though Powers is not in the end zone. By returning in bounds, Powers must establish two feet in bounds before touching the loose ball; otherwise he makes the ball out of bounds just as if he was touching the sideline. It is irrelevant that Powers's entire body is in bounds until that second foot comes down. It is also irrelevant that the ball is not physically touching the sideline. The Texans also lost possession of the ball, giving the Colts a first-and-10 on the 20.

26. On the fumble by Moats, how does the call change if Moats touches the ball while on the sideline or if Powers touches the ball prior to it touching the goal line?

As long as the ball has not broken the plane of the end zone, a touch by an out-of-bounds Moats or Powers makes the ball dead, and it would be Texans ball inside the 1-yard line. The player touching the ball can even have a part of his body in the end zone, but the ball does not get extended into the end zone by touching.

27. On the fumbles by the Packers, Eagles, and Texans illustrated here, how does the ruling change if the play is after the two-minute warning?

To answer this question, we go to a play that occurred on September 10, 1978, at San Diego Stadium. The Chargers had a 20–14 lead over the visiting Oakland Raiders with 10 seconds remaining in the game. The Raiders had the ball at the Chargers' 14-yard line. Faced with an imminent sack by Chargers linebacker Woodrow Lowe, quarterback Ken Stabler pitched the ball out to look like an unintentional fumble. Stabler later admitted his fumble was deliberate, but since covering referee Jerry Markbreit was screened by Lowe, he could not assess whether the fumble was deliberate and had to let the play continue as a legitimate fumble. Running back Pete Banaszak also misplayed the recovery of the fumble in an action that gave the ball extra momentum toward the end zone. Receiver Dave Casper clumsily attempted to scoop up the ball until it rolled into the end zone, at which point he fell on the ball.

Despite the intentional efforts to get the fumbled ball into the end zone, it was ruled a legal play. Despite the fact that it *looked* like a deliberate fumble and an intentional batting of the ball, there was a high standard to be met to judge that. Markbreit did not get any contrarian opinion from any of the other officials on the fumble call, so it was not ruled an incomplete pass. The batted ball by Banaszak involved two hands, so he was given the benefit of the doubt that he was making a recovery effort. Even though the Chargers protested vehemently, the touchdown stood, and it forever became known as the Holy Roller play.

The rules were changed in the next off-season to curb any advantage on such a fluke play in a desperate situation. What continues to be referred to as the Holy Roller Rule to this day restricts the ability of the offense to re-cover fumbles that occur after the two-minute warning. By rule, any fumble by the offense in the final two minutes must be recovered by the player who fumbled in order for the ball to be advanced. If another offensive player picks up the fumble, the ball is dead immediately and returned to the spot of the fumble or the spot of recovery, whichever is more disadvantageous to the offense.

In addition to fumbles inside two minutes, the Holy Roller Rule applies to the offense on a fourth-down play at any time during the game.

In the three fumble scenarios presented, there is no change to the Eagles' or Texans' fumbles if the two-minute fumble rule applies, because the ball was declared to have gone out of bounds without a recovery. In the case of the Packers' fumble, the play would be whistled dead as soon as Jarrett Boykin secures possession of the ball. The Packers would retain possession, but it would be second-and-16 from the 23-yard line—the spot where Rodgers fumbled. If it was a fourth-down play, the Bears would have possession at the 23.

28. The Packers were visiting Ralph Wilson Stadium in Orchard Park, New York, for an interconference game against the Buffalo Bills on December 14, 2014. Trailing 19–13, the Packers were starting a drive from their own 10-yard line at the two-minute warning. On the first play from scrimmage, Aaron Rodgers was hit by defensive end Mario Williams and fumbled at the 3-yard line. The ball came to rest just inside the end zone, where running back Eddie Lacy picked up the ball and ran with it. The play was whistled dead. What is the correct spot?

The efforts of Stabler, Banaszak, and Casper in 1978 wound up trapping the Packers with an unusual set of circumstances. When Rodgers fumbled the ball with less than two minutes remaining in the game, he was the only player on the Packers who could recover the ball and keep the play alive. Lacy's recovery made the play dead immediately, and referee Bill Leavy did not hesitate to kill the play.

Once the play has ended, the ball is spotted at either the spot of the fumble or the spot of the recovery, whichever is farther back. If the recovery was in advance of the fumble, the Packers would have the ball at the 3-yard line, but Lacy's recovery created a declared dead ball in the end zone. According to Rule 11-5-1(b), because the Packers' fumble put the ball in the end zone, it is a safety when "the ball is dead in the end zone in its possession or the ball is out of bounds behind the goal line."

The Bills scored two points and the ball was spotted at the 20-yard line for a safety kick by the Packers.

Usually, these fumble rules are invoked relatively undetected by the casual fans, as many times there is a recovery without an advance (which means the ball would have been dead anyway) and the spot of the ball seems reasonable under the circumstances.

29. At a September 22, 2013, game at Cincinnati's Paul Brown Stadium, the Packers—yes, the Packers again—were leading the Bengals 30–27 with 4:01 remaining in the fourth quarter. The Packers had the ball at the Bengals' 30-yard line, with a fourth down and inches to go. Rodgers handed off to running back Johnathan Franklin, who fumbled. Being that it was fourth down, Franklin was the only Packers player who could recover the ball. Bengals free safety Reggie Nelson recovered the loose ball at the 29, and Nelson fumbled the ball at the 35. Bengals cornerback Terence Newman recovered the ball at the 42 and ran to the end zone. How is the Bengals' fumble handled under the fourth-down fumble rules?

As the rules added in the wake of the Holy Roller play were written, fumbles on fourth down and fumbles after the two-minute warning are handled nearly identically. However, once a fumble is recovered by the defense, the fourth-down fumble rules are no longer applicable. Since the defense does not have to reach the first-down marker, there is no advantage that needs to be offset by the rules.

Therefore, once Nelson recovers the ball, there is no restriction on who recovers Nelson's fumble. Newman's possession of the ball is legal, and the touchdown counts.

If the same play occurs on fourth down *and* after the two-minute warning, the fourth-down fumble rule does not apply, but the two-minute fumble rule is still applicable. While the downs are irrelevant once the defense recovers the ball, the clock affects both teams equally. In this under-two-minute scenario, the recovery by Newman kills the play, and the ball is returned to the 35—the spot of the Nelson fumble. The Bengals would keep possession, but would have a first-and-10 play from there, and Newman cannot score the touchdown.

Back to the actual play, which is fourth down with four minutes remaining. Once Nelson fumbles the ball, who on the Packers is eligible to recover, since the Packers had previously fumbled?

While Johnathan Franklin was the only player eligible to recover his own fumble on fourth down, that restriction ends for the remainder of the down once the Bengals recover the ball. When the ball is loose a second time, any player on the Packers is eligible to recover the ball. If there is a double change of possession on the play, the first-down line is no longer applicable to the team that snapped the ball. Any recovery of the second fumble by the Packers would give the Packers a first-and-10 at that spot, and it is treated as a new possession by the Packers, even though their offense never leaves the field.

As indicated previously, the two-minute fumble rule remains in effect through the completion of the down if the fumble occurs after the two-minute warning. But in the case of multiple changes of possession on the same play, only the last player to fumble is considered for the two-minute fumble rule.

Incidentally, on the two-fumble play in Cincinnati, referee Clete Blakeman tossed a blue beanbag to mark the spot of the first fumble, as required.

When the Bengals fumbled the ball, according to standard officiating mechanics, Blakeman threw his hat to mark the second fumble.

The Holy Roller Rule also has a special signal. In order to remind officials that the fourth-down fumble rule is in effect, the umpire, after spotting the ball, will make a rotating fist-over-fist signal, just like the signal for a false start—or a roller.

EIGHT

PENALTY ENFORCEMENT

Because of the magnitude of this call, I want you all to pay attention!

> —*Referee Bernie Kukar, announcing a penalty that
> negated a last-second touchdown, Baltimore Ravens at
> Tennessee Titans, November 12, 2001*

In the early days of the NFL, a penalty was signaled by an official sounding a horn at the end of the play. Although the games were sparsely attended by modern standards, it was difficult for the fans to know there was a penalty without a visual cue. The first penalty flag to be thrown in an NFL game was at a venue not readily associated with football—Fenway Park—during a Friday night game between the Green Bay Packers and the Boston Yanks on September 17, 1948. The officials must have liked the red-colored flags, as they assessed both teams with 22 penalties for 215 yards. In 1965 the NFL switched the penalty flags to the familiar gold color they are today—although with more than 90 percent of households watching the games on black-and-white televisions, few people outside of those in the stadium noticed.

The referee has a compendium of signals to communicate which foul is being called. For many decades this was the only communication from the officials to the fans. The referee's wireless microphone was introduced in 1975, which gave rise to the folksy witticisms of Ben Dreith, the punctuated Texas drawl of Red Cashion as he bellowed "first dooooowwwn!", and the voluble elucidations provided by Ed Hochuli. Despite the fact that the referee has been able to announce penalties for years, the hand signals remain a throwback of the game's silent era.

PENALTIES AT THE SNAP

On October 26, 2014, the Detroit Lions and Atlanta Falcons played a regular-season game at Wembley Stadium in London. In an effort to accommodate the spectators, the NFL scheduled the game for 1:30 p.m. local time. Viewers in the United States had to arrange their schedules for the earliest kickoff time to date: 9:30 a.m. on the East Coast, 6:30 a.m. on the West Coast, and 3:30 a.m. in Hawaii. While viewers in the Pacific and mountain time zones are accustomed to watching football on a Sunday morning, it was a whole new experience for fans in the eastern and central time zones to have football at breakfast time. The fact that the Sunday pregame shows were showing highlights of a game in progress was not the only oddity with this game.

With seconds remaining in the fourth quarter, the Lions were lined up to kick a field goal. As the kick was in the air, a penalty flag was thrown by the back judge. The field goal was wide to the right and no good.

The penalty was on the Lions for a delay of game. The penalty moved the Lions back 5 yards to have another shot at the field goal, which was successful and gave the Lions the victory.

1. Why didn't the officials allow the Falcons to decline the delay-of-game penalty?

Any foul—as long as there aren't fouls by both teams—can be declined. While the Falcons certainly had that option available to them, it wouldn't have helped them in the least.

Even though the play seemed to continue after the snap, a delay-of-game penalty prevents the snap from happening. The whistle may be late or not heard, but it does not reverse the fact that there is no legal snap after a delay-of-game penalty. If the Falcons decline the penalty, they cannot take the supposed result of the play of a missed field goal because the play was already dead.

This serves as a perfect introduction to an essential penalty enforcement resource. NFL referee Ed Hochuli wrote the *Hopperbook*, a reference book that distills penalty enforcements down into manageable categories. It is based on a longstanding officiating parlance of metaphorical "hoppers," one of 15 mental containers an official places a foul into and then enforces the penalty belonging to the hopper. Each foul has a yardage assessment, but the *Hopperbook* defines where on the field the foul should be assessed.

In the *Hopperbook*, Hochuli warns his colleagues about jumping ahead too quickly when assessing a penalty. "The key to penalty enforcements," he writes, "is to first get the penalty into the correct hopper, and then apply the enforcement. Most of our confusion arises because we start in the wrong hopper. Therefore, always be careful to first decide on the hopper before you start thinking about the enforcement."

The 15 hoppers are illustrated in Figure 8.1.

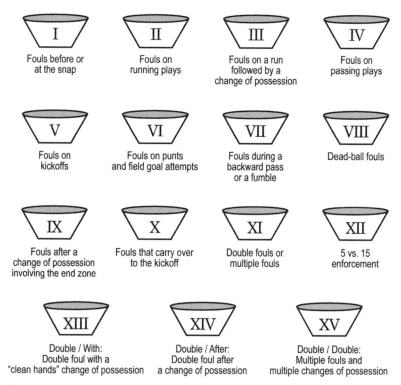

Figure 8.1.

In the Falcons–Lions game, the delay-of-game penalty is one of the penalties that belong in Hopper I: fouls at or before the snap. These fouls are ones that prevent the snap from happening:

A. Delay of game
B. False start
C. Neutral-zone infraction
D. Illegal substitution (12 men in the offensive huddle)
E. Too many men in formation (only if the snap is imminent)
F. Encroachment.

Also in Hopper I are fouls at the snap that allow the play to continue; if accepted, the penalty is enforced from the line of scrimmage and the down is replayed. Those fouls include:

A. Offside (offense or defense)
B. Too many men on the field (but not in formation)
C. Illegal motion
D. Illegal formation
E. Illegal shift
F. Illegal substitution.

The numbers on the hoppers are shown just as they are assigned in the *Hopperbook*. The hoppers have no hierarchy, so a higher-numbered hopper doesn't override a lower number. For the sake of discussion, we will look at them in a different order. Forgive the pun, please, but we will hop around.

FOULS BY BOTH TEAMS

When fouls are committed by both teams, the general principle that applies is that the fouls offset each other. There is no limit as to how unbalanced the penalties are on a particular play—one team could have three while the other has only one. As long as each team committed a foul, the penalties offset.

This does not mean that the hopper principles are completely ignored. Depending on the type of foul and the kind of play, the penalties can offset before the down or after the down. When there is a kick or change of possession involved, it can get really tricky, depending on when each foul occurs.

Without any other complications, a simplified example of offsetting penalties would be a first-and-10 running play where there is a flag for offensive holding and a second flag for illegal contact on the defense. Since we have two live-ball fouls, the two fouls offset and the down is replayed, erasing any advance by the offense.

During a game against the Giants on November 20, 2011, Philadelphia Eagles wide receiver DeSean Jackson caught a 50-yard pass along the sideline. While the ball was in the air, the defense of the New York Giants committed a foul for illegal use of hands. At the conclusion of the play, Jackson ran out of bounds and then tossed the ball to Giants defensive coordinator Perry Fewell, which, by rule, is a taunting foul on Jackson.

2. The play was a first-and-10 from the Eagles' 2-yard line, and Jackson went out of bounds at the Giants' 48. The Giants foul was a live-ball foul, and the Eagles foul was a dead-ball foul. How do you assess the penalties, and where is the ball next spotted?

Despite the fact that Jackson's foul comes after the play, the entire play is lost, and the Eagles will repeat the down, first-and-10 from the 2.

According to Rule 14-4-9-Item 3, any time there are both live- and dead-ball fouls in the same down by both teams, the fouls combine as if they are all live-ball fouls. By combining the two fouls as the rule states, the taunting foul by the Eagles and the contact foul by the Giants offset each other, and there is no play. The ball returns to the original line of scrimmage, even though it seems to disproportionately punish the offense.

3. Would the play be any different if, instead of the illegal contact, the Giants were guilty of a foul that occurred at the snap, such as a defensive 12-men-on-the-field foul?

All fouls that occur at the snap or before the snap are, for practical purposes, treated as live-ball fouls. Changing the foul from illegal contact to defensive 12 men still has the taunting foul being combined with a live-ball foul. The result remains the same: combine, offset, and replay the down. Of course, if there was a foul that killed the snap, such as a neutral zone infraction, the play would be whistled dead before we get to the part of the play when Jackson commits the taunting foul.

Another key example of offsetting fouls occurred on September 10, 2013, opening day of the final season of San Francisco's storied Candlestick Park. The 49ers hosted the Packers, who they would later meet in Green Bay for a Wild Card Playoff game. On a third-and-6 from the Packers' 10-

yard line, 49ers quarterback Colin Kaepernick rolled to his left and ran out of bounds at the 6-yard line. Clay Matthews hit Kaepernick as he stepped out, drawing a late-hit penalty on the Packers linebacker. A fight broke out over the hit, and 49ers offensive tackle Joe Staley was assessed an unsportsmanlike conduct foul.

4. The crew offset both fouls and repeated third down. Was this the correct call?

Even though there are offsetting 15-yard fouls, there is still the matter of enforcement. In this case, the crew combined the two fouls as live-ball fouls, which erased the down, just as the crew had done on the DeSean Jackson 50-yard catch in 2011. To determine if the crew assessed this properly, we should place these fouls in their respective hoppers.

The penalty on Staley is clearly after the play, so this goes in Hopper VIII: Dead-Ball Fouls. The Matthews late-hit foul came as Kaepernick was going out of bounds, but, by definition, a late hit can occur only after the play was dead. If the hit happened a fraction of a second earlier, with Kaepernick in bounds, it could not be a late hit, but can be ruled as unnecessary roughness (a live-ball foul). But, Matthews's foul is also placed in the dead-ball hopper. After the game, referee Bill Leavy acknowledged that the crew realized, a few plays later, that they had made an enforcement error, but it was too late to make a correction.

"The down should have counted," Leavy said. "The penalties were both dead ball, and they should have offset at the spot where the runner went out of bounds. And it would have been fourth down."

Compounding the error, instead of facing a fourth-and-2 and likely a field goal attempt, the 49ers scored a touchdown on the replayed third down.

5. Later that season, on December 15, Kaepernick threw an incomplete pass in the direction of receiver Michael Crabtree. Well after the play was over, Crabtree picked up the ball and heaved it several yards in frustration. Referee Scott Green was announcing an offside penalty against the Tampa Bay Buccaneers when Crabtree threw the ball. Green's crew assessed the penalty against the Buccaneers and then a 15-yard unsportsmanlike conduct penalty against the 49ers. Was that correct?

To determine how this call was made, there is a third class of penalties in addition to live-ball and dead-ball fouls: penalties that are assessed between downs. Live-ball fouls and dead-ball fouls are assessed before any between-downs fouls are considered. Since Green was announcing the penalty on the Buccaneers, the officiating crew counted Crabtree's action as a between-downs foul. The dead-ball period following the play encompasses any continuing action after the play, but Crabtree threw the ball long after the play was over, placing the foul clearly in between-downs territory.

This was correctly assessed by the crew. Once the live-ball and dead-ball fouls are sorted out, the officials establish the new down and distance before the between-downs fouls are assessed. In this case, the incomplete pass happened on a first-and-10. This means the Buccaneers' offside is enforced (it may also be declined, because it is being handled alone), giving the 49ers a first-and-5. Then, the between-downs unsportsmanlike foul is 15 yards from that spot, leading to a first-and-20.

If the same situation happened on a third-and-4 play, the defensive foul would have given the 49ers a first down, then the 49ers' penalty would go 15 yards back from the new first down spot, giving the 49ers a first-and-25 situation.

With that in mind, assess these two plays for the correct enforcement.

Play No. 1: Harvey Dahl, an offensive lineman for the St. Louis Rams, became a little too animated while protesting a fourth-quarter holding call during a game at the Edward Jones Dome against the Cincinnati Bengals on December 18, 2011. While referee Jerome Boger was announcing the penalty over the public-address system and on television, Dahl was overheard grousing, "I know you didn't call me for holding?" As Boger paused in his announcement, Dahl blurted out for the masses to hear, "That's not fucking holding!" Boger turned off his microphone and threw a flag.

Play No. 2: During a game on December 23, 2007, in Jacksonville, the Oakland Raiders defense let their frustrations with the officials show. On a third-and-10, Jaguars quarterback David Garrard threw an incomplete pass, but offensive tackle Tony Pashos was flagged for a 10-yard penalty for illegal use of hands. After that penalty was announced, Raiders defensive tackle Warren Sapp complained to the officials too much, and he was flagged for unsportsmanlike conduct. Referee Jerome Boger (yes, again!) announced that penalty, and then Sapp and teammate Derrick Burgess continued to berate the officials, each being assessed an unsportsmanlike conduct penalty. During the same dead-ball period, Sapp confronted line judge Jerry Bergman, who threw another flag and immediately gave Sapp an ejection signal. In total, there is one penalty flag on the Jaguars and four against the Raiders.

6. For both plays, which fouls are assessed and which ones are disregarded?

Usually if multiple penalties happen during a play, only one can be assessed, or if it involves a penalty on both teams, they offset. There is an exception for fouls that are committed against the officials. These are automatically enforced as between-downs fouls, regardless of when they occur.

For Dahl's infraction, he was penalized twice, and both were marched off separately. First, the holding penalty was assessed, 10 yards against the Rams from the 31-yard line to the 21. Then, the unsportsmanlike conduct for disrespecting an official would have been another 15 yards, but was assessed half the distance to the goal line, since it was inside the 30. Dahl was not ejected, because the infraction did not elevate to the level of inflammatory language that would warrant ejection.

As for the Oakland game, all five penalties were enforced. After the Jacksonville penalty was assessed, each of the unsportsmanlike conduct fouls was enforced sequentially from the 35-yard line, starting with a 15-yard penalty, and then half-distance penalties of 10, 5, and 2½ yards.

"Warren was upset because they tried to make the call before we made our decision," linebacker Thomas Howard said after the game. "So then a flag was thrown and then it was just wild commotion after that. They threw another flag and then another. Everybody's arguing and asking why these flags got thrown."

The penalty that ultimately got Sapp ejected from the game was for unnecessary physical contact with an official.

7. Should Sapp have been ejected after the second unsportsmanlike conduct foul, before he was allowed to get a third one?

Basketball has an automatic ejection rule after two technical fouls on the same player, and a third one cannot be assessed. Soccer, similarly, has a red-card ejection for a player who is assessed two yellow cards. Football (the American version, that is) does not have this rule, and ejections are always a matter of officials' discretion.

FIVE VS. FIFTEEN ENFORCEMENT

The San Diego Chargers and the Oakland Raiders met at Oakland's O.co Coliseum on October 6, 2013, for a game that set the record for the latest kickoff—8:35 p.m. Pacific time, or just before midnight on the East Coast. Because the stadium was the site of a home game for baseball's Oakland Athletics in the American League Divisional Series on Saturday night, the grounds crews needed 24 hours to convert the stadium from a baseball configuration to a football configuration. The league decided to move the game from its scheduled kickoff at 1 p.m. local time to the unprecedented late time slot.

Since it followed the conclusion of the regularly scheduled *Sunday Night Football* game, the Chargers–Raiders game was then televised nationally. But by the fourth quarter, many football fans had already gone to bed, and they missed one of the more unusual enforcements in football.

Chargers quarterback Philip Rivers completed a touchdown pass to receiver Vincent Brown. The Chargers committed a 5-yard illegal formation foul on the play, and Raiders cornerback Mike Jenkins shoved Brown after the touchdown catch in the end zone.

8. How should the penalties be assessed on the play?

This is a multistep process, but one that Jeff Triplette's crew sorted out with little delay.

The Chargers infraction is a live-ball foul, since it occurred at the snap. The Raiders infraction is a dead-ball foul, since the touchdown ended the play, and the late hit, by definition, came after the play was dead.

Ordinarily, this would make the penalties offset, and the down would be replayed from the previous spot. However, this is a special situation where one team has committed a 15-yard penalty and the other has what is called a "simple-5"—a 5-yard penalty that doesn't also include an automatic first down, a loss of down, or a 10-second runoff. This situation is a 5 vs. 15 enforcement, and it enforces the 15-yard penalty and ignores the simple-5, rather than the penalties canceling each other out. In a 5 vs. 15 enforcement, the play doesn't count, so on this play, the Chargers' touchdown was nullified, even though their illegal formation penalty was thrown out.

Since the play is nullified, the 15-yard penalty is enforced from the previous spot, even if it would have ordinarily been enforced from a different point. It also means if the defense commits the 15-yarder, it is an automatic down, but if the offense commits the major penalty, the same down is repeated after the penalty is marked off.

With a lone exception, the team committing the simple-5 may not decline the penalty.

Incidentally, the 5 vs. 15 enforcement is in effect if there are multiple fouls against the team that also commits the 15-yard penalty. On the other side, if a team commits multiple simple-5s and no other foul, the 5 vs. 15 enforcement is also applied. Also, if the rules require a half-distance penalty, this has no bearing on whether the 5 vs. 15 enforcement is used.

9. In a situation where the defense commits a 15-yard live-ball foul, such as roughing the quarterback, and the offense commits a 5-yard delay of game by spiking the ball after a nonscoring play, how is this ruled?

This is the only exception to being allowed to decline a penalty in a 5 vs. 15 enforcement. In this situation, the offense is allowed to decline the defense's live-ball foul and have only their 5-yard penalty be assessed from the dead-ball spot. (This means that the down counts.) They may also opt to have a 5 vs. 15 enforcement. This exception was made because the ball-spiking penalty was deemed a very minor infraction.

If the roles are reversed—say the offense commits the 15-yard live-ball foul, and suppose a defensive player picks up the loose ball and spikes it in frustration—the defense is allowed the same options: to assess only the 5-yard penalty and allow the down to count or apply a 5 vs. 15 enforcement.

Two other provisions apply to the 5 vs. 15 enforcement: (1) one of the fouls must be a live-ball foul, because no result can go back to the previous spot if there are no live-ball fouls, and (2) any 5 vs. 15 situation at the end of the half does not extend the quarter by an untimed down.

FOULS ON A PUNT

The final season at Candlestick Park once again enters into the penalty enforcement discussion in a 49ers game against the Seattle Seahawks on December 8, 2013. The Seahawks were faced with a fourth-and-24 at their own 17-yard line in the first quarter. The punt by Jon Ryan was blocked by Kassim Osgood of the 49ers. While the ball was rolling around behind the line of scrimmage, Seahawks special teams player Chris Maragos bats the ball in desperation at the 16-yard line, with the ball going out of bounds at the 34.

10. There was no question that Maragos was guilty of an illegal bat penalty, but where is it enforced from?

The penalty for an illegal bat is contained in Rule 12–4–1, which states that it is a "loss of 10 yards. For enforcement, treat as a foul during a backward pass or fumble (see 8–7–7)." Going to Rule 8–7–7, the instruction is as follows, with Team A being the team that snaps the ball: "When the spot of a backward pass or fumble is behind the line of scrimmage, all fouls committed by either team, including a foul by Team B in Team A's end zone, are enforced from the previous spot."

This leads to an enforcement that repeats fourth down with the penalty assessed from there. The crew gave the 49ers the option of accepting the foul at that spot, or they could decline the penalty and take the ball at the spot where it went out of bounds. But this omits a key part of the puzzle: the ball was loose not because of a fumble, but from a blocked punt.

The foul occurred after the blocked punt, before the ball crossed the line of scrimmage, and before a change in possession. Once the ball is punted, the play is considered a kicking play, and it remains a kicking play until someone takes possession of the ball or the ball becomes dead. In this case, Maragos only bats the ball, so as the ball is going down the field, it is still a kick, even though it was his batting action that sent the ball moving. Therefore, we are going to place the illegal bat foul in Hopper VI: Fouls during Scrimmage Kicks, and the *Hopperbook* states, "Fouls by [Team] A during the kick, but before possession by Team B (other than kick-catch interference or fair-catch interference, which are spot fouls) can be enforced from either the previous spot or tacked on from the dead-ball spot."

This gives the 49ers three options:

A. Accept the penalty from the previous spot (half-distance), Seahawks ball, fourth-and-32 from the 9.
B. Accept the penalty from the dead-ball spot, 49ers ball, first-and-10 from the 24.
C. Decline the penalty, 49ers ball, first-and-10 from the 34.

The 49ers should have been given the option to get the ball at the 24-yard line with the proper enforcement. As it so happened, the 49ers were unable to advance the ball on the ensuing drive and kicked a field goal, which did not affect the ultimate result.

11. If Maragos had batted the ball at the 19-yard line instead of the 16, would this affect the penalty enforcement?

It is important to remember that, even though the punt was blocked, the play retains all of the attributes that apply to a standard punt. Once a kicked ball crosses the line of scrimmage, in many respects it is considered that the kicking team has surrendered the possession of the ball. The kicking team cannot take possession of a punt that crosses the line of scrimmage unless it is first touched by the receiving team. But a punt that is still behind the line of scrimmage, whether it is shanked by the punter or blocked, is a free ball for either team.

In this hypothetical scenario, with the Seahawks batting the ball beyond the line of scrimmage, it is treated the same as any punt that is touched by the kicking team downfield. In the enforcement of the penalty, the 49ers would also have the option of taking the ball at the spot of the Seahawks' first touch (the 19-yard line). Then, the 49ers can tack on the illegal bat penalty from that spot, which would be half the distance to the goal line.

12. Does the original scenario change if the blocked punt lands beyond the line of scrimmage, the backspin on the ball causes it to return behind the line of scrimmage, and then the ball is batted at the 16-yard line?

As long as the ball is not touched beyond the line of scrimmage, a punt that returns behind the line actually regains many of the properties it ordinarily would lose. This means that the original penalty options are still applied, and the Seahawks are not ruled to have a first-touch violation like the case was in the previous scenario.

One rule that does not change is the option to pass after a short or blocked kick. The rules for a legal forward pass state that the ball cannot cross and return over the line of scrimmage. If the Seahawks threw a forward pass instead of batting the ball in the original scenario, it is a legal play, but not if the backspin brings the ball back behind the line.

13. The Dallas Cowboys were hosting the Philadelphia Eagles on Thanksgiving in 2014. The Eagles punted from midfield in the fourth quarter with a comfortable lead and a chance to pin the Cowboys deep in their own territory. Cowboys kick returner Dwayne Harris decided not to make a play on the ball; rather he deliberately plowed into Eagles special teamer Nolan Carroll. Carroll was unable to prevent the ball from going into the end zone, resulting in a touchback. Harris was flagged for unnecessary roughness at the 5-yard line. Where is the ball spotted?

Referee Clete Blakeman announced this as a "dead ball personal foul," but this had clearly occurred during the action of the play. However, Blakeman was correct, as it effectively is enforced from the dead-ball spot.

While kicking plays are treated as changes of possession much the same as fumbles and interceptions, the point at which possession is deemed to have changed hands is slightly different. On an interception play, as soon as the pass is caught, there is a physical change of possession, but on kicking plays, possession is deemed to be surrendered once the ball is kicked.

There is one overriding consideration as to why the change of possession precedes the physical change. Because kicking plays tend to have a higher rate of injury, the rules have evolved over the years to reduce the number of re-kicks. One example of this trend is a rule that once allowed teams two chances to attempt an onside kickoff if the first one was not legal. A rule change in 2003 gave possession of the ball to the receiving team in most cases of an invalid onside kick.

In the punting situation, the kicking team is determined to have surrendered the ball to the receiving team at the point of the kick. Therefore, this is considered a post-possession foul, as long as the Cowboys do not subsequently lose possession during the down. Rule 14-4-8 states, "The penalty shall be enforced from whichever of the following spots is least beneficial to the receiving team: (a) the end of the kick; or (b) the spot of the foul."

This is actually slightly misleading in this situation, because the touchback is clearly more beneficial to the Cowboys than the foul at the 5. In fact, a case can be made that Harris's actions prevented the Eagles from downing the ball near the goal, and the violent act is rewarded with a touchback. To clarify the enforcement spot, the rules then state, "If the least beneficial spot is in the end zone, the spot of enforcement is the 20-yard line." This is a "20/10 enforcement," which spots the ball for a touchback and assesses the penalty half the distance to the goal line, to the 10-yard line.

While seemingly unusual, enforcing from the 5-yard line to the 2½ was not an option available to the Eagles.

FOULS CARRIED FORWARD TO THE KICKOFF

During a game on September 28, 2014, Bears tight end Martellus Bennett was stopped short of the goal line by the Packers as time ran out in the second quarter. Bears guard Kyle Long was shoving after the play and drew an unnecessary roughness foul.

14. Is this penalty enforced or ignored?

Any dead-ball personal foul in the continuing action of the final play of the half carries forward to the second-half kickoff. This includes dead-ball fouls by the defense; the half is not extended by an untimed down for the defensive infraction, since the half expired prior to the penalty. The foul does not carry forward, however, if it is part of a multiple-foul situation. Long's foul moved the second-half kickoff from the 35 to the 20.

If these fouls occur at the expiration of regulation in a tie game, the foul carries forward to the overtime kickoff.

15. On December 14, 2014, Washington quarterback Robert Griffin III scored a touchdown on the last play of the first half against the Giants. A replay review showed that Griffin lost possession of the ball before scoring the touchdown, so the score was reversed and the half was over. As the teams began to clear the field for halftime, Griffin's teammate, Santana Moss, confronted referee Jeff Triplette and drew a flag from him. In the chaos Moss also confronted side judge Alex Kemp, who flagged Moss for improper contact with an official. How are these flags assessed?

The two unsportsmanlike conduct fouls that Moss incurred are infractions against officials, which are always enforced as between-downs fouls. Because there are two separate actions against Moss in the intermission period, both are assessed, moving the Giants' kickoff from their 35 to Washington's 35-yard line. With such a short field, the Giants attempted an onside kick and wound up recovering the ball.

For contacting the official, Moss was ejected from the game.

16. What are the situations where a penalty is assessed on the ensuing kickoff?

There are a number of infractions in which a team may delay or ignore the rules of the opening coin toss. This is very unlikely to ever happen, but it is an instance where a foul can be assessed on the kickoff.

More often, personal fouls and unsportsmanlike conduct fouls by either team that occur on scoring plays are carried forward to the kickoff, except for live-ball fouls against the scoring team that negate the score. Fouls on scoring plays where the score stands are covered in Hopper X: Carry-Over Fouls.

Hopper X does override some of the principles of live- and dead-ball fouls combining, such as the double foul and the 5 vs. 15 enforcement. The purpose of this is to avoid the harsh sanction of the scoring team's post-score, dead-ball foul combining with the opponent's live-ball foul and negating the score. The score stands, but there is a compromise that still penalizes the scoring team. As long as the score is with clean hands—in other words, no foul is committed by the scoring team before the score—then the scoring team must decline the opponent's penalty to make the score count, and the dead-ball foul (invariably, 15 yards) is assessed on the ensuing kickoff.

This applies to touchdowns, field goals, and safeties. On safety plays, it depends how the foul is assessed as to whether the foul carries forward. A foul that creates the safety (such as a chop block in the end zone) does not carry forward to the kickoff, because the penalty for the foul is used to get the two points. In a situation where a quarterback is sacked in the end zone and a personal foul is committed by the offense in the end zone, the sack creates the safety, and the personal foul moves the kickoff from the 20- to the 10-yard line.

Finally, Hopper X also includes defensive fouls on the point-after-touchdown conversion as bridging to the kickoff, at the option of the team scoring the touchdown. If a conversion kick fails, a defensive foul would cause the conversion to be retried instead of assessing the foul on the kickoff. A successful kick also may be taken off the board by a defensive foul if the scoring team wishes to attempt a two-point try from the 1-yard line after assessing a half-distance penalty against the defense. Any defensive foul not triggering a retry is carried forward to the kickoff. Fouls by the team attempting the conversion result in a retry, unless the conversion failed (the defense will decline the penalty) or the foul is a loss of down (the try fails by rule).

In summary, the fouls that carry forward to the kickoff include 15-yard fouls on scoring plays and any defensive foul on a successful point-after-conversion attempt.

DOUBLE FOUL AND A CHANGE OF POSSESSION

Returning to the 2014 London game between the Falcons and Lions mentioned at the beginning of this chapter, a third-quarter pass by Matt Ryan was intercepted in the end zone by Lions cornerback Rashean Mathis, who ran the ball back 102 yards to the opposite end zone. Mathis was penalized for pass interference, but during Mathis's return, Ryan attempted to dive for Mathis and wound up tackling another Lions player low. Ryan drew a penalty for a low block.

17. What is the correct enforcement of the fouls, and does Mathis get the touchdown?

Whenever a team forces a change of possession and commits a foul in the same down, the official must determine if that team acquired possession with "clean hands." In other words, was the foul committed prior to the change of possession? When double fouls and a change of possession occur in the same play, there are two relevant hoppers: Hopper XIII (Double Foul with a Change of Possession, or "Double/With") and Hopper XIV ("Double/After"). The Double/With enforcement is applied when the team does not gain possession with clean hands. Since the pass interference foul on Mathis obviously had to occur prior to the interception, there is no way that the interception will stand, much less the touchdown.

Ryan's foul for an illegal block below the waist was unusual, as he was essentially on defense after the change of possession and therefore would not be blocking for Mathis. However, after a change of possession, any hit below the waist by either team is considered an illegal block, as long as the ball carrier isn't one of the players involved in the hit (either administering or receiving the hit).

Since the Lions cannot keep the ball—because the interception was not with clean hands—the two fouls offset at the previous spot, and the down is repeated. The announcement from referee Pete Morelli to explain the enforcement is all the time that Mathis gets to catch his breath.

That's not to say Ryan's penalty wasn't costly. Had he not committed the illegal low block, the defensive pass interference penalty would have been the only foul on the play, which would have given the Falcons the ball on the 1-yard line.

Compare this play to a punt by the San Diego Chargers on November 23, 2014, when they played the St. Louis Rams. Mike Scifres punted to Rams return specialist Tavon Austin in the fourth quarter. Just after the ball was kicked, a Rams defender was flagged for a holding penalty. Austin caught the ball at his own 22-yard line and ran the punt back 73 yards to the Chargers' 5-yard line. During the return, Scifres committed an illegal low block at the Chargers' 40-yard line.

18. What is the correct enforcement of the two penalties on this play?

The elements of this play seem to line up with the events of the double foul on the interception in the Lions–Falcons game, but, remember, the rule on punts is that the change of possession for penalty enforcement begins at the kick.

On the punt by the Chargers, the Rams penalty at or after the kick is determined to be a post-possession foul, so the Rams are entitled to possession. Before the Chargers commit their penalty, this is shaping up to be a foul on a scrimmage kick, Hopper VI. However, the Chargers penalty creates a double foul.

Since the Rams penalty is reckoned to have occurred after the change of possession, this is a Double/After enforcement instead of a Double/With. While Double/With nullifies the change of possession, Double/After keeps the change of possession and assesses the penalties at an appropriate enforcement point. That enforcement point is when the Chargers committed the penalty, because that is the instant when there is a double foul. As long as the Rams retain possession throughout the rest of the play, any advance by the Rams after the double foul is ruled will be erased by the penalty.

The Chargers low block occurs at the 40-yard line, and the two fouls will offset at that spot, with the Rams having first-and-10 from there.

19. If the Chargers had a foul for a 12th man leaving the field at the snap and the low-block foul later in the play, would this affect the enforcement at all?

It is important to note that the *After* in a Double/After enforcement refers to the fouls committed by both teams.

With a foul by the Chargers at the front of the play, the double foul takes effect once the Rams commit the holding penalty. The play would continue as usual, but the low-block foul would not create a Double/After enforcement—a Double/With enforcement takes precedence over a Double/After. That means the enforcement takes effect at the point where the second foul is, but since the ball is in the air at that point, the enforcement carries to the spot where the Rams catch the ball. The penalties offset at the Rams' 22-yard line, with the Rams having a first-and-10 from there. (If the foul by the Rams occurs behind the spot of the catch, the enforcement is from the spot of the foul, just as if there was a single foul against the Rams.)

20. Returning to the original scenario—a Rams holding penalty occurs after the kick and a Chargers low-block penalty on the return—what is the enforcement if the Chargers recover a fumble by the Rams on the punt return?

This falls into the final hopper, Hopper XV: Double/Double, or a double foul and a double change of possession. Hopper XV exists to capture any combination of multiple penalties against both teams and multiple changes of possession.

Until there was a refinement in the rules in 2013, the ball went to the point of the previous clean-hands recovery, if the last recovery was not with clean hands. This would have the crew step back to multiple recovery points to make a spotting determination. This proved to be too complex, particularly when there were so many elements to keep track of.

The rule is simplified as such: The team that finishes the play with the ball must have finally acquired possession with clean hands in order for the play to count. The determination of the proper enforcement depends on when the Chargers commit the low-block foul. If the foul occurs after the final change of possession, the Chargers keep the ball. If the Chargers do not have clean hands on the recovery, it is a simple offset and the down is replayed.

This hopper can accommodate any number of fouls and changes of possession. If there is a punt followed by two fumbles, that means the receiving team would have ended the play with the ball. As long as the receiving team has not committed a penalty at the point of the final change of possession, they keep the ball, and everything offsets at the recovery point.

NINE

UNSPORTSMANLIKE CONDUCT AND PERSONAL FOULS

There's a personal foul on number 99 of the defense. After he tackled the quarterback, he's giving him the business down there. That's a 15-yard penalty!

—Referee Ben Dreith, announcing a penalty against Jets linebacker Marty Lyons for unnecessary roughness on Jim Kelly, Buffalo Bills at New York Jets, October 5, 1986

Football was on the precipice of being banned outright in the United States after numerous reports of serious injuries and deaths occurring across the country. In December 1905, President Teddy Roosevelt convened a meeting at the White House with athletic representatives from Harvard, Yale, and Princeton universities to urge reform in the football rules for safety's sake. Although football lore may be overstating the president's influence, the rules of the game were revised in 1906 to spread the formations out and to allow for the forward pass. Today, reforms to the rules are largely concerned with reducing the number of concussions to key players and devastating knee injuries to linemen.

Most violations of these safety-minded rules incur a major 15-yard penalty, sharing a link to similar penalties of unsportsmanlike conduct fouls.

In Super Bowl X, played in the Orange Bowl on January 18, 1976, Steelers kicker Ray Gerela missed a 33-yard field goal in the third quarter. Cowboys safety Cliff Harris offered mock praise for Gerela and patted him on the helmet. This so enraged Steelers linebacker Jack Lambert that he knocked Harris to the ground. Ordinarily this would be an ejectable offense, but officials realized that it was in retaliation for Harris's taunting, which was legal at the time, and did not throw a flag. To avoid these confrontations and to improve the general fan experience, the NFL expanded its unsportsman-like conduct rules in 1978 to include baiting an opponent without using physical contact.

TAUNTING AND TOUCHDOWN CELEBRATIONS

During the national showcase that is *Monday Night Football*, Jets receiver Keyshawn Johnson taunted the Patriots' home crowd after a touchdown he scored on November 15, 1999. Television networks broadcast an image of Johnson giving a throat-slash gesture, with his index finger slowly dragging across his throat.

1. Johnson wasn't taunting an opposing player, but is this a penalty?

Johnson's throat-slash gesture was only a few years removed from the trial that graphically detailed the fatal stabbings of Nicole Brown Simpson and Ronald Goldman, crimes of which one of the league's former stars, O. J. Simpson, was acquitted. Packers quarterback Brett Favre returned the gesture toward Lions players during another 1999 game. Favre drew an unsportsmanlike conduct penalty on the second instance.

The league then started to tighten down on taunting. This included a wide swath of behaviors they were looking to curtail, based on video review of what was deemed acceptable and unacceptable by league standards. The league, if anything, is always hypervigilant about brand image.

In various parts of the rulebook and in policy memos distributed to play-ers, this is a partial list of the taunting behaviors that draw a 15-yard penalty if they occur anywhere on the field: the throat-slash gesture, machine-gun salute, sexually suggestive gestures, prolonged gyrations, stomping on a team's logo, and gang signing.

Taunting gestures that are directed at an opponent include, quoting Rule 12-3-1, "sack dances; home run swing; incredible hulk; spiking the ball; spinning the ball; throwing or shoving the ball; pointing; pointing the ball; verbal taunting; military salute; standing over an opponent (prolonged and with provocation); or dancing." These all must involve an action directed at an opponent in order to be a flag. Spinning the ball, for instance, is not a foul unless it is directed at the feet of an opponent.

The taunting rule extends further into "prolonged and excessive celebrations" after an official warns the player. However, a flag is issued without warning if there is a premeditated or choreographed celebration involving multiple players or if the ball, pylon, or goalposts are used as a prop. In 2014 an interpretation of the existing rule was expanded to include dunking the ball over the crossbar on the goalposts—after a dunk by Saints receiver Jimmy Graham left the goalposts slightly askew on November 21, 2013, against the Falcons. Finally, in order to cast a wide net on certain celebrations the Competition Committee felt were unsportsmanlike, an odd admonition was added: any celebration involving a player going to the ground is considered a foul.

Even the league's disciplinary memos acknowledge that the list is not complete, stating, "Obviously, it is not possible to identify in advance every action that may constitute taunting, and final judgment on this is left to Game Officials and/or video review."

2. There are two exceptions to the celebration penalty when the player goes to the ground. What are they?

First, a player who drops in prayer in the end zone is exempted from a penalty. This became subject to judgement on September 29, 2014, when Chiefs safety Husain Abdullah scored a touchdown on an interception return. Abdullah, a devout Muslim, went to both knees in a prayerful gesture of prostration following the score. Abdullah was flagged not for his prayer, but because he slid on his knees for three or four yards into the prayer. Although this could technically go either way—using a higher power to absolve one's self of the unsportsmanlike conduct—the league instructed the officials to have a little more leniency in interpreting these actions.

The second exception to the rule is if a player, in the act of celebrating with his teammates, is tripped or inadvertently falls. It is up to the official to determine whether the act of going to the ground was intentional.

3. Isn't the Lambeau Leap considered a taunting penalty?

The Lambeau Leap—originating in Green Bay, but also occurring in many other stadiums with end zone walls low enough—is a jump and flop into the first row of the stands following a touchdown. Obviously, this celebratory tactic is recommended only for home games. Because the league saw this as a player–fan engagement celebration, it was "grandfathered in" according to the Competition Committee. Perhaps a better assessment is that the wording of the taunting rules was specific to avoid including this action as a penalty.

Contrast that to a celebration by Kansas City Chiefs receiver Dwayne Bowe following a 75-yard touchdown reception on December 26, 2010, against the Tennessee Titans. Bowe leaped into the front row of the Arrowhead Stadium end zone, and fans and players were confused when officials let the flags fly. Running back Jamaal Charles followed Bowe with his own leap, which made it a group celebration, with the penalty correctly marked off on the ensuing kickoff. Referee Scott Green explained the ruling over the public-address system in amusing fashion, saying, "Only one man is permitted to jump into the stands."

Compare these two plays.

Play No. 1: Seahawks receiver Golden Tate had just caught a pass at the 40-yard line in the open field from Russell Wilson against the Rams in an October 28, 2013, Monday night game. Realizing he was likely to score, he raised the ball in his left hand. Then he made a hand gesture at safety Rodney McLeod that could only be interpreted as Tate communicating that McLeod is all talk and no action. Tate was nearly caught at the goal line, but he was able to score the touchdown. Tate was flagged for taunting at the 35.

Play No. 2: In college football, Louisiana State was hosting Florida on October 8, 2011. On a fake punt near the end of the first quarter, LSU punter Brad Wing sprinted down the left sideline. As Wing's touchdown became apparent, he started celebrating early by slightly extending his arms. Although it was a minor spontaneous moment of exuberance by a punter who would rarely score a touchdown, there was no ambiguity in the college rules that this was taunting. A flag was thrown at the 8-yard line.

4. How are these penalties assessed?

Wing's touchdown run became the unwitting test case for the NCAA's new taunting rules passed before the 2011 season. The sanction was especially harsh for Wing, as it is enforced 15 yards from the spot of foul. This meant that the redshirt-freshman punter had his only touchdown taken off the scoreboard, with LSU getting a first-and-10 from the 23-yard line.

The NFL does not often flag an early celebration or "showboating" as a taunting foul. This includes raising the ball, high-stepping, deliberately slowing down, and walking backward or somersaulting into the end zone. However, any of the actions listed in the taunting rules are penalized even if the play is in progress. Because Tate was pointing at his opponent, it is a rare live-ball taunting foul. However, all taunting fouls in the NFL are assessed as if they are dead-ball fouls with the 15 yards enforced from the succeeding spot; on a scoring play, the succeeding spot is the ensuing kickoff.

While Wing lost his touchdown, Tate's was able to stand.

5. On October 14, 2002, receiver Terrell Owens caught a touchdown pass for the 49ers against the Seahawks on Monday Night Football. Owens reached into his sock and pulled out a marker to autograph the touchdown ball on the spot. Is this an unsportsmanlike conduct foul against Owens?

At the time, there were limited criteria as to what constituted an "excessive celebration" under the rules. Owens was not flagged for his actions.

This was likely one of many increasingly elaborate celebrations that the Competition Committee reviewed for the rule change, including Saints receiver Joe Horn pulling out a cell phone he stashed under the goalpost padding in pregame and Chad Ochocinco pantomiming a golf swing with the pylon. Under the current rules, any use of the ball, pylon, goalposts, or any other object as a prop in a celebration is an immediate unsportsmanlike conduct foul.

In addition to the foul under today's rule, Owens's instant autograph would cause him to be ejected from the game. Possessing a foreign or extraneous object that is not part of the uniform, if it is deemed a safety hazard, is subject to disqualification regardless of whether the player uses the object.

Owens did not completely escape punishment, as the league fined him for a uniform violation that week: $5,000 for having his shirt untucked.

UNNECESSARY ROUGHNESS

On November 23, 1986, Packers defensive lineman Charles Martin drilled Bears quarterback Jim McMahon a good two seconds after McMahon released his pass. Martin then landed on McMahon as part of the tackle, further injuring his arm and ending McMahon's season. Bears lineman Jimbo Covert hit Martin, who was standing over and taunting the writhing McMahon on the turf. The ball was intercepted by the Packers on the play.

6. What is the result of the play after penalty enforcement?

The hit by Martin came so late, it was determined to have occurred after the interception. The Packers were able to keep the ball after the 15-yard penalty was marched off. Covert was not assessed a foul.

Referee Jerry Markbreit had a decision to make. Players have been ejected for throwing punches after a play was over, but there was no precedent for a flagrant hit during a play. This became the template, as Markbreit ejected Martin for the hit. Many of Markbreit's peers believe that his decisive action to eject Martin led to his assignment that year to his second of a record four career Super Bowls as a referee.

Commissioner Pete Rozelle also took unprecedented action. Martin was the first player to be suspended multiple games for an on-field incident. Through the 2014 season, this has happened to only three other players, as shown in Table 9.1.

7. If 20 yards from the line of scrimmage a defensive back commits pass interference that also qualifies as unnecessary roughness, which foul is called, and where is it assessed from?

This scenario has been in the rulebook since 2009, but there is no record of it ever being called. In this case, both fouls are called, and the unnecessary roughness is tacked on to the spot of the foul. Assuming a half-distance penalty is not involved, this would be a 35-yard penalty. The player making the hit also may be subject to ejection if the hit is flagrant enough.

8. On October 5, 2014, Jets linebacker Quinton Coples tackled Chargers running back Donald Brown, initiating contact at his chest and sliding up under Brown's chin. Brown was stopped so suddenly, his feet left the ground momentarily and his helmet came off. Coples was flagged for unnecessary roughness. Was this the correct call?

This was not a foul for a so-called clothesline tackle; in fact, Coples had taken down Raiders running back Maurice Jones-Drew in similar fashion in the season opener a few weeks earlier. In the case of the tackle on Brown, it was a violent but legal tackle that drew a flag anyway.

A clothesline tackle is a swinging arm or strike to the head, neck, or face, even if the contact begins at the chest and moves up to the neck area. There

Table 9.1. Players suspended for multiple games for on-field incidents

Date	Player	Team	Opponent	Incident	Suspension
Nov. 23, 1986	Charles Martin	Green Bay	Chicago	Forcibly threw quarterback Jim McMahon to the ground after a pass	2 games
Oct. 1, 2005	Albert Haynesworth	Tennessee	Dallas	Stepped on center Andre Gurode's head when his helmet was off	5 games
Nov. 24, 2011	Ndamukong Suh	Green Bay	Detroit	Stomped on lineman Evan Dietrick-Smith	2 games
Aug. 23, 2014 (preseason)	Brandon Meriweather	Washington	Baltimore	Illegal hit on defenseless player; multiple prior violations of illegal hits	2 games

must be a deliberate, separate act from a standard tackle to call a clothesline tackle. The force of the tackle alone is not enough to create a clothesline tackle.

The irony for Coples is that the season began with the enshrinement of the 2014 class to the Pro Football Hall of Fame—a class that included Chris Hanburger, a linebacker for Washington who was so well known for the clothesline tackle, he earned the nickname "the Hangman." In Hanburger's day, the clothesline tackle was legal, but a rule change in 1980, a year after his retirement, made the tactic unnecessary roughness.

Hanburger's clothesline tackle brings up a more recent signature tackle by Cowboys safety Roy Williams that, while legal at the time, sent three players to a season-ending injured reserve in 2004. It is known as the horse-collar tackle, in which a runner is pulled down from behind or the side by the top of the

Figure 9.1. Ravens cornerback Lardarius Webb takes down Saints receiver Joe Morgan in a 2014 game with a horse-collar tackle. A ball carrier in the open field cannot be forcibly pulled downward by the collar of the jersey or the in-side of the pads along that same collar-line. The top of the shoulder pads also may not be used in this type of tackle. Essentially the off-limits area on Morgan's body is facing the camera for this maneuver. Webb is putting the weight of his body into this tackle, which can cause season-ending knee and leg injuries.
Jonathan Bachman/AP Images

shoulder pads, causing the runner to twist backward as his knees buckle from the excess weight. That excess weight is disproportionately concentrated in the legs and the knees, causing ruptured ligaments and leg fractures.

The horse-collar tackle quickly became illegal for the 2005 season, a rule that the media anointed Williams the namesake of. By 2007 his repeated violations of the Roy Williams Rule eventually earned him a one-game suspension.

In addition to grabbing a player from the top of the shoulder pads, the rule expanded a year later to make it illegal to pull an open-field runner down by grabbing the inside of the shoulder pads or the jersey collar along the same semicircular line. A horse-collar tackle cannot occur with the defender reaching to the front of the runner's pads or jersey, so the axis line is essentially the top surface of the shoulder pads around the collar of the pads and jersey.

Examine these two plays for potential fouls.

Play No. 1: In a game played in London on September 29, 2013, the Pittsburgh Steelers were trailing the Minnesota Vikings 34–27 with 19 seconds remaining in the game on a third-and-goal from the 6. Quarterback Ben Roethlisberger dropped back and stood in the pocket as he was pulled down by Vikings defensive tackle Everson Griffen, who had grabbed the uniform collar right above the "Roethlisberger" sewn on the back. Roethlisberger fumbled the ball, and the Vikings recovered.

Play No. 2: Four weeks after the London game, the Vikings were at MetLife Stadium in East Rutherford, New Jersey. On a first-quarter Giants punt by Steve Weatherford, Marcus Sherels returned the ball 86 yards for a Vikings touchdown. Weatherford was the last player who could have stopped Sherels. Weatherford, in desperation, was able to leap and grab Sherels on the back collar of the jersey and pull him down. Sherels's knees bent, but he was able to shake the tackle and score the touchdown.

9. Are these illegal horse-collar tackles?

Griffen was not flagged for a horse-collar tackle, because a quarterback who is in the pocket does not get protection from these types of tackles. It is unusual that a player-safety rule actually exempts an action against a quarterback, but there is a recognition that this type of tackle poses less risk of injury to a player who is not running at full speed, because there is no momentum from running that is transferred to the legs and knees. Similarly, a runner who is still in the tackle box—an area as wide as the space the interior linemen occupied at the snap and extending from the offensive backfield to 3 yards beyond the line of scrimmage—has not had the opportunity to build a running momentum to contribute to significant injury and does not get relief from the horse-collar tackle rule.

Even though Weatherford does not finish the tackle to the ground, there is still a risk of injury. There are three elements that must be present for a horse-collar tackle foul: (1) grabbing the runner from the indicated collar regions, (2) putting a downward force on the runner, and (3) causing the runner's knees to buckle *or* pulling him to the ground. Since Sherels's knees buckled, this was assessed as a 15-yard penalty on the kickoff following the touchdown.

GIVING THE OFFICIALS AN EARFUL

In another game featuring the Vikings and the Steelers—this one at the old Three Rivers Stadium in Pittsburgh on September 24, 1995—Vikings kicker Fuad Reveiz was attempting a 48-yard field goal with two seconds remaining in the second quarter. As the kick sailed wide right of the goalposts, a yellow flag from line judge Ben Montgomery fluttered to the ground. Montgomery had counted 12 players on the Pittsburgh defense. Since the half could be extended due to the defensive foul, Reveiz connected from 43 yards after the penalty was marked off.

Steelers coach Bill Cowher was livid. He insisted that there were only 11 Steelers players on the field, and he was right. The Steelers used a sideline photo printer to produce pictures of the offensive and defensive formations for coaching purposes. Cowher grabbed the picture of the formation showing the Steelers had the correct number of players and chased down referee Gordon McCarter as he went to the exit tunnel at the end of the half. The television broadcast showed Cowher talking sternly and then stuffing the photo in Mc-Carter's shirt pocket, as the referee refused to look at the evidence.

10. How is this situation to be handled?

Before addressing Cowher's actions, there are two facts worth noting. First, at the time of this game, there was no replay review, so there was no way to reverse the call unless another official counted 11 players and was able to convince Montgomery to pick up the flag. When the replay system was reinstated in the 1999 season, this play may very well have influenced the decision by the Competition Committee to include in the list of reviewable calls "whether more than 11 players were on the field at the snap." Under the current rules, Cowher still could not issue a coach's challenge to review the number of players, but the replay official could have called for a review. (It wasn't a scoring play, but it was after the two-minute warning.) That would have resulted in the flag being picked up and the half ending on a missed field goal.

The second item to consider is that the officials are not permitted to use any external sources to decide, correct, or refine their calls, with the obvious exception of the replay system. The most obvious outside source would be a replay on the scoreboard. Many times, coaches argue a call with an official when a replay is shown on the scoreboard. If a coach implores an official to look at the screen, the official must not reflexively act. It is imperative that the official not give anyone the impression he stole a glance at the behemoth video board that takes up a major part of one of the stadium's walls. Similarly, McCarter refused to look at Cowher's photographic evidence, not only because it would not have changed the call, but also because it avoided even the tiniest whiff of impropriety.

In addition to the incorrect foul on the Steelers, there was a second missed call. Cowher's heated actions were improper contact with an official, and McCarter should have ejected Cower and assessed a 15-yard unsportsmanlike conduct penalty on the second-half kickoff. Players who make that type of contact in protest are immediately disqualified, and the same standard applies to nonplayers. In fact, the NFL's casebook illustrates an extraordinarily similar situation in Approved Ruling 13.14:

> After the end of the first half (or second half if the game is going into over-time), Team A's coach contacts an official while arguing with him as they leave the field, or in the tunnel.
>
> **Ruling:** Enforce the 15-yard penalty against Team A on the ensuing kickoff. Disqualify the coach. The officials' jurisdiction continues during intermissions.

McCarter and Montgomery were each fined the equivalent of a game check—$4,009 and $2,826, respectively—for the erroneous 12-men penalty. Cowher was fined $7,500, but he dodged an ignominious distinction: in the years before and since, a referee has never disqualified a football coach, despite examples of officials tossing baseball managers (frequently), basketball coaches (occasionally), and hockey coaches (rarely).

TEN

REPLAY

It was a tough call. And this is a place where an instant replay would be important.

—NBC announcer Dick Enberg, on an erroneous incomplete pass call to receiver Mike Renfro before replay reviews were enacted, 1979 AFC Championship Game, Houston Oilers at Pittsburgh Steelers, January 6, 1980

In planning network coverage for the annual Army–Navy game in 1963, Tony Verna, a 29-year-old television sports director, was hoping to show the audience some of the action that he was seeing from his multiple camera angles during the live play. He was able to convince CBS Sports president Bill MacPhail to authorize a 1,200-pound videotape machine to be transported to Philadelphia Municipal Stadium for an experiment in instant replay.

Verna had some technical gremlins to overcome. Videotape machines took a few seconds to sync up on playback, especially a machine that had bumped around in the back of a rental truck down the New Jersey Turnpike. Also, videotape was expensive: an hour's worth of tape was $300. Verna used a five-minute piece of 3M Scotch 179 two-inch videotape full of splices pilfered from the engineering department that contained snippets of *The Lucy Show* and a Duz soap commercial. In the fourth quarter, after about six aborted attempts to show a replay through the game, everything came together and a clean shot of quarterback Rollie Stichweh running for an Army touchdown became the first use of instant replay.

Verna did not show another replay during the game, but a month later he used it several times for the Bert Bell Benefit Bowl—a now-defunct playoff game for third place in the NFL. Tex Schramm, the Cowboys' general manager, said at the time that instant replay "will have such far-reaching implications, we can't begin to imagine them today." When Schramm worked at CBS, he hired Verna; while on the NFL Competition Committee, Schramm was instrumental in ushering in the instant replay system as an officiating tool.

1. On the fourth play of the 1986 season, Chicago Bears center Jay Hilgenberg snapped the ball wide of quarterback Jim McMahon. Cleveland Browns safety Al Gross recovered the ball just as it went out of bounds. There was hesitancy from referee Ben Dreith on the call, and after the game, he told a pool reporter, "The call was made, but we wanted to confirm it with them upstairs. The call was a touchdown. I told the umpire [Dave Moss] to call upstairs and make sure they couldn't switch it on us." Was this use of replay correct?

This was the first use of replay in a regular-season game, so it is understandable that Dreith did not have the protocol down. At the time, the replay official—who was a supervisor in the league office, and not specifically hired as a replay official—was the only person who could call for a review. In this case, replay official Nick Skorich contacted Moss before Moss was able to call upstairs.

Under the first generation of replay, the replay official made the final decision, taking the ultimate call outside of the crew for the first time. In 1999 the referee was responsible for making the decision using a field-level monitor. A rule change in 2014 allowed a designated individual in the officiating headquarters to consult with the referee—namely, vice president of officiating Dean Blandino and senior supervisor of officiating Al Riveron. As the 2014 season progressed, the consultation process was clearly more of an interventionist role in the final decision. It seems fairly certain the NFL is moving toward a centralized replay system similar to the National Hockey League.

After reviewing the play in the Browns–Bears game, Gross was determined to have recovered the ball before going out of bounds on the third replay angle. This confirmed the Browns touchdown instead of a potential safety on a reversal.

The terms *confirmed* and *reversed* were not part of the replay protocol from the start. Early in that inaugural season for replay, an unfortunate miscommunication between the replay official and the umpire led to a change in mechanics that endures today.

Mark Heisler of the *Los Angeles Times* opened his October 6, 1986, column on the Los Angeles Raiders–Kansas City Chiefs game with, "The boys in the replay booth botched another one here Sunday." A touchdown catch by Raiders wide receiver Dokie Williams was being reviewed by replay official Jack Reader. Williams's second foot touched out of bounds, so the touchdown was clearly going to be taken off the board. Umpire John Keck was using the standard-issue walkie-talkie to communicate with Reader when Reader issued his ruling: "incomplete." Keck thought the call was "complete." The Raiders lined up for the extra point while Reader frantically tried to contact the field; once the kick was made, the crew could not change the touchdown call. Under improved communication procedures (and being outfitted with better transmission equipment), Reader's call would have been "reversed, reversed, reversed, over."

The instant-replay system introduced in 1986 was fraught with technical issues, long delays, and questionable rulings. At the annual league meetings in Phoenix in March 1992, the owners voted 17–11 in favor of continuing replay for another season. Since replay was approved incrementally, one year at a time, the extension into the 1992 season required a two-thirds vote by the owners, so this meant the vote failed. The system was scrapped, and it didn't return until the 1999 season.

The current system allows two replay challenges by a coach, with a third one granted if the first two lead to reversals. The coach cannot challenge if he is out of timeouts. He also cannot challenge any play that is a score, is a turnover, or occurs after the two-minute warning.

2. Which of these plays can a coach legally challenge before the two-minute warning and are not in the exclusive jurisdiction of the replay official to initiate a review?

A. Quarterback sack that occurred in the end zone for a safety, when the ruling on the field was that it was at the 1-yard line

B. Any fourth down that fails due to not achieving the first-down line to gain (turnover on downs)

C. Recovery of an onside kick

D. A play that includes an intercepted illegal pass

E. Runner ruled down at the 1-yard line, short of a touchdown, in overtime.

The replay official is given sole jurisdiction over all scoring plays, but notably absent from the rules are plays that are *potential* scores, such as a player who is ruled short of a touchdown or out of bounds in the end zone. The sack scenario in the list above (A) would have to be challenged by the coach as long as it isn't after the two-minute warning in regulation. When flipped around—a safety call is made on the field, but video shows it is dead at the 1-yard line—the replay must come from the replay official, because it is a scoring play. A denied touchdown (E) could be challenged by the coach in regulation time; however, the replay official has exclusive authority over the reviews in overtime, making this potential score solely under the replay official's authority.

The types of turnover plays that the replay official may look at are:

• Fumbles and backward pass recoveries
• Fumbles and backward passes out of bounds in the opponent's end zone
• Interceptions
• Muffed scrimmage kicks recovered by the kicking team.

Not included in this list is a change of possession due to the offense not gaining the first down in four downs. If there is a reviewable aspect of the fourth-down play, the coach must use a challenge to have the play reviewed (B). The onside kick recovery is not a scrimmage kick (punt or field goals only), so the coach would have to challenge that play (C) as well.

The interception of an illegal forward pass is still considered a change of possession by interception, so the replay official would have to initiate the view for that play (D).

Reviewing the choices, the coach may challenge the plays marked A, B, and C. The other two would be challenged by the replay official.

3. With 32 seconds remaining in the fourth quarter, the Tampa Bay Buccaneers are trailing the Cincinnati Bengals 14–13. The Buccaneers complete a 21-yard pass, putting them in field goal range. However, they have 12 players on the field and are lining up for the next play when Bengals coach Marvin

Lewis throws a challenge flag. This play occurs after the two-minute warning and may not be challenged by the coach. What happens?

Lewis, a member of the Competition Committee, obviously knew the penalty against his team would wind up helping his team in the long run. Anytime a coach challenges a play, it costs him a timeout. If the challenge is successful, then he gets the timeout back; if the challenge is not successful or if he is not authorized to challenge, then he does not get the timeout returned.

Going back to Thanksgiving Day 2012, Detroit Lions coach Jim Schwartz attempted to challenge a touchdown run by Houston Texans running back Justin Forsett. Forsett was clearly down by contact earlier in the play, and the replay review would have reversed the touchdown. Under the rules of the time, the unauthorized challenge of a scoring play froze out the replay official from reviewing the play with an outcome that favored the Lions. The touchdown call stood, and there was nothing to do but stare at the TV screen with your mouth wide open.

The Competition Committee felt that a wrong call should not stand if there is an opportunity to correct it. Similarly, the penalty of points is an extraordinarily harsh sentence for the challenge infraction. In the off-season following Schwartz's gaffe, the rule was changed to penalize a timeout. When Lewis made the challenge, he was aware that he would get the timeout, but that the replay official was still permitted to review the play. (The replay official is not compelled to do so, but in this case, vice president of officiating Dean Blandino said that replay official Larry Nemmers was already in the process of stopping the game for a review.)

The Buccaneers penalty for 12 players on the field was enforced, nullifying the 21-yard gain on the play.

4. *What is the penalty if the Bengals did not have any timeouts left?*

If a coach throws a red flag when he is not permitted to do so and is out of timeouts, the team is assessed a 15-yard penalty. That penalty is enforced between downs, so, in the case of the 12-on-field foul, the 21-yard pass is still nullified, and the 5-yard penalty on the Buccaneers is assessed. Then the 15-yard foul for the Bengals challenge is marked off, which nets 10 yards in the Bucs' favor from the previous spot.

5. *During a November 15, 2009, game against the Cowboys, Packers coach Mike McCarthy challenged a down-by-contact ruling in the beginning of the fourth quarter, but replay did not reverse the call, resulting in a failed*

challenge. It was his second challenge, so he was out of challenges for the re-mainder of the game. With timeouts remaining, McCarthy attempted a third challenge in the fourth quarter. What is the penalty?

Just as a situation where a coach challenges when only the replay of-ficial is permitted to challenge, the penalty for a challenge in excess of the two allotted is a charged timeout. There is also an unsportsmanlike conduct penalty of 15 yards if the team does not have any timeouts to use.

6. Is there any situation where the coach may legally challenge and the replay official also may call for a review on the same play?

The rules strictly divide the plays that coaches or the replay officials may challenge. There is only one instance where both are authorized to challenge the same play: whether a loose ball in play has touched any object suspended over the field, such as a scoreboard or a television camera. The replay official is allowed to initiate a booth review even if it is outside of the two-minute warning window of his jurisdiction. The coach also may chal-lenge whether the ball struck an object, but he is still not permitted to do so after the two-minute warning.

On October 13, 2013, punter Brian Moorman played his first game after he re-signed with the Buffalo Bills. The former Pro Bowl punter spent 12 seasons with the Bills before being released in 2012 and spending the rest of that season with the Dallas Cowboys. After Moorman's replacement struggled in 2013, the Bills were able to bring Moorman back because he was a free agent. The first punt of the day was met with uncharacteristically loud cheers before the Bills even snapped the ball.

Moorman did not disappoint. The punt dropped inside the 5-yard line, bounced along the sideline, and bounded past the outside of the pylon in the corner of the end zone. The ball brushed the pylon ever so slightly, and field judge Craig Wrolstad ruled that it was a touchback, since the pylon is considered out of bounds and in the end zone when touched by a loose ball.

7. This play was after the two-minute warning in the half, so the replay official initiated a review to see if the ball was out of bounds prior to touching the pylon. Is this a valid review?

Replay is allowed if the ball touched a player, a sideline, the end line, the goal line, or the pylon, in addition to the overhead objects previously men-tioned. This can be a reviewed play either way—to determine that a touch has occurred or has not occurred—but there must be incontrovertible video evidence to overrule the on-field call.

In this case, the pylon was determined to be contacted slightly, but the ball touched the sideline inside the 1-yard line before touching the pylon. The Bengals were given the ball at the out-of-bounds spot, reversing the touchback call.

8. How would the play be called if the ball did not touch the sideline?

The actual play was very easy to reverse when subjected to a slow-motion replay, because of the clarity of the evidence. It would be very difficult to get the conclusive evidence to determine the pylon was not contacted and where to spot the ball. To understand this better, let's take a broader look at the rules regarding punts that go out of bounds.

An airborne punt is dead when it lands out of bounds, but the spot reverts back to the point where the ball crossed the sideline. Where a punt crosses the sideline in the air is not subject to review, because the video cannot show the three-dimensionality of the call. In this case, the field judge can determine where the ball crossed the sideline, and the referee would have to announce this fact, saying, for example, "The ball crossed the sideline at the 1/2-yard line, then it touched the pylon, creating a touchback." The referee would have to announce this ruling prior to going in for a review. If the evidence shows that the pylon was not touched, then it effectively strikes the "touched the pylon" segment of the announcement from the record, which leaves "The ball crossed the sideline at the 1/2-yard line."

One other note: even though the ball crosses the sideline at the 1/2-yard line, the ball is not dead at that point. If the ball does, in fact, contact the pylon before touching anywhere else out of bounds, the ball is dead at that point. Then, the touchback ruling trumps the spot where the ball crosses the sideline.

9. During the fourth quarter of a game on October 1, 2012, Bears quarterback Jay Cutler threw a pass to receiver Brandon Marshall in the end zone on a third-and-goal from the 4. The Cowboys were penalized for defensive pass interference in the end zone, which would give the Bears a first-and-goal from the 1. Cowboys coach Jason Garrett challenged the ruling, arguing that the ball was tipped prior to the interference, which means that a foul cannot be called by rule. Is this a challengeable call?

Part of the objective criteria of reviewable calls is to determine when the ball touches a player, object, or a line, but subjective criteria, such as pass interference, is not reviewable. To break this paradox, the *Instant Replay Casebook* provides several examples of plays and how they are to be ruled.

In this case, Approved Ruling 15.151 provides the necessary guidance, which reads, in part:

> Pass to A2 is incomplete, but B1 is called for defensive pass interference at the A40. Replays show the pass being tipped at the line of scrimmage by B2 prior to the interference.
>
> **Ruling:** Reviewable. No foul. . . . In order for the foul to be negated, the ball must be touched prior to the interference and by a player away from the action that creates the foul.

Garrett was allowed to challenge the call, and referee Walt Anderson reversed the pass interference penalty. In this case, Anderson determined the tip was enough distance away from where the interference occurred and that the tip preceded the foul.

Incidentally, the next entry of the casebook allows for the reverse to happen. Approved Ruling 15.152 states that if a pass interference flag is picked up because of a tipped ball, a replay review can reverse the flag pickup if there is clear evidence the ball was not touched in flight. In that case, there must be an announcement of the flag pickup and the reason. This does not mean there must be a flag on the field. An announcement stating that the covering official did not call a foul because it was tipped is equivalent to a literal flag pickup. Replay cannot make the assessment of a pass interference; it can only negate the flag or an announced flag pickup.

On a related note, a replay review can negate or enforce a running-into-the-kicker or roughing-the-kicker foul that involves the determination of the defender touching the ball. If a player is ruled to have not touched the ball, replay can void the foul. If the announcement is that a foul is not called because of a defensive touching, the "announcement" can be reversed on the touched-ball aspect.

REPLAY BLOWS A FUSE

The Dolphins were hosting the New Orleans Saints on October 25, 2009, at Miami's Land Shark Stadium. On the Dolphins' first possession of the game, quarterback Chad Henne connected with receiver Davone Bess for an 8-yard gain. Saints coach Sean Payton challenged the call, as it was clearly not a complete pass. Referee John Parry went to the replay equipment and found that it was not working.

10. What happens to the Saints challenge in this situation?

If the problem is isolated to the on-field equipment, the referee can use an alternate sideline replay monitor to review the play. In outdoor stadiums, this alternate monitor is set up in the field access tunnel to protect it from the weather. In this case, there was a switch malfunction, which required the replay technician to reboot the system. Therefore, both sideline monitors were down as well.

Parry is required to wait two minutes to see if the replay equipment will become active. After two minutes, the replay review is abandoned, and the call on the field stands. Neither the replay official nor a designated senior staffer at the officiating command center may act as a proxy for the referee. The challenge is not taken from the coach, and the play resumes as if there was no interruption.

If either side decides to challenge the next play, they may do so, and wait the requisite two minutes if the system is not yet functional. Even though one team is technically disadvantaged, there is no equitable offset to the opposing team. Neither coach wound up challenging that game, although two reviews were initiated by the replay official later in the game.

REVIEWING THE ENTIRE PLAY

On November 1, 2009, the Philadelphia Eagles had a commanding lead over the New York Giants in the third quarter. Eagles quarterback Donovan McNabb was attempting to pass when his arm was hit by cornerback Bruce Johnson, causing McNabb to fumble. Defensive tackle Fred Robbins recovered the fumble and lateralled to linebacker Osi Umenyiora during the runback. Umenyiora took the ball the rest of the way for a touchdown.

At the time, turnovers and scoring plays were not subject to an automatic review, so Eagles coach Andy Reid had to challenge the call. Reid challenged the fumble ruling. After reviewing the play, the fumble was confirmed, but Robbins's lateral to Umenyiora was actually an illegal forward pass.

11. How is this review properly handled?

When a play is under review, all reviewable aspects of the entire play are subject to scrutiny. The only caveat is that the review may take only 60 seconds from when the referee goes under the hood of the replay equipment, with no extension allowed even if there are multiple aspects to review. The replay official and the referee are allowed to communicate prior to the referee going under the hood to discuss what is going to be reviewed; that discussion does not count against the 60-second limit.

In this case, referee Carl Cheffers checked the fumble ruling first, which was probably determined fairly quickly. With a confirmed fumble, attention turned to the latter segment of the play. The determination of a pass being forward or backward is reviewable, so Cheffers is allowed to assess the illegal forward pass penalty as part of the replay review.

Even though Reid challenged the fumble ruling, which was confirmed, he is not charged with a failed challenge. Since a reviewable aspect of the play had been reversed, the challenge is deemed to be successful, even though it was not part of the challenge request. The reversal does not even have to have a benefit for the challenging team; as long as there is some element on the play that is reversed, the team is not charged with a timeout.

TAKING BACK A CHALLENGE

Baltimore Ravens coach John Harbaugh threw a challenge flag during the second quarter of a game on November 22, 2009, against the Indianapolis Colts. Quarterback Peyton Manning had just converted a third-down pass to Colts receiver Reggie Wayne at the sideline, and Harbaugh felt that Wayne was out of bounds. While discussing the challenge with the referee, Harbaugh wanted to withdraw the challenge, because replays were showing that Wayne was able to drag his toe in bounds, giving him a catch with both feet down.

12. Can Harbaugh cancel the challenge?

The officials granted the request to cancel the challenge by Harbaugh, but they should not have done so without penalty. Under the current rules, Harbaugh can use a timeout to cancel his challenge, or he may proceed with the challenge as originally called.

There are some exceptions that allow a coach to pick up a challenge flag once a situation is explained to him or if he is challenging a nonreviewable aspect of the play. In a podcast on *Football Zebras*, I asked vice president of officiating Dean Blandino to explain when a coach can pick up his challenge flag free and clear.

"We've given our referees some discretion that if the coach is genuinely confused and does not understand that the play is not reviewable, then we're going to allow him to pick up the flag," Blandino explained. "Obviously, if the referee feels he is using the flag to manipulate the clock, then we'll charge a timeout."

The example given during the interview was a coach that challenges a noncall of a fumble when the officials ruled that the runner's forward progress was stopped prior to the fumble. A coach that does not realize there was a ruling that freezes out any chance of a reversal will be able to take back the challenge without the loss of a timeout or a challenge. If the ambiguity is tied to a reviewable aspect, such as whether Reggie Wayne got his second foot down in bounds, the challenge must go forward or the team is charged a timeout.

ELEVEN

CREWS

"Make Super Bowl calls only, no Woolworth calls." That means it's got to be big. If it's a call that could determine a Super Bowl, call it. I don't want Woolworth calls, nickel and dime kind of stuff.

—Jerry Seeman, NFL senior director of officiating 1991–2001, on his number one commandment of officiating

Seventeen crews of seven, plus a replay official and a replay assistant for each, are assembled each year on May 15 like clockwork. Following the Super Bowl, the officials go into a "dark period" of no contact from the league office. This allows them a guaranteed stretch of time without having to tend to league matters, so that they can plan vacations and not be interrupted at their full-time, year-round jobs.

As soon as May 15 hits, the officials will get a packet welcoming the new officials and announcing the retirements. The new rules passed by the team owners at the March annual meeting are also included, as is a lengthy rules test. May 15 also marks the day that the officials may not have contact with the media without prior league permission.

Once the dark period has ended, the league office will send videos and official interpretations of existing rules and new rules for review. In July all officials will meet for their annual clinic—a two-day training camp for the officials that involves intense video study, additional rules testing, physical conditioning tests, and break-out meetings by position. It is the only chance to get all of the officials together at the same time during the year, and this allows incoming officials to meet the veterans as well.

Officiating attracts people from all walks of life. At the beginning of the 2013 season, I included a list on the *Football Zebras* website of the occupations of the various officials, grouped into manageable categories. The job sector with the most officials was education, with 21 current or retired educators, including teachers, principals, and professors. There are also a fair number of lawyers and even corrections and probations officers. If anything, these fields are all about enforcing rules.

There weren't always seven officials on the crew. When the league began in 1920, the referee, umpire, and linesman were the only officials on the field. There were a lot of short running plays, so it worked. By 1929 the passing game still had onerous restrictions—for example, all passes had to originate from 5 yards behind the line of scrimmage—but the league added a field judge to cover receivers. Passing became increasingly a part of the game, and after World War II, the back judge was added for deep coverage. Vikings quarterback Fran Tarkenton and his scrambling tactics pushed the calls at the line of scrimmage, so the line judge was added in 1965. Shortly after Chargers coach Don Coryell unveiled his "Air Coryell" passing-assault offense, the league added more eyes in the secondary by the addition of a side judge.

After the 1998 season, the designations of back judge and field judge were swapped to match the titles at all other levels of the game. Finally, the umpire was moved from his position behind the defensive linebackers to behind the quarterback, opposite the referee, due to repeated injuries suffered by umpires. However, the umpire returns to his traditional position during the last two minutes of the first half, the final five minutes of the second half, and when the ball is inside the defense's 5-yard line.

During the third quarter of a Panthers–Giants game on December 28, 2003, the Giants blocked a punt by Todd Sauerbrun. The trajectory of the blocked punt put referee Bernie Kukar square in the middle of the play. He was watching the ball go out of bounds at the 1-yard line, focusing on a potential goal-line call. Giants safety Clarence LeBlanc was running for the loose ball and rolled up on Kukar's leg, knocking him out of the game.

1. Who takes the place of the referee?

There is no single designated position that assumes the referee's duties. Each crew has one official who has prior experience as a crew chief in college. The crew determines before the season who would take the reins in the referee's absence.

During the regular season, there are no alternate officials on the sideline to fill in. When the crew is down an official, they revert to six-man mechanics. There is no set procedure in the NFL, but most crews will sacrifice the back judge position to get to six. The back judge will either move to the vacated position or be part of a two-position move—for example, the side judge fills in for the head linesman who shares the same sideline, and the back judge goes to the side judge position. These moves are all planned in advance.

In the Panthers–Giants game, the field judge was a rookie official named Gene Steratore who would ascend to the referee position permanently three years later. Kukar handed his white hat to Steratore, but Steratore initially declined. Perhaps fueled by the pain from his injury, Kukar insisted with a sharp-tongued response. Steratore obliged.

In an article in *Referee* magazine some years later, Steratore admitted his reservation to wear the white hat was out of respect for the man who would continue to be their crew chief, albeit from the locker room. "For me, that was sacred ground," Steratore said, referring to the symbolism of the white hat.

In the postseason, there are three alternates assigned to a game. Generally, there is one that can work as a referee or umpire, one for the line of scrimmage, and one deep official. Super Bowls have five alternates: a referee, an umpire, a line official, a deep wing, and a back judge.

During postseason games, alternate officials assist the crew by managing the sidelines to prevent altercations or interference. They may assist with communication to and from the replay booth and to the chain crew to allow for more efficient administration of the game. Because of the magnitude of the game, alternates can interject if a crew is remiss in a rule or an enforcement, but must exclude themselves from any discussion or judgement of a call.

Alternates are rarely pressed into service on the field, but occasionally it does happen. On December 28, 1975, the Cowboys faced the Vikings for a divisional playoff game. Cowboys quarterback Roger Staubach completed a deep touchdown pass to receiver Drew Pearson in the waning seconds of the game, and Staubach's postgame comments about the play gave birth to the football term "Hail Mary." Protesting the fact that there was no pass interference penalty on the play, a hailstorm of debris emanated from the old Metropolitan Stadium stands, and a half-full bottle of Corby's whiskey struck field judge Armen Terzian in the head. Terzian was momentarily knocked unconscious and needed 11 stitches to close the gash. Alternate official Charlie Musser replaced Terzian for the final two plays of the game and earned a full game check of $5,500.

ONE MAN DOWN

On November 8, 2014, side judge Jeff Lamberth checked into an emergency room in Green Bay with severe stomach pains a day before his assigned Bears–Packers game on Sunday night. Lamberth made a full recovery and returned to the field just a few weeks later. However, at the time, the NFL had to make a decision about the crew for the game.

2. Can the game start with only six officials?

The crew very well could have officiated the entire game in six-man mechanics. The NFL will, however, go to great lengths to avoid this happening.

Occasionally, the league carries a small number of officials as "swing" officials to substitute. Swing officials are generally used when an official is recovering from an injury or surgery in the off-season, and his status for Week 1 is not known when the crews are formed on May 15. In the 2014 season, there were no swing officials when the regular season started.

When time is not critical, the league can pull someone from a crew who has the week off. At least one crew is off each week, and when teams have bye weeks, more crews are scheduled an off week. If for some reason that does not work, someone from the Thursday night crew will be called in to do a second game.

When substituting, the league will try to go to the same position, but if there are still conflicts and shortages, a substitute might play in a mirrored position to his regular assignment, such as a head linesman filling in at line judge, or a field judge working as side judge.

On the day Lamberth got sick, there was little time to get a substitute flown in to Green Bay—a city known for its football, but not for its abundance of direct flights. Umpire Tony Michalek was just a car drive away from Green Bay and was available, but Lamberth was a side judge that season. Since Michalek was also a line judge when working in college games, he worked as line judge in the Sunday night game and the originally scheduled line judge moved out to side judge.

Scheduling can get tight in Week 17, because every team plays on Sunday and there is only one crew that has the week off. In 2011 field judge Terry Brown worked the season finale at the umpire position because two umpires were sidelined, and only one umpire was available.

GAME ASSIGNMENTS

3. Is it possible for a crew to see the same team twice in a season?

Just based on the number of games in a season, it is impossible for crews to avoid seeing the same team during the season. However, there are restrictions to make sure that they do not get the same team too often or within the same month.

The crew assigned to a game will not be scheduled for either of those two teams for the next five weeks of the season. So, the earliest the Week 1 crew can see either team again is Week 7. A team will not have the same crew more than twice in one season, and a crew is not assigned to work two home games for any team. Rarely, these parameters may rule out a crew from working any game on a particular weekend, in which case an assignment would be allowed to conflict with the scheduling criteria.

Each crew works the 21-game preseason and regular-season schedule with no more than two off weeks. Once the playoffs start, it would be too difficult to maintain any of the regular-season restrictions. However, when making playoff assignments, the officiating department will be aware of potential controversies. For example, in the 2012 playoffs, head linesman Dana McKenzie was assigned to a game in Washington. He was quickly moved off of that game, since he had ejected Washington cornerback DeAngelo Hall in a heated discussion during the regular season; Hall insisted that McKenzie said insulting and disrespectful things to him.

The playoff assignment procedure changes from time to time, but basically the top tier of officials—as determined by an aggregate score of accuracy for every call made on every play and other factors—is assigned to later rounds of the playoffs.

4. Can an official request to be scheduled to work only certain teams?

The officiating department does maintain a small do-not-schedule list for some of their officials. Most of the entries on the list are at the request of the official himself.

When the NFL brought an expansion Houston Texans to replace the Oilers franchise that relocated to Nashville, referee Walt Anderson requested to not be assigned to Texans games, as he lives in the nearby city of Sugar Land, Texas. Officials do not have to avoid teams that live near them, and in many cases the league will assign those officials less often to a local team or assign them for preseason games. However, when the NFL hired temporary officials during the 2012 stalemate with the referees' union, the league had to have a heightened awareness of potential integrity issues.

Replacement side judge Brian Stropolo was a fan of the New Orleans Saints, and even attended a preseason game during an off week. He did not report this to the league when they assigned him to a regular-season Saints game; rather an ESPN reporter's question brought it to the league's attention. Stropolo was apparently dressed for the game and was pulled during pregame warmups. Every NFL official grew up as a football fan and had a favorite team. Because of the length of the hiring process, referees have a few years to mentally detach from their favorite team, something the hastily hired replacement officials did not have a chance to do.

Former referee Mike Carey took exception to the name of the Washington team as being derogatory, long before many scribes began omitting that name from their works. Carey, as a man of color, felt it was inconsistent with his beliefs to work a game that openly made references to men of a different color. The league office obliged his request because of his strong convictions.

Occasionally, the league will impose a do-not-schedule order on an official with a certain team when an officiating controversy arises in connection with the referee. In some cases, the referee is unfairly conflated with the rest of the crew; other times, the controversial call was the correct call, but the powers that be decide to still reroute the official to other teams. Sometimes, this may be a season or two just to avoid a potential controversy. The longest-running do-not-schedule order is between referee Walt Coleman and the Oakland Raiders. Coleman was the referee who correctly invoked the "tuck rule" that reversed a Raiders fumble recovery to an incomplete pass in the 2000 AFC Divisional Playoff against the New England Patriots. As of the end of the 2014 season, Coleman has officiated 202 regular season games and 8 postseason games since that snowy day in Foxborough, Massachusetts, but none of those games featured the Raiders. The ban has even outlived the tuck rule itself, which was repealed from the rulebook before the 2013 season.

TWELVE

OVERTIME

I've never been a part of a tie. I didn't even know it was in the rulebook.

—*Eagles quarterback Donovan McNabb, after a 13–13 tie, Philadelphia Eagles at Cincinnati Bengals, November 16, 2008*

Tie games were very common in the early days of the NFL. In the 1930s an average of approximately 1 in 13 games resulted in a tie, and there was no overtime period to determine an ultimate winner. The 1932 season saw an unusual spike in stalemates: more than one-fourth of the games were ties, which, for the purposes of determining the league's standings, were ignored when calculating a team's win percentage. Those tie games in the 1932 season caused an unusual circumstance at the end of the season.

The Chicago Bears had as many ties as wins at 6–1–6. The Portsmouth Spartans (today's Detroit Lions, originally from a small industrial city centered on Ohio's southern border) were 6–1–4 and determined to have a win percentage identical to the Bears'. Since there were no title games, the league bylaws stated that the Bears and Spartans would be declared cochampions. However, both teams agreed to determine a solo champion by playing an impromptu championship game; the idea was so popular, there has been a title game played every year since.

But it would be more than 40 years before the league would address tie games in the regular season.

1. In 1940 the American Association, a rival league to the NFL, had a tie for the fourth and final playoff position. The Newark Bears and the Long Island Indians played an extra tiebreaker game, but that game ended in a scoreless tie. How did the league resolve the tie?

Because there was no overtime rule in the American Association, they scheduled a Thursday "replay" game, a tiebreaker method common in some European soccer leagues. The Thursday game had to be canceled due to snow, and a new game could not be rescheduled. The league resorted to a series of coin flips to determine the final playoff spot, with Newark winning three out of a possible five.

Another minor professional league had an unusual provision in case of a tie. The Dixie League Championship game in 1936 was nearing the end, deadlocked in a scoreless tie between the Washington Pros and the Baltimore Orioles. Washington scored a field goal with 13 seconds remaining, but if they had not, they still would have prevailed. Washington would have won the league championship by virtue of having more first downs than Baltimore in the game.

In 1941 the NFL amended its bylaws to allow a provision for overtime in divisional playoff games, likely as a reaction to the American Association's difficulties a few months earlier. In the pre–Super Bowl era, the top teams in the two divisions played each other in the NFL Championship game. Divisional playoff games were played only if necessary to break a tie at the top of the division standings to determine which team would advance to the championship game. Divisional playoffs were similar to baseball's one-game playoff, and the game could not end in a tie, since only one team could advance to the championship game. (Today, the term *divisional playoffs* is still used to identify the second round of the postseason, even though it has lost any connection to the concept of divisions.) The new overtime rule was a sudden-death format: overtime would begin a new quarter at the conclusion of the fourth quarter and would end on the first score by either team—touchdown, field goal, or safety.

The NFL Constitution and Bylaws still carry the original text in Article XX, complete with the archaic hyphenated use of *over-time*:

> The sudden-death system to determine the winner shall prevail when the score is tied at the end of regulation playing time of a Division Playoff game.

Under this system the team scoring first during over-time play herein provided for, shall be the winner of the game, and the game is automatically ended on any score (including a safety) or when a score is awarded by the referee for a palpably unfair act. Other provisions in respect to the sudden death system shall be as provided in the Rule Book of the League.

2. The 1941 provision in the bylaws applied only to divisional playoff games tied at the end of regulation. What would happen in a championship game if there was a tie score after four quarters?

Initially, the NFL Championship game could end in a tie, resulting in the two teams being declared cochampions. That never wound up happening because, in 1947, the league owners extended the sudden-death rule to championship games, and 11 years later the Baltimore Colts and the New York Giants needed an extra period to decide the league title. The Colts beat the Giants 23–17 on a 1-yard touchdown run by running back Alan Ameche in the 1958 NFL Championship.

Although it was a simple modification at the time, that rule change in 1947 wound up having far-reaching effects. The 1958 championship game became widely known as the Greatest Game Ever Played, largely because of the exciting finish. Soon after that game, football's popularity soared, and it quickly overtook baseball as the nation's favorite sport—a designation it has held ever since. Who knows what might have been if the Colts and Giants finished the game tied and shared the league title.

Despite the excitement generated by that 1958 NFL Championship game, the league played another 15 seasons before it added sudden-death overtime to the regular season. Beginning in 1974, regular-season games would play one 15-minute overtime period, which would end if either team scored before the 15 minutes expired. On September 22, 1974, the first regular-season overtime game was played between the Pittsburgh Steelers and the Denver Broncos. After 15 minutes of overtime, that game ended in a 31–31 tie. The first decisive overtime game in the regular season happened in the non–professional football city of New Haven, Connecticut. The New York Giants needed a temporary home since Yankee Stadium was being completely refurbished and Giants Stadium in East Rutherford, New Jersey, was still being built. On November 10 of that season, the Giants hosted their in-name-only crosstown rivals, the New York Jets, at the Yale Bowl—the Ivy League university's stadium. Jets quarterback Joe Namath found halfback Emerson Boozer on a 5-yard touchdown pass after eight minutes and seven seconds of overtime, and the Jets won, 26–20.

The NFL altered the sudden-death procedure in 2010 so that a team could not immediately win the game if it scored a field goal on the first possession of overtime.

SUDDEN-DEATH OVERTIME

3. Fill in the blanks: Regular-season overtime periods follow the timing rules of the ___ quarter, and postseason overtime periods follow the timing rules of the ___ quarter.

Because the game will end at the conclusion of one overtime period, a regular-season game follows the fourth-quarter timing provisions. But since a playoff game can play indefinitely until the tie is broken, overtime in the postseason will begin under first-quarter timing provisions.

Since only one extra period is played in the regular season, each team is allotted two timeouts. In the postseason, timeouts follow the regulation rules, with three timeouts for every two extra periods played.

4. Six postseason games have needed a second overtime period to decide the game. What is the procedure to start the second overtime period?

At the conclusion of the first overtime period, teams will switch sides of the field, and the second overtime begins just like the second quarter of a regulation game. This applies only to playoff games; a regular-season overtime game ends in a tie if the single 15-minute overtime period expires.

5. On June 30, 1984, the Los Angeles Express and the Michigan Panthers of the United States Football League (USFL) met in the spring football league's Western Conference Quarterfinal Playoff game. Tied at 21 at the end of regulation, the game went to sudden-death overtime. After two overtime periods, the game remained tied, 21–21. Under current NFL rules, what happens next?

Rule 16–1–5(b) provides for a two-minute break between each overtime quarter, but "there shall be no halftime intermission after the second period." As much as fans might want to see the Frisbee-catching dog from halftime again, it's not going to happen.

Under NFL rules, the third overtime period begins with a kickoff, just like the third quarter in regulation. The team that lost the coin toss at the beginning of the overtime period receives the first option for the start of the third overtime period. In the USFL game, however, the teams just switched sides of the field, and play continued from the dead-ball spot in the same manner as between the first and second overtime period.

The 1984 USFL game is the only time a game in a major football league needed a third overtime period.

6. If a game goes scoreless for four overtime periods, what happens?

A new coin toss and a kickoff start the ninth period of play. It's like starting a new game—but it would be the equivalent of a third game for the two teams.

Even though the fifth overtime period follows the first overtime period rules, there is no provision to restart the modified sudden-death process, so the first score wins, even if it is a field goal on the opening possession.

MODIFIED SUDDEN DEATH

In 2010 the Competition Committee recommended to the NFL owners a slight revision to the sudden-death overtime procedure. Because the kicking game had vastly improved since the first overtime game in 1958, the Competition Committee saw a distinct advantage for the team that won the overtime coin toss.

"We really felt like you wouldn't want that game to end—a Super Bowl, a conference championship game—where there's a kickoff, one pass, field goal, game over," said Rich McKay, the chairman of the Competition Committee.

This was a reaction to the overtime game between the Saints and the Vikings in the 2009 NFC Championship game, although McKay commented at the time that this game had little impact on the decision. With the game tied 28–28, the Saints took the first possession of overtime 39 yards in 10 plays, ending with Garrett Hartley kicking a 39-yard field goal, and sending the Saints to the Super Bowl. The Vikings offense, including perennial all-star quarterback Brett Favre, watched the overtime from the sideline, completely helpless to change the result.

For the following postseason (and for regular-season games beginning in 2012), the only exception made to the sudden-death procedure was to extend the overtime period if the team that possessed the ball first kicked a successful field goal at the end of the drive. In the case of the 2009 championship game, this would have given Favre and the Vikings the ball following a kickoff after Hartley's field goal. Under the new rules, if the Vikings tied the game again, the game would continue as a regular sudden-death overtime. However, if they scored a touchdown, they would have won, and they would have lost if they failed to score on that possession.

The Vikings, not ones to sour on their own fate, voted down the modified-sudden-death proposal, but the new rule was passed by a vote of 31–2.

7. If the opening kickoff of overtime is an onside kick recovered by the kicking team, would they have to kick off again if they scored a field goal on the first possession?

No. The game would be over when they score the field goal. Rule 16–1–3(b) states that the modified sudden-death provision gives a team "the opportunity to possess the ball once during the extra period," but not a *guaranteed possession*. Therefore, the opening kickoff was the receiving team's failed opportunity to possess.

In addition to an onside kick recovered by the kicking team, the overtime reverts to standard sudden-death rules if there is a punt, an interception, a fumble recovery, a missed field goal, or a failure to get a first down on a fourth-down play. If any of these things happen when the score is not tied in the overtime period, the game ends, and the team in the lead wins.

8. The first game under the modified sudden-death rules was a 2011 Wild Card Playoff game between the Pittsburgh Steelers and the Denver Broncos. Broncos quarterback Tim Tebow completed an 80-yard touchdown to receiver Demaryius Thomas on the first play of overtime. What happens next?

In all overtime scenarios, the game ends on a touchdown or a safety, regardless of whether the other team had an opportunity to possess the ball. The Tebow–Thomas touchdown ended the overtime in 11 seconds, an NFL record.

Overtime is the only time a touchdown is not followed by a point-after-touchdown attempt. Even when a team has scored a game-winning touchdown as time expires in the fourth quarter, making an extra point unnecessary to win the game, the conversion attempt must be made.

9. On September 9, 2012, the Vikings and Jacksonville Jaguars played the first overtime game where the modified sudden-death rule was invoked. After the Vikings scored a field goal on the first possession of overtime, they kicked off to the Jaguars. On that possession, the Jaguars attempted a pass on fourth down that fell incomplete. What happens next?

Since the Jaguars failed to convert a fourth down, it ended their possession. The game ended immediately with the Vikings earning the win.

10. In a November 18, 2012, regular-season game, the Houston Texans scored a field goal on the opening drive of overtime. The Jaguars followed up with a field goal of their own, tying the score again at 37–37. When the Texans receive the ensuing kickoff, what rules apply?

Overtime is then played under the standard sudden-death rules through the end of the game. Once each team has had one possession, the team that is next in the lead will win the game. In this game, the Texans scored a touchdown on that next possession, allowing them to score a total of nine points in overtime, which would have been impossible under the standard sudden-death rules. The combined 12 points by both teams is the most that can be scored in overtime.

11. The Green Bay Packers hosted the Vikings for the second matchup of the season for the two teams on November 24, 2013. After finishing regulation time tied at 23–23, the Packers received the kickoff in overtime and scored a field goal on the opening drive. The Vikings tied the score again on the next possession with only 3:54 remaining in overtime. Neither team could score in the remaining time. What was the result of the game?

The game ended in a 26–26 tie. This was the first instance where there would have been a decisive result under the standard sudden-death format and the modified sudden-death rules changed that result. In this case, what would have been a win for the Packers reverted back to a tie.

This same scenario occurred October 12, 2014, when the Cincinnati Bengals and Carolina Panthers traded field goals in overtime. The third possession ended with the Bengals missing a field goal attempt, which occurred as the clock expired. The game ended in a 37–37 tie, the highest-scoring NFL game to end in a tie.

12. Let's say a ball-control offense runs an extra-long opening possession and scores a field goal on that possession, leaving only 2:45 on the clock. The opponent gets the ball after the kickoff, but the time expires before they are able to score or get in range for a field goal attempt on that second possession. Does the overtime period get extended?

It depends if it is the regular season or the postseason. In the postseason, overtime would extend into a second overtime period to complete the necessary extra possession. But since there is no provision for a second overtime in the regular season, the 15-minute limit is firm, meaning the game ends as a win for the team that controlled the ball. Even if a team kicked a first-possession field goal at the expiration of the overtime period (which would shatter the NFL record for the longest duration of a single possession), the game would also end as a win for that team in the regular season, but a playoff game would begin a second overtime with the kickoff that follows a successful field goal.

There are not many games that have been played under the modified overtime system, so there are few examples of the rules in practice. To better illustrate the overtime scenarios, here are hypothetical situations under the modern rules, for which I have used the names of defunct NFL franchises for ease of expression.

In the first hypothetical game, the Pottsville Maroons have won the overtime toss and will receive the kickoff from the Muncie Flyers. During the first possession, the quarterback for the Maroons is intercepted, but before the play is over, the Flyers fumble the ball back to the Maroons.

13. What happens if the Maroons score a field goal on that possession?

Since a change of possession occurred during the play, it is considered a new possession for the Maroons after the fumble recovery. When there is a double change of possession, the original down and distance do not apply; even though the offense keeps the ball at the end of the play, it is a new first-and-10 at the dead-ball spot.

The Flyers had possession of the ball in the overtime period, even though they never had the ball on offense. By the rules, the criteria for the Flyers to have an opportunity to possess the ball is satisfied, so the field goal by the Maroons will end the game.

14. In that same situation, if the Flyers have 12 players on the field at the snap, does that change anything?

A defensive penalty can wind up saving the team in this case, but it depends on a few circumstances.

First, since the foul is for too many players on the defense, this foul happens as soon as the ball is snapped. That means that the foul precedes the interception, which is an important distinction. If the Maroons get better field position by accepting the penalty, then the double change of possession never happened, because the entire play would be wiped out by the penalty. The first possession would continue after the assessment of the penalty, and the field goal by the Maroons would not end the game.

However, if the Maroons decline the penalty, the change of possession counts, so there would be no change to the previous answer.

The Flyers would not get any advantage if they commit a foul after fumbling the ball back to the Maroons. The penalty assessment, as long as it was the only foul on the play, would not be assessed from the previous spot; it would be tacked on to the end of the play. When a penalty is tacked on, the down counts, and if the down counts, the Flyers have used their opportunity to possess the ball.

15. In another situation, the Providence Steam Roller score a field goal on the first possession of overtime. On the second possession, the Franklin Yellow Jackets are intercepted, but the Steam Roller fumble the ball back to the Yellow Jackets on the play. What happens next?

Because it is considered a new possession, the Yellow Jackets failed to score on their first possession of overtime. It does not matter that the Yellow Jackets regain possession before the end of the play. Even if the play continues with the Yellow Jackets scoring an apparent touchdown off of the fumble recovery, the score does not count, because the Yellow Jackets had a new possession in the middle of the play.

After the interception, the game is over at the conclusion of the play, and the Steam Roller win. This is due to specific wording of the overtime rule. Although the play will continue until a dead ball is declared, the additional play will not affect the result.

16. On that same play, if it is third-and-10, assume the Steam Roller commit two fouls: one is a defensive offside penalty at the snap, and the other is a personal foul after the interception. Which option are the Yellow Jackets allowed?

A. Accept the 15-yard personal foul from the previous spot, and it is an automatic first down.
B. Accept the 5-yard offside foul, and it is third-and-5.
C. Accept the penalty that nets the best field position.
D. Accept the 15-yard penalty from the dead-ball spot.

In this case, the Yellow Jackets must select option B according to the rules. The offside penalty negates the interception, and negating the interception is the only thing that allows the previous drive to continue. If the Yellow Jackets accept a penalty that happens after the interception, it doesn't erase the interception. In fact, the rules specifically prohibit the Yellow Jackets from making a decision that would end the game, presumably because of the unusual enforcement.

If this play happened at another time of the game without the complications of the sudden-death rules, option A would not be offered because the personal foul can't override the interception that preceded it. It could only be enforced to a post-possession spot.

17. Assume the Staten Island Stapletons score a field goal on the opening possession and kick off to the Orange Tornadoes (from Orange, New Jersey— Google it). The Tornadoes have a first-and-10 at their own 5. The Tornadoes quarterback fumbles the ball in the field of play, and it comes to rest on the 2-yard line. A Stapletons linebacker tries to jump on the ball but knocks it out of bounds in the end zone. What happens next?

Since the Stapletons are charged with the impetus that puts the ball out of bounds, it is ruled a touchback, and the Tornadoes get the ball first-and-10 at the 20. However, even though there is no physical change of possession, the touchback is considered the start of a new possession. It is treated just the same as if a Stapletons player recovered the ball; the opportunity to possess has ended and the Stapletons win the game.

18. What is the maximum margin of victory possible in overtime? What is the minimum a team can win by?

A team may win by nine points, but only in a very specific way: A team that scores a field goal on the opening possession may also score a touchdown on defense by intercepting the ball or recovering a fumble in the end zone. It *must* be a change of possession in the end zone. If the defense intercepts or recovers the ball in the field of play and then runs it back to the end zone, it is not a touchdown under specific wording of the overtime rule. Although the play will continue until a dead ball is declared, the additional play will not affect the result. Only when the change of possession and the touchdown occur at the same instant will the touchdown score.

As for the minimum, conventionally a defense can score a safety and win by two. However, in a very unusual situation, a team can win by one point. First, there would be a field goal on the opening possession. Then, the offense of the second possession would have to be awarded a safety. In most circumstances, the defense scores on a safety, but it is possible for the offense to also score two points.

One way an offense can get a safety: the team on offense (who would be trailing by three) would need to be near the opponent's end zone and fumble the ball. Taking the example earlier with the Stapletons and the Tornadoes, let's flip it around and give the ball to the Tornadoes first-and-goal on the 2. If the same fumble occurs, but instead the Stapletons provide the impetus to put the ball into *their own end zone*, it would be a safety against the defense, not a touchback.

This means the Tornadoes would get two points, the Stapletons would have had the field goal on the previous possession, and the game would be decided by one point. In this example, the defense, again, never possesses the fumbled ball; as in the nine-point example above, the rules preclude a safety call resulting in any points if there is an actual change of possession.

While seemingly unfair, the fact that a team scores and loses the game by one point is offset by the fact that they fumbled the ball in order for this unusual chain of events to happen.

In summary, the only possible outcomes for overtime are a win by one point (with a lot of help), two points (safety), three points (field goal), five points (field goal, then a safety), six points (touchdown), or nine points (field goal and a touchdown)—or a tie.

THIRTEEN

EXTRAORDINARY SITUATIONS

We have been blessed with almost springlike weather here . . .
sunny skies forecast for the remainder of the afternoon.

—*CBS announcer Verne Lundquist, opening the broadcast
of the game to be known as "The Fog Bowl,"
1988 NFC Divisional Playoff Game, Philadelphia Eagles
at Chicago Bears, December 31, 1988*

The rulebook of the NFL is very thick compared to those for other major sports. The myriad of rules and official interpretations that have been explored throughout these chapters explore just a portion of the rulebook. The rules have evolved over time to account for nearly every conceivable situation in a game.

Despite the comprehensiveness of the rules, there still are circumstances that go beyond the pages of the rulebook.

1. Has an NFL team ever forfeited a game?

Technically, a forfeit has never happened. However, on December 4, 1921, a game between two now-defunct teams, the Rochester Jeffersons and the Washington Pros, was not played as scheduled in the nation's capital after a snowstorm. Rochester did not want to take the field and demanded to be reimbursed for travel expenses. A *Washington Post* article tells what happened next:

> ROCHESTER ELEVEN FORFEITS TO PROS
> Washington's local professional football team was awarded yesterday's contest by Referee C.A. Metsler when the Rochester Jeffersons refused to take the field on account of weather conditions. Manager [Leo] Lyons, of the visiting team, had all of the advertised stars on hand, but would not risk their injuring themselves on account of slipping on the snow-covered field.
>
> The contract signed by the visitors contains a clause to the effect "that if both teams have arrived on the field of play, and it is found that said field is too wet for play, the question of cancellation shall rest solely with the manager of the home team."
>
> As Manager [Tim] Jordan had his Washington team on hand, [he] felt that he should not disappoint the 400 or so faithful fans who were on hand. In view of the Jeffs' refusal to take the field, there was nothing left for Referee Metsler to do but give the locals the game, 1 to 0, which he did after 40 minutes of argument.

The reported "forfeit" game was between two member clubs of the American Professional Football Association—the organization would adopt the name "National Football League" the next season. However, the NFL record books do not list this game, or *any* game for that matter, as a forfeit. The official record keepers, the Elias Sports Bureau, decided this was a *cancellation* instead of a forfeit, as cancellations due to weather did occasionally happen in that era. While the league did not keep official records at that time, a vote at its 1922 meeting required the Pros to reimburse the Jeffersons for the $800 in travel expenses that were part of the disagreement. The Pros chose to withdraw from the NFL rather than pay $800.

The word *forfeit* popped up again almost three-quarters of a century later, and ice and snow were again a part of the equation. On December 23, 1995, Giants fans took out their frustrations about their team's performance by throwing icy snowballs on the field during the second half at Giants Stadium. An assistant equipment manager for the visiting Chargers was knocked unconscious on the sideline from a snowball that hit him in the head. Some NBC Sports camera operators were removed so that they didn't become targets themselves. Bob Sheppard, the euphonious public-address announcer for the New York Yankees who also worked Giants home games, pronounced this stern warning to the fans: "Ladies and gentlemen: You have been advised—and admonished—about throwing snowballs. Now we have been informed that *unless* the referee can give the 'all clear' and the snowballs stop, this game could be forfeited to the San Diego Chargers."

2. Referee Ron Blum used a sideline phone to talk to a game supervisor in the press box. What recourse did he have?

Longtime league executive Val Pinchbeck was the point person in the press box. He communicated with commissioner Paul Tagliabue during the game. Tagliabue said that Pinchbeck and Blum should keep the game going, but that they would have to reevaluate the situation as the game progressed.

Blum was also authorized to suspend the game and even remove teams from the field for 15 minutes to allow stadium security to take control of the stands behind the Chargers' bench. Under current league policies, fan interference is not grounds for forfeiture, and a team may not be assessed a yardage penalty for fan misconduct.

While the game is suspended, the authority to resume becomes a league decision. The commissioner is allowed to terminate the game short of its conclusion if there is reasonable certainty that the result will not change or that some other interteam competitive issue is affected.

At Cleveland Municipal Stadium on December 16, 2001, a controversial replay decision by referee Terry McAulay caused the final 48 seconds of the game to devolve into chaos. McAulay reviewed a play after the snap of the next play, which is not permitted under the rules. However, McAulay insists that the replay pagers he and the umpire wore signaled before the snap, so the replay was allowed to continue. The Browns' bench and the fans did not accept that explanation. After McAulay reversed the call, the visiting Jacksonville Jaguars were given possession and just had to kneel down twice to run the remaining time off the clock.

3. A hail of debris and bottles littered the field, and McAulay declared the game over. Officials and players tried to exit the field without being pelted. Since the game was in hand and the result pretty much determined, could the game be terminated?

The game could have been terminated, but it was not McAulay's decision to make. In fairness, he had the largest bull's-eye on him in the entire stadium. Commissioner Tagliabue contacted Dick McKenzie, the officiating observer on-site, and ordered that the game be completed. In Tagliabue's opinion, the game could be completed once order was restored, and therefore the effort should be made to do so. The players and even some officials were changing at the time they were told the final 48 seconds had to be played out. With just a few lingering fans, the Jaguars kneeled down twice to run out the clock.

4. Each preseason begins with the Hall of Fame Game played at Fawcett Stadium in Canton, Ohio. On August 2, 1980, the Chargers and Packers were scoreless with 5:24 remaining in the fourth quarter when a severe lightning storm came in. The game was suspended. What did the league do?

Commissioner Pete Rozelle, recognizing the game was an exhibition game in addition to the teams' normal preseason slate, terminated the game without it being completed. The same thing happened when the Packers faced the Chiefs in the 2003 Hall of Fame Game; after a thunderstorm halted the game with 5:49 remaining in the third quarter, the game was suspended. As ABC scrambled to air an episode of *World's Funniest Commercials* to fill the rain delay, the cameras returned live to Canton shortly thereafter to declare the game terminated, with the Chiefs winning, 9–0.

On October 10, 1998, Kansas City's Arrowhead Stadium was subjected to an absolute quagmire. The heavy rain in the Sunday night game soon brought lightning close to the stadium. Officiating supervisor Art McNally got referee Phil Luckett on a sideline phone and shouted, "Get 'em off the field, get 'em out of there! I'll take responsibility." Although McNally was not in the chain of command to suspend the game, he is so well respected that no one would ever think to challenge him on that decision. It was, at the time, only the second game in modern league history suspended due to weather; the previous occurrence in the regular season was a Colts–Jets game at the New Jersey Meadowlands in 1996 that was halted for half an hour in the fourth quarter.

5. If one team does not take the field out of protest, what happens?

The referee is not allowed to declare a forfeit; in fact, he is not permitted to use the word *forfeit* or *cancellation* over his public-address microphone. Even the commissioner cannot unilaterally declare a forfeit, except, in this case, he may do so as a disciplinary measure if a team has withdrawn its players from the field. A forfeit is recorded if one team fails to or refuses to play *and* the other team is "ready and willing to play," according to league policies. If a team refuses to play but does not forfeit, the commissioner may declare it a forfeit in this limited circumstance.

At the time of the previously mentioned Rochester–Washington game in 1921, the league used the college rulebook, which fixed the score of a forfeit at 1–0, the only method by which a team could have scored only a single point. The current NFL rulebook states that a forfeit is recorded as 2–0, but the points do not count "for purposes of offensive production or tie-breakers."

POSTPONEMENTS AND CANCELLATIONS

Two preseason games were cancelled outright when there was an issue with the field. Due to an "unfit playing surface" at the Astrodome, the commissioner's office canceled a game between the San Diego Chargers and the Houston Oilers on August 19, 1995. At Philadelphia's Veterans Stadium on August 13, 2001, the turf inserts that covered the baseball infield were uneven. The Eagles' game against the Baltimore Ravens was initially postponed, but due to the preseason schedule having games scattered from Thursday through Monday each week, an equitable makeup date could not be found. In both cases, there was no significant disadvantage to either team competitively, other than the ability to evaluate players in a game situation who were vying for the final roster. During the regular season, this can complicate matters.

While transporting the Washington team to TCF Bank Stadium for a November 2, 2014, game against the Vikings, the team buses were involved in a traffic accident. A few players were shaken up, and backup running back Silas Reed was placed on the inactive list for the game so that he could be evaluated for a neck injury. Luckily, the accident was not severe, despite shaking up a few players and causing significant damage to the two buses. The game started as scheduled.

6. If an accident occurs that is more severe, what can the league do?

In cases of unforeseen circumstances that do not allow the game to be started or started on time, the kickoff may be postponed. Slight delays can be made under the referee's authority, but long delays require the commissioner or an appointee to make an evaluation. In the case of extensive or severe injuries that cause a competitive issue, Rule 17 guides the procedure for rescheduling a game at a later date. For any general emergency not involving injuries, the rules state that the commissioner "will make every effort to set the game for no later than two days after the originally scheduled date." There are provisions for potential Tuesday games in a subsequent week if necessary.

Frequently when a natural disaster occurs, the league attempts to reschedule a game by giving the teams an unplanned week off in exchange for their bye week. Table 13.1 shows the games since 1982 that have been cancelled, postponed, or relocated due to some emergency situation or stadium conflict. Also of note, the American Football League postponed games that were scheduled on November 24, 1963, two days after President John F. Kennedy was assassinated. NFL commissioner Pete Rozelle, on the advice of Kennedy press secretary Pierre Salinger, opted to play the scheduled games, which were not televised.

ACCIDENTS AND TRAGEDIES

It is quite a sensitive subject, so the league does not like to address it publicly too often. The reality is that with teams traveling by air every week, the league must have a contingency plan in case of a team calamity. In order to avoid making decisions after such a horrific event, the league has a written procedure, complete with an uncomfortable, but necessary, calculus of assessing the toll on the team.

After the games immediately surrounding a tragic accident are at least postponed, the grim task of continuity would be carried out by the league. If a team has lost fewer than 15 players to season-ending injury or worse, it is classified as a "near disaster" and the season will continue for that team. The team will have priority over any other team on waiver claims, and if the team lost a quarterback, it may draft any team's third-string quarterback.

If 15 or more players are incapacitated or killed, the commissioner will decide if the team's season could continue under the "near-disaster" plan or if the team's schedule should be abandoned. Under the "disaster" plan, that team would get the first pick in the next NFL draft and a restocking draft—similar in procedure to a redistribution of veteran players for an expansion team—would be conducted. The games that were cancelled would not count in the standings, and any unequal number of games in the standings or tiebreakers would be figured by percentages. Contract incentives for players on the opposing teams, such as a certain number of yards gained in a season, would be automatically prorated to 16 games.

Table 13.1. NFL Postponements, Relocations, and Cancellations, 1980–2014

Date	Teams	Incident	Resolution
Nov. 23, 2014	Jets–Bills	State of emergency due to lake-effect snowstorm	Game moved to Monday night at Ford Field in Detroit
Oct. 6, 2013	Chargers–Raiders	Stadium crews needed 24 hrs. to reset after baseball playoff game	Kickoff moved from 4:25 local time to 8:35 local time (11:35 p.m. Eastern)
Dec. 26, 2010	Vikings–Eagles	Incoming blizzard	Kickoff moved from Sunday night to Tuesday night
Dec. 13, 2010 Dec. 20, 2010	Giants–Vikings Bears–Vikings	Roof of the Metrodome collapsed due to weight of snow	Giants game moved to Monday night at Ford Field in Detroit. Bears game played at TCF Stadium at the Univ. of Minnesota
Sept. 14, 2008	Ravens–Texans	Damage to Reliant Stadium by Hurricane Ike	Both teams took a bye week in Week 2, the rescheduled game was played later, also requiring a Titans–Bengals game and the Bengals bye week to be moved
2005 season	Saints home games	Destruction of the Louisiana Superdome and the city of New Orleans by Hurricane Katrina	The Saints first home game was moved to Giants Stadium (and remained a Saints home game in the records); the remainder of the home schedule was split between Baton Rouge, La., and San Antonio, Texas
Oct. 23, 2005	Chiefs–Dolphins	Hurricane Wilma threatening Florida	Kickoff was moved to Friday night
Sept. 26, 2004	Steelers–Dolphins	Hurricane Jeanne threatening Florida	Kickoff was moved from a night game to 1 p.m.

(continued)

Table 13.1. (continued)

Date	Teams	Incident	Resolution
Sept. 12, 2004	Titans–Dolphins	Hurricane Ivan threatening Florida	Kickoff was moved to Saturday
Oct. 27, 2003	Dolphins–Chargers	Qualcomm Stadium used for emergency response due to wildfires	Game was moved to Sun Devil Stadium in Tempe, Ariz.
Oct. 21, 2001	Cowboys–Raiders	Potential conflict with baseball playoffs	Game was moved to Oct. 7, when both teams had a bye. In the end, the Oakland A's did not have a playoff game that day.
Sept. 17–18, 2001	All NFL teams	Terrorist attacks on Sept. 11	Week 2 games were moved to the end of the schedule; playoff games and the Super Bowl all pushed back one week
Oct. 26, 1997	Bears–Dolphins	Conflict with Game 7 of World Series	Game moved to Monday night
Sept. 6, 1992	Patriots–Dolphins	Cleanup from Hurricane Andrew	Game postponed to Oct. 18 when both teams were scheduled to have a bye week
Oct. 22, 1989	Patriots–49ers	Damage to Candlestick Park from Loma Prieta earthquake	Game moved to Stanford Stadium at Stanford Univ.
Oct. 8, 1989	Saints–49ers	Conflict with baseball playoffs	Teams swapped dates of their home games
Oct. 25, 1987	Broncos–Vikings	Conflict with Game 7 of World Series	Game moved to Monday night
Sept. 27–28, 1987	All NFL teams	NFL player's union strike	Week 3 games were cancelled
Sept. 26–Nov. 14, 1982	All NFL teams	NFL player's union strike	Several weeks cancelled, schedule and playoff format modified

This table does not reflect games that are rescheduled to a different time in the same day, with the exception of the 2013 Raiders–Chargers game, which was moved out of the standard Sunday football time period.

We all hope that this plan remains on paper and not something that needs to be carried out.

SUSPENDING PLAY

On the shores of Lake Michigan in Chicago, Soldier Field hosted a divisional playoff game on December 31, 1988, that most of the fans in the stadium and watching on television never saw to its conclusion—in a literal sense.

After the two-minute warning of the second quarter, the field became enveloped in a thick fog. "This is a spotter's nightmare," said CBS Sports play-by-play announcer Verne Lundquist as the camera struggled to find the ghostly shadow of a kick returner in the haze. A whistle gave an indication that the play was over. It would only get worse for the television crew.

Andy Kindle, the director in the television production truck, repurposed the cameras dedicated for the halftime show and shot the remainder of the game from field level. Referee Jim Tunney announced the down and distance over his wireless microphone after each play. On-screen graphics to

Figure 13.1.   Field judge Jack Vaughn looks up to rule on a field goal attempt by the Philadelphia Eagles in the fog during a 1988 Divisional Playoff Game against the Chicago Bears. The players are barely visible about 30 yards away.
Photo by Heinz Kluetmeier/Sports Illustrated/Getty Images

help orient the home viewer (in the era before it was a computer-automated operation) were feverishly entered with the typing sometimes visible on the air in the chaos. Kindle even considered giving halftime show host Brent Musburger the play-by-play duties from the field level, but Musburger admitted he could not see all the way to the other sideline.

7. Could Tunney have suspended the game?

He was authorized to do so, but neither Bears coach Mike Ditka nor Eagles coach Buddy Ryan requested that the game be stopped. With both iconic coaches chiseled from the bedrock of the ironman image of the sport, it is likely that neither coach wanted to be the first to blink. Ryan was further motivated to win a playoff game against his former master. Could he claim true victory if he pulled his team in the face of harmless fog?

Tunney did not need authorization from the coaches to continue, but, so long as there was no threatening hazard, there was no need to stop the game. Football is played in all sorts of conditions, including blizzards (1947 NFL Championship) and temperatures below −15 degrees (1968 NFL Championship, the "Ice Bowl"). There was no precedent for halting a game, in fact. It would be eight years before a modern-era nonexhibition NFL game was suspended due to weather, when lightning struck a little too close to the stadium during the aforementioned Colts–Jets game in 1996.

Further complicating matters was the uncertainty of when the fog would lift, and the fact that any delay would complicate the rigid broadcast schedules of other playoff games that weekend, which were not intended to overlap.

8. Since the Eagles were wearing white, and presumably were harder to see than the Bears in their dark blue uniforms, could an equipment manager apply colored tape to the Eagles' uniforms?

For the most part, no, a team cannot enhance the color of the jersey by using tape. According to Rule 5-4-4(f), a player may not use "contrasting-color tape that covers any part of the helmet, jersey, pants, stockings, or shoes; transparent tape or tape of the same color as the background material is permissible for use on these items of apparel."

The Eagles could have placed tape on the arms and hands of the wide receivers with white (not helping), black (very close to the Bears' dominant color), or a team color. The same color restrictions apply to the receivers' gloves as well.

Although fluorescent gaffer tape did not exist at the time of the Fog Bowl, a team cannot use a color outside of the team's color palette for a visual enhancement.

UNFAIR ACTS

In the 1954 Cotton Bowl, the Alabama Crimson Tide had their hands full trying to contain Rice Owls halfback Dicky Moegle, who racked up 265 yards rushing in the New Year's Day game. That's when one player went to extraordinary lengths to stop Moegle.

With Rice at the 5-yard line, leading 7–6, quarterback LeRoy Fenstemaker handed off to Moegle, who broke free along the Alabama sideline en route to a potential 95-yard touchdown run. Alabama running back Tommy Lewis came off the bench and tackled Moegle at the Alabama 42-yard line, and then returned to the bench as if nothing happened. Only one Alabama defensive player had an angle to tackle Moegle on the play; the rest had been outrun. Referee Cliff Shaw—a sales manager at the family dairy of future NFL referee Walt Coleman (a toddler at the time)—convened his crew to determine how to rule the play.

9. What rule did Shaw invoke on the play?

The officials ruled that Lewis committed a *palpably unfair act*—a catch-all category of actions that are undefined but blatantly outside the norms of the game. The current NFL rulebook states the following: "For a palpably unfair act [the] offender may be disqualified. The Referee, after consulting his crew, enforces any such distance penalty as they consider equitable and irrespective of any other specified code penalty. The Referee may award a score."

In this Cotton Bowl, Shaw and his crew felt Moegle was likely to score, so they awarded the touchdown to Rice. Oddly, Lewis was not ejected from the game, but this conduct would unquestionably be ruled a disqualification today. Lewis apologized to the Rice coach for his actions and told reporters after the game, "I guess I'm just too full of Alabama. He just ran too close."

Analyze the following four plays and what actions should be taken.

Play No. 1: San Francisco 49ers kicker Ray Wersching was attempting a "gimme" 19-yard field goal near halftime of a November 11, 1985, *Monday Night Football* game against the Denver Broncos. Right before holder Matt

Cavanaugh caught the snap, a snowball landed near him. Cavanaugh mishandled the ball, and the resulting broken play ended with an incomplete pass.

Play No. 2: On September 15, 2013, the Seahawks were about to punt to the 49ers in a game at Seattle's CenturyLink Field. Some Seahawks linemen were standing up, reacting to a whistle, but the whistle came from the stands. The ball was snapped, and the punt was blocked.

Play No. 3: In a 2013 Thanksgiving night game in Baltimore, Ravens receiver Jacoby Jones was returning a punt along the Pittsburgh Steelers' sideline. Steelers coach Mike Tomlin was watching the play unfold on the video screen, not realizing his right foot was out on the field. When Tomlin saw himself on the screen, he darted to the sideline but did a stutter step with his on-field foot. Jones cut into the field of play, likely a reaction to avoid Tomlin, and was tackled shortly thereafter by a pursuing Steelers player. In Jones's words, "It broke my stride a little bit; I still shouldn't have gotten caught."

Play No. 4: On a punt by the Miami Dolphins on December 12, 2010, Nolan Carroll was running along the sideline of the New York Jets. The player in the "gunner" position will run that route and frequently gets knocked out of bounds. Several Jets substitutes were lined up in a flank, but were within the legal limits of the designated bench area. At one end of the flank, Sal Alosi, an assistant coach, stuck his knee out to trip the out-of-bounds Carroll, and Carroll had to leave the game with an injury.

10. These four plays illustrate a disadvantaged team, but are they palpably unfair acts?

The first two involve actions from nonparticipants, or people not "entitled to sit on a team's bench." A team is not going to be penalized for the actions of the fans. Jim Tunney was the referee for the 49ers–Broncos contest, and he stated after the game to a pool reporter that the play could not be overturned. "We have no recourse in terms of a foul or to call it on the home team or the fans," Tunney said. "There's nothing in the rule book that allows us to do that."

Similarly, the Seahawks may have been confused by an external whistle, but the case could be made that the 49ers were, too. When the Seahawks players stood at the line, this could have further distracted the defense, but they played through. The Seahawks were not flagged with a false start (which would have killed the snap) because players that are in a three-point stance—as the Seahawks were—may move to a two-point stance as long as the movement is not abrupt. If the officials called an illegal shift (which it wasn't), the 49ers would have declined the penalty anyway.

The other two examples are very problematic examples of interference.

Alosi's actions were not seen by the officials; they only saw that Carroll was legally pushed out of bounds and that he fell. No foul was called on the Jets bench. Had the trip been seen, the least that could have been done was to assess an unsportsmanlike conduct foul on the Jets bench and have Alosi removed. There does not appear to be any other remedy the officials could have made to address the situation, because the disadvantage really could not be quantified. Alosi was fined $25,000 and suspended for the remainder of the season by the team. The Jets organization was fined $100,000. Alosi has not worked on an NFL sideline since that game.

Tomlin's actions are just as troubling, even though, if taken at his word, the actions were inadvertent. By Jacoby's admission, Tomlin did not affect him too much, so the referee really could not have attached any meaningful distance penalty other than an unsportsmanlike conduct foul. (The punt return was inside the 30, so it would have been a half-distance enforcement.) No flag was thrown on the play, although officiating vice president Dean Blandino said that an unsportsmanlike conduct foul should have been called. Tomlin was fined $100,000 for what the league described as "interfering with a play in progress." The Steelers were threatened with a possible forfeiture of a draft choice or other draft-day penalty when Tomlin was fined, but the league ultimately did not take that recourse.

As for the palpably unfair act, it remains in the rulebook, but it has never been used in an NFL game.

SNOW

Football continues to be played no matter what the conditions are, and fans often root for a game played in the snow—usually from the warmth and comfort of their living rooms. The Miami Dolphins obviously wouldn't be ones cheering about snow, especially when they faced the New England Patriots on December 12, 1982.

After Schaefer Stadium had been soaked with rain, the artificial turf froze solid, and a heavy snowstorm made conditions even worse. Treacherous footing rendered the passing game essentially null and void—both teams had a combined 72 yards passing that day. With the game still scoreless with 4:45 remaining in the fourth quarter, the Patriots were set to attempt a field goal, with the ball at the 16-yard line and a potential kicking spot at the 23. The Patriots called timeout, at which time snowplow operator Mark Henderson, who was on a work furlough from jail, serving a 15-year sentence for burglary, seemingly stole a victory for the Patriots. He drove a modified John Deere tractor onto the field to clear the lines. While rolling up the 20-yard line, Henderson banked a left turn and cleared the snow over the spot where the Patriots were going to kick. Dolphins coach Don Shula furiously protested to the officials.

11. What did referee Bob Frederic do to rectify the situation?

There was nothing Frederic could do, as there was no rule or league policy that governed the clearing of snow from the field. In fact, prior to the game, Shula and Patriots coach Ron Meyer agreed to an emergency ground rule that the yard lines could be cleared during a timeout.

New England's field goal attempt was successful. The Dolphins were able to get the ball to the Patriots' 19-yard line on the next drive, but quarterback Dave Woodley was intercepted with 30 seconds remaining in the game.

The league adopted policies in the wake of the "Snowplow Game" that dictate the restrictions for clearing the field of snow:

A. Sidelines, goal lines, and end lines should be kept as clear as possible. Ten-yard intervals are also to be cleared according to the restrictions below.

B. Snow cannot be cleared in front of the offense once a drive has started, except the referee can request that the goal line be cleared if it is obscured. (The goal line remains covered if it is still visible.)

C. Snow can be cleared well behind the offense, but never a spot that could be a potential field goal placement once the offense is in the red zone.

Just to make it absolutely clear, the policies state, "Under no circumstances will a Referee permit clearing by the grounds crew of a spot for a [point-after-touchdown] or field goal attempt. It is permissible for players to clear such spots by hand or foot." The coaches also cannot mutually agree to override that provision.

The referee will decide, based on the snowfall rate, if the grounds crew should be clearing while play progresses at the other end of the field or if timeouts and quarter intermissions need to be extended. Any clearance procedure must come at the direction of the officials or a designated league representative.

One additional modification that occurs when there is an accumulation of snow: the surface of the snow is the new "ground" for the purposes of the rules. So if a pass is caught but the ball makes an impression in the snow partially to the field surface before the receiver establishes control, it is an incomplete pass. Similarly, a ball carrier's knee that grazes the surface of the snow is down if he is contacted by a defender, even if no part of his body touches the actual playing surface of the field.

PROTESTS

12. Returning to the snowplow incident in the 1982 Dolphins–Patriots game, can the Dolphins protest the result and have the game (1) replayed from the beginning, (2) replayed from the point where the Patriots kicked the field goal, or (3) declared a scoreless tie?

The suggestion to overturn the result of a game will cause some to immediately invoke a scene from a baseball game that played out a few months later on July 24, 1983, in the warmth of the summer in the Bronx. Kansas City Royals third baseman George Brett hit a two-run homer with two outs in the top of the ninth to give his team a 5–4 lead. New York Yankees manager Billy Martin complained that Brett's bat had pine tar too far up the shaft of the bat. Home plate umpire Tim McClelland agreed, reversed the home run, and declared Brett out. Being the third out, this ended the game immediately with the Yankees winning 4–3, as an enraged Brett stormed out of the dugout and charged at McClelland before being restrained. The Royals protested, and American League vice president Lee MacPhail later overturned the out and restored the home run, which required the final four outs to be played in order to complete the adjusted game. The controversial game was completed on August 18, with the Royals prevailing 5–4.

But, back to the snow-covered Schaefer Stadium outside of Boston: The Dolphins are absolutely allowed to protest the result of the game . . . but it won't do them any good. Rule 17, Section 2 says the result of the game is final:

Article 1. The Commissioner has the sole authority to investigate and take appropriate disciplinary and/or corrective measures if any club action, non-participant interference, or calamity occurs in an NFL game which he deems so extraordinarily unfair or outside the accepted tactics encountered in professional football that such action has a major effect on the result of the game.

Article 2. The authority and measures provided for in this entire Section 2 do not constitute a protest machinery for NFL clubs to avail themselves of in the event a dispute arises over the result of a game. The investigation called for in this Section 2 will be conducted solely on the Commissioner's initiative to review an act or occurrence that he deems so extraordinary or unfair that the result of the game in question would be inequitable to one of the participating teams. The Commissioner will not apply his authority in cases of complaints by clubs concerning judgmental errors or routine errors of omission by game officials. Games involving such complaints will continue to stand as completed.

In addition to allowing the final score to stand, commissioner Pete Rozelle repeated what the referee had told the Dolphins sideline during the game: there was no rule that could have changed the situation.

As a member of the league's Competition Committee, Shula raced to remedy that loophole. The snow-clearing policies were clearly spelled out in the following off-season to prevent this incident from happening again. And, for the next 10 years, the schedule makers showed mercy on the Dolphins by not scheduling them for a game in New England in the month of December.

Henderson, the snowplow driver, served a two-and-a-half-year sentence before he was paroled for good behavior. He has since turned his life around and become a folk hero in New England. The John Deere tractor he drove, with the rotary brush still attached to the front, is on display at the Patriots' current home stadium.

APPENDIX

FIVE-YARD PENALTIES

Delay of game
Illegal substitution (unless classified as unsportsmanlike conduct)
Twelve players in offensive huddle (enforced between downs)
Twelve players in formation (whistled dead before the snap or kickoff)
Twelve players on the field (ball remains in play)
Illegal formation
Illegal formation by defense on a scrimmage kick
Offside
Encroachment
Neutral zone infraction
Illegal motion
Illegal shift
Illegal snap
False start
Illegal forward pass (second forward pass from behind the line)
Illegal forward pass (on a change of possession)
Illegal forward pass beyond the line of scrimmage (also **loss of down**)
Illegal forward handoff beyond the line of scrimmage (also **loss of down**)

Illegal touching of a forward pass
Ineligible player downfield on a pass
Ineligible player downfield on a kick
Kicking team player voluntarily out of bounds during a punt
Invalid fair-catch signal (also **ball is declared dead on catch**)
Defensive holding
Defensive illegal use of hands
Illegal contact with receiver before pass
Running into the kicker
Illegal touching of a scrimmage kick (if inside the 5-yard line, **award a touchback** plus the penalty)
Illegal touching of a free kick that has not traveled 10 yards (or **award possession at the spot of foul** to the receiving team)
Illegal touching of a free kick by player who steps out of bounds and is first to touch
Short free kick (also **requires a rekick**)
Free kick violation (using the wrong type of kick)
Excess timeout for injury (starting with second excess timeout)

TEN-YARD PENALTIES

Offensive pass interference
Offensive holding or illegal use of hands, arms, or body
Illegal block in the back above the waist
Tripping
Assisting the runner
Interlocking interference
Illegal bat
Intentional grounding less than 10 yards from line of scrimmage (also **loss of down**)
Illegally kicking the ball (also **loss of down**)
Illegal scrimmage kick

FIFTEEN-YARD PENALTIES

Fair-catch interference (and **fair catch is awarded**) as long as catch isn't first muffed

Kick-catch interference

All unnecessary roughness, including late hits, head slaps, striking an opponent, kicking, kneeing, and piling on

Defenseless player hit in the head or neck area

Face mask foul (grasping or pulling)

Blocking below the waist on a kick or change of possession (offense or defense)

Roughing the passer, kicker, or holder

Leg whip

Leverage (on a kick-block attempt)

Leaping (on a kick-block attempt)

Initiating contact with the crown of the helmet

Clipping

Illegal crackback

Peel-back block

Blindside block

Illegal chop block

Illegal cut block

Horse-collar tackle

Illegal block after a fair-catch signal

Illegally forming a wedge block on kickoff

Punt team player out of bounds during kick (voluntarily or involuntarily) and does not make immediate effort to return

Unsportsmanlike conduct, including taunting, contact with an official, bench foul, team personnel in boundary areas

Using abusive, threatening, or insulting language or gestures

Use of the ball, goalpost, pylon, or any other object as a prop

Possession of a foreign object

Disconcerting acts or signals

Illegal hideout near bench area

Lingering by outgoing substitutes

Illegal simulated substitution

Offensive failure to have 11 players inside hashmarks to make ball ready for play after change of possession (after a warning)

Illegal entry onto field by personnel other than substitutes, attendants, or trainers

Player reports ineligible, but does not line up in the "core" of the formation

Concealing the ball under uniform

Goaltending (or option to **award a field goal**)

Icing the kicker with an unavailable timeout (does not kill the snap)

Sideline interference with officials or chain crew

Illegal return of ejected player

Delaying the start of the half

Failure to comply with coin toss procedure (and **surrender kickoff options** for both halves and overtime)

FIFTEEN-YARD PENALTY
AND DISQUALIFICATION

Use of the helmet as a weapon

Flagrant striking, kicking, or kneeing

Flagrant blow to the head with heel, hand, wrist, elbow, or forearm

Flagrant roughing the passer, kicker, or holder

Flagrant unsportsmanlike conduct

Unnecessary physical contact with an official

Possession of a foreign object that is a safety hazard

Illegal return of withdrawn player (equipment violation)

SPOT OF THE FOUL

Defensive pass interference (if in the end zone, then spot at 1-yard line)

Intentional grounding more than 10 yards behind line of scrimmage (also **loss of down**)

Fair-catch interference if catch is muffed (and **fair catch is awarded**)

HALF-DISTANCE-TO-THE-GOAL PENALTY

Any penalty that moves the ball greater than half the distance to the goal, except those listed under "spot of the foul"

Defensive pass interference in the end zone (if the line of scrimmage was inside the defense's 2-yard line)

AUTOMATIC FIRST DOWN

Any defensive foul except for one that occurs at or prior to the snap, excess injury timeout, or running into the kicker
Any defensive penalty that moves the ball beyond the line to gain

PLAYER WITHDRAWN

Injury stoppage except if either team is charged timeout, two-minute warning occurs, quarter ends, or injury was caused by a foul (withdrawn for one down)
Equipment violation (player may return after corrected, minimum one play)

TIMEOUT CHARGED

Injury stoppage after two-minute warning
Coach's challenge does not result in reversal
Coach's challenge not permitted (**15-yard penalty** if no timeouts remain)

TEN-SECOND RUNOFF

Illegally conserving time with less than one minute in the half with the clock running, in addition to other penalties specified:
False start or other snap-killing foul
Intentional grounding
Illegal forward pass beyond line of scrimmage
Substitution violation
Fumble or backward pass out of bounds (also **5-yard penalty**)
Intentional offensive fouls causing the clock to stop
Replay reversal under one minute that changes the clock from stopped to running
Injury stoppage for the offense after two-minute warning and with no timeouts remaining

SAFETY AWARDED

Any offensive penalty enforced from the spot of the foul when that spot is in the team's own end zone (offensive holding, illegal use of hands, illegal bat, illegal kick, etc.)
Intentional grounding in the end zone

DISTANCE PENALTY ASSESSED ON THE KICKOFF

Any 15-yard foul committed by the non-scoring team during a scoring play (except if the foul is used to award a safety)
Any 15-yard dead-ball or between-downs foul by either team after a score
Any foul by the defense on an extra-point conversion (unless offense elects to assess on the conversion attempt)
Any 15-yard dead-ball foul on the last play of the half

MISCELLANEOUS SITUATIONS

Kickoff out of bounds (possession awarded **25 yards** from the spot of kick or **at out-of-bounds spot**)
Safety kick out of bounds (possession awarded **30 yards** from the spot of kick or **at out-of-bounds spot**)
Defensive foul that conserves time or prevents the snap with less than one minute in the half (**play clock reset to 40** or, if less than 40 seconds on game clock, **end the half**)
Live-ball defensive fouls (or offsetting fouls and at least one is a live-ball foul) or first-touch violation as time expires in the quarter (option for offense to run an **untimed down**)
Fair catch as time expires in the quarter (option for offense to **attempt a fair-catch kick**)
Fumble through opponent's end zone with impetus charged to the fumbler (award possession to opponent, **touchback**)
Palpably unfair act (referee makes **any equitable ruling** and may **award a score**)
Repeated fouls to prevent a score (after warning, **award the score**)

INDEX

ABOUT THE AUTHOR

Ben Austro has been an armchair official since he wrote to the league office in 1988 and received a copy of the official NFL rulebook. From there, he founded *Football Zebras*, a website dedicated to rule interpretations and the 33rd team in the NFL: the officiating crews. When he is not writing about football, he is a regulatory specialist in food labeling. He lives in New Jersey with his wife and three children.